Marcuse

Marcuse

From the New Left
to the Next Left

Edited by John Bokina and Timothy J. Lukes

 University Press of Kansas

Published by the University Press of Kansas (Lawrence, Kansas 66049), which was organized by the Kansas Board of Regents and is operated and funded by Emporia State University, Fort Hays State University, Kansas State University, Pittsburg State University, the University of Kansas, and Wichita State University

Library of Congress Cataloging-in-Publication Data

Marcuse : from the New Left to the next left / edited by John Bokina
  and Timothy J. Lukes.
    p. cm.
  Includes bibliographical references and index.
  ISBN 0-7006-0658-0 (hardcover)
  ISBN 0-7006-0659-9 (pbk.)
    1. Marcuse, Herbert, 1898- —Contributions in political science.
  2. Marcuse, Herbert, 1898- —Contributions in sociology.
  I. Bokina, John. II. Lukes, Timothy J., 1950- .
  JC251.M25M37 1994
  300'.1—dc20   93-40249

British Library Cataloguing in Publication Data is available.

Printed in the United States of America
10 9 8 7 6 5 4 3 2 1

The paper used in this publication meets the minimum requirements of the American National Standard for Permanence of Paper for Printed Library Materials Z39.48-1984.

Contents

Contents

John Bokina

Marcuse Revisited: An Introduction

" 'Our' Western Marxist"

The phrase is Martin Jay's,[1] and it could not be more apt. Not only does it characterize Herbert Marcuse's (1898–1979) nearly sixty years of work within its proper theoretical tradition, but the possessive also links the fate of that work to a particular generation and a particular era.

It would be foolish, in retrospect, to overestimate the theoretical sophistication of sixties and seventies radicalism. For better and worse, New Left ideas and actions were characterized more by emotion, circumstance, and improvisation than they were by any self-conscious theoretical orientation. Yet it would also be a mistake to dismiss entirely the influence of theory in general and Marcuse in particular. During this period, Marcuse's lifelong appropriation and synthesis of classical German thought—from Kant, Schiller, and Hegel through Marx and Freud—burst the confines of academia and acquired a striking political resonance.

Marcuse's books articulated the new discontents within Western liberal capitalism. He attacked the system at its points of strength: economic prosperity, personal contentment, political freedom. In contrast to the self-congratulations of the affluent society, Marcuse's description of a prosperity based on selective deprivation, the creation of false needs, waste, needless duplication, and weapons production appealed to a generation of radicals who found themselves in economic circumstances far removed from those of Marx's proletariat. A life scenario of school, work, marriage, and the split-level was the dearly won achievement of their parents' generation, hardened by depression and world war. New Left discontent with this scenario was verbalized by Marcuse's condemnation of "comfortable, smooth, reasonable, democratic unfreedom,"[2] even if much of the rest of *One-Dimensional Man* remained opaque to his young readers. The assumption that relatively prosperous middle-class life fostered happiness and satisfaction was undermined by Marcuse's *Eros and Civilization*, in which that life was understood as the product of

1

the excessive repression of sensuality and sexuality. In this context, advanced technology was not the precondition for the elimination of toil and misery but rather the means of widening and intensifying the worst aspects of late capitalism. Likewise, Marcuse exposed the sham of political liberalism: freedom of choice, but no meaningful alternatives; freedom of speech, but only when the effect of radical speech is negated by the conservative chorus of the ruling majority.

The situation was exacerbated by the theoretical and political bankruptcy of the traditional alternatives to liberal capitalism. Marcuse analyzed the transformation of Soviet-style Marxist theory from a form of critical thinking designed to guide revolutionary practice to an ideological legitimation of the status quo. Emancipation, for Marcuse and his readers, was understood as more than the seizure of state power and the transference of the ownership of the means of production. By the adjective "New," the radicals declared their independence from the old Leftist conceptions of socialism and communism. "Really existing socialism" was the realm of the proverbial dour men in ill-fitting suits rather than Spartacus reborn.

A chance for emancipation remained. As Marcuse stripped the liberal capitalist view of history of its aura of progress, he provided a vision of liberation that abandoned the notion of historical inevitability. The connection to a flexible, Western Marxism was never completely severed. But instead of sequential *stages* of capitalism-socialism-communism, Marcuse wrote of the *possibilities* of liberation, possibilities predicated on the same material and technological achievements that led to one-dimensionality. In the words of Tim Lukes, Marcuse's "mechanisms of qualitative change, whether psychic or political or cultural, are based consistently on the prospects of an escalating tension between the consciousness of enhanced possibilities and ever more formidable conventional obstacles." Despite these obstacles, there was the possibility of a "pacification of existence," in which the economic prosperity and technological achievements of advanced industrial societies would be redirected to the creation of more benign and satisfying forms of life: the liberation of sensuality and sexuality, of animate and inanimate nature.

The New Left received more from Marcuse than particular critical and emancipatory ideas. Marcuse also gave the radicals an intellectual legitimacy and an intellectual tradition. To the mandarins of academia, the

2

protests and hopes of the New Left were nothing more than the mewlings of spoiled middle-class children. Marcuse, however, armed the radicals for intellectual combat. He provided an alternative understanding of the great thinkers and the great books, an understanding that challenged the ideological props to the status quo. And at the same time, for the theoretically inclined, he opened the doors to previously unknown thinkers. We learned that his ideas were related to those of critical theory and the Frankfurt School: Adorno, Horkheimer, Benjamin, Fromm, Lowenthal, Neumann, and, later, Habermas. We learned that the Frankfurt School itself was but one tendency within a diverse tradition known as Western Marxism: Lukács, Korsch, Bloch, Gramsci, among others. Through Marcuse, we learned how to think politically.

Marcuse's theoretical work began long before the rise of the New Left, and it continued after its demise. The handful of years of New Left activism gave Marcuse's ideas a public vibrancy that has rarely been equaled, yet this period also clouds the meaning of Marcuse's theoretical legacy. Was "our" Western Marxist merely a thinker for a particular generation at a particular point in its development? Are Marcuse's ideas so tightly tied to the peculiar circumstances of the sixties and seventies that they should be rightly consigned to a place in the history of intellectual fads? To use one of his own favorite epithets, is Marcuse "obsolete?"[3] Or do his ideas address the new-old conditions of the nineties? If it is too soon to tell whether Marcuse will join the philosophic pantheon, it is not too soon to determine whether he is a thinker for our *fin de siècle* age.

The essays in this book open a new stage of thinking about Marcuse. The heated polemics of the sixties and seventies are long gone, as are the explications of Marcuse's ideas; we finally do understand *One-Dimensional Man*. Nor is this book still another analysis of the relation of Marcuse's ideas to his significant intellectual predecessors and contemporaries. Douglas Kellner's essay on the Marcuse Archive attests to the need for more research on these subjects, but this research will not be found here. The goal of this collection of commissioned essays is, rather, the reassessment of Marcuse's themes and ideas in light of contemporary political and intellectual developments.

The contributors to this book reflect the catholicity of Marcuse's interests. Political scientists—always eager for significant if unremunerative tasks—are overrepresented. There are also philosophers, literary scholars, a historian, an urbanist, and a sociologist. The contributors selected their own topics and were free to take any critical perspective on Marcuse. Some are still enthusiasts, some are dismissive, and the rest fall somewhere in between. Contributions from scholars who previously worked on Marcuse would seem to bias the book in his favor, but the range of perspectives is surprising.

The first part of this book examines important themes in contemporary theory and philosophy. Ben Agger's "Marcuse in Postmodernity" and Paul Breines's "Revisiting Marcuse with Foucault: *An Essay on Liberation* Meets *The History of Sexuality*" address the relationship between Marcuse's theoretical legacy and postmodern theories. Peter Marcuse's "Herbert Marcuse on Real Existing Socialism: A Hindsight Look at *Soviet Marxism*" and Terrell Carver's "Marcuse and Analytical Marxism" explore the implications of Marcuse's ideas for aspects of contemporary socialism and Marxism.

The second part focuses on feminism and feminist perspectives in psychoanalytic theory. Trudy Steuernagel's essay, "Marcuse, the Women's Movement, and Women's Studies," traces the relation of Marcuse's ideas about women to the various stages and trends within the women's movement. Isaac Balbus's "The Missing Dimension: Self-Reflexivity and the 'New Sensibility,'" Gad Horowitz's "Psychoanalytic Feminism in the Wake of Marcuse," and Fred Alford's "Marx, Marcuse, and Psychoanalysis: Do They Still Fit after All These Years?" reconsider the Freudian component of Marcuse's theories in light of more recent developments in psychoanalytic theory—developments produced by the heightened awareness of women's issues.

The third part looks at contemporary issues in art and aesthetics. Shierry Weber Nicholsen's "Persistence of Passionate Subjectivity: Eros and Other in Marcuse, by Way of Adorno," focuses on *The Aesthetic Dimension*. Nicholsen proposes a new understanding of the relation between Marcuse's and Adorno's works, as well as the renewed relevance for the nineties of Marcuse's notion of an aesthetic sensibility. Carol Becker's "Surveying *The Aesthetic Dimension* at the Death of Postmodernism" also discusses the implications of Marcuse's last book and analyzes the dilemmas of postmodern and post-postmodern art.

The fourth part surveys current developments in the theory and practice of ecology and advanced technology. Tim W. Luke's piece, "Marcuse

4

and Ecology," situates Marcuse's ideas about nature within the various schools of ecological theory. Andrew Feenberg's "Critique of Technology: From Dystopia to Interaction" and Tim J. Lukes's "Mechanical Reproduction in the Age of Art: Herbert Marcuse and the Aesthetic Reduction of Technology" emphasize the more optimistic aspects of Marcuse's theory of technology.

In the last part, Doug Kellner's "Marcuse Renaissance?" provides an overview of the unpublished material in the Frankfurt Marcuse Archive. These materials furnish the foundation for a more accurate understanding of the genesis of Marcuse's ideas and are also the basis for new Marcusean work on contemporary politics.

The contributors dutifully explore the relevance of Marcuse to their chosen subjects, but the net result is something more than a mere collection of discrete and disparate essays. This book is, rather, an intellectual stock taking, a tracing of the trajectory of radical ideas from the sixties and seventies to the present. For veterans of the New Left, this book will subject the Marcusean assumptions of their ideas to self-conscious and critical analysis. And younger scholars—confident that their theoretical approaches are somehow "beyond" Marcuse—will discover some hitherto unsuspected connections.

Part I: From New to Post

A reborn Marcuse would certainly recognize the crucial landmarks of political debate in the nineties. The issues are similar to those of the sixties and seventies, but they are posed from new perspectives. Marcuse discussed the progressive and regressive implications of advanced technology for commodity production. But what is the meaning of Marcuse's analysis when the burning high-tech questions of the nineties revolve around issues of information rather than production? Marcuse characterized the Marxism of the Soviet Union as fatally flawed, a pseudo-alternative to the liberal-capitalist West. But what are the implications for Marxism, pseudo or not, of the collapse of communism in the USSR and Eastern Europe? Marcuse heralded environmentalism as an essential part of a new revolutionary consciousness that went beyond the traditional economic and political concerns of socialism and communism. But what is the political content of environmentalism when the recently defeated Republican incumbent could even claim to be "the environmental president?" Marcuse applauded the revolutionary significance of the feminist movement. But what is the relationship between feminism and revolution when a feminist can write of her abhorrence of the "properly masculinist business of revolution?"[4] Marcuse argued for the preferential treatment of progressive ideas in an era of conservative intellectual domination. But what is the status of this recommendation when intellectual debate is constrained by left-liberal notions of political correctness?

In the realms of philosophy and political theory, the intellectual pillars of the New Left—Marcuse, critical theory, and Western Marxism—are alleged to be surpassed by postmodern perspectives: poststructuralism, deconstruction, multiculturalism, semiotics, and various feminisms. Nietzsche and Heidegger are again in fashion, but the Germanic heroes of the New Left have been replaced by thinkers with a decidedly Gallic accent: Foucault is the towering figure, but also prominent are Derrida, Lacan, and Baudrillard.

The relation of Marcuse and Western Marxism to the postmodern theoretical tendencies is subject to radically different interpretations. In the night vision of the conservative culture warriors, where all Leftist cows are gray, a direct line of succession connects Marcuse and postmodern theorists.[5] He is therefore partly responsible for the pernicious attacks of these theorists on the canonical texts of Western philosophy. From this perspective, Marcuse is faulted not so much for his occasional espousal of noncanonical thinkers like Babeuf and Fourier but rather for his irreverent treatment of the core thinkers of the Western philosophical tradition.

Unlike the conservative culture warriors, Marcuse never viewed Western philosophy as the ahistorical, politically neutral repository of permanent and eternal truth. For Marcuse, Western philosophy was embedded in Western history, and this history was and is nothing less than the history of domination: class over class, West over non-West, mind over body, man over nature, men over women. Marcuse, however, did not reject Western philosophy outright but exposed its hidden presumptions, then mined its legacy for those atypical bits and shards that could provide the foundation for a nondominating, liberating alternative. The culture warriors, for their part, see Marcuse's *Ideologiekritik* as the essential precondition for the withering relativism of poststructuralism and deconstruction.

There is in fact an important element of truth in the assertion of a link between Marcuse and postmodern theories. Neither the deconstruction of the latent forms of domination nor the semiotic analysis of political signs is imaginable without the work of Marcuse and the other Western Marxists. Several essays in this volume attest to this link, albeit in less tendentious and more subtle forms. Postmodern theorists, however, reject or ignore this connection.

The postmoderns emphasize the differences rather than the similarities between their theories and those of Marcuse and Western Marxism. According to postmodern theorists, the ostensible opposition of Marcuse to the dominating tendencies of Western philosophy merely cloaks his "hidden orthodoxy,"[6] as revealed in his inadequate relativism, his continued attachment to the idea of historical development, and his Eurocentrism. Marcuse demystified Western philosophy by dividing it into a manifest tradition of domination and a latent tradition of emancipation, but the postmoderns eschew all truth claims. Philosophy itself is just another form of subjective discourse and narrative. Marcuse detached the idea of emancipation from any connection to an inevitable developmental course of history, but his concepts are said to be tainted by Marxist residues. He may have written about the pacification of existence rather than socialism, about the Great Refusal rather than revolution, but he is still tied to the "metanarrative" of total transformation rather than microlevel moments of resistance. Marcuse lauded the political aspirations of women and other outsiders, but he remains just another "pale penis"[7] person reconfiguring the ideas of a bevy of other pale penis persons. His critique and reinterpretation of Western philosophy try to redeem a tradition irredeemably contaminated by sexism, racism, and heterosexism.

Agger's "Marcuse in Postmodernity" concurs with the main line of the conservative culture warriors' thesis: that postmodern theories are the successors to the work of Marcuse and his contemporaries. And he proposes a new synthesis. According to Agger, the theoretical work of Marcuse and the classical critical theorists remains sound, but it is excessively abstract. Although Marcuse put the issues of the lifeworld, discourse, and the body on the theoretical agenda, the postmoderns have explored these themes in concrete studies.

Within Agger's synthesis, the relationship between Marcuse and postmodern theories is not purely reciprocal, because Marcuse contributes more than the postmoderns. In order to reestablish a connection between scholarly work and radical political practice, studies of the lifeworld, discourse, and the body must restore Marcuse's sense of history, his critique of ideology, and his vision of totality. Without these elements, postmodern theories are only the sources of "playful frissons," trendy and ironic studies that are hopelessly disconnected from any possibility of emancipatory political practice. The concepts of lifeworld, discourse, and the body are distinctly postmodern, but Agger's synthesis recalls the Frankfurt School's original research program.

Breines's "Revisiting Marcuse with Foucault: *An Essay on Liberation* Meets *The History of Sexuality*" traces the relationship between Marcuse and poststructuralism. Written at the peak of New Left activism, *An Essay* articulates Marcuse's most utopian hopes. Foucault's *History*, on the other hand, is the critique of these hopes. Yet Breines sees more than opposition linking the two books. In the seventies, the New Philosophers attacked Marcuse and the New Left from the standpoint of hostile theoretical and political principles. Foucault's critique is different; it is internal, a New Left critique of the New Left. While Breines retains a sympathy for Marcuse, he is also attracted to elements of Foucault's position: that the argument for sexual emancipation was but another stage in the inherently dominating discourse of sexuality; that the New Left perpetuated the privileged position of theory and theorists; that liberation is the outcome of numerous resistances at the microlevel rather than a grand event; that the New Left—if not Marcuse himself—retained elements of heterosexism and homophobia.

Breines is more ambivalent than Agger about the continued vitality of Marcuse and critical theory in the era of the postmoderns. This ambivalence is the strength of the essay, as it documents the struggle of a New Left intellectual to come to terms with poststructuralism. If Marcuse had lived for another ten years, he would have faced the same task.

Postmodern criticism is but one aspect of the recent assaults on socialism and Marxism. Marcuse and Western Marxism continue to be the subjects of attacks by the conservative culture warriors. And although Marcuse's vision of pacified existence was never predicated on Soviet socialism, the demise of communism in the Soviet Union and Eastern Europe lends an aura of credibility to the latest declarations of the death of socialism.

In "Herbert Marcuse on Real Existing Socialism: A Hindsight Look at *Soviet Marxism*," Peter Marcuse uses his father's writings to analyze first the reform, then the demise of Soviet socialism. First published in 1958, Marcuse's *Soviet Marxism* delineated the objective and subjective factors that would incline the Soviet Union toward the reform of the Stalinist system. Objectively, competition with the West necessitated a liberalization of intellectual life in order to facilitate technological innovation. Subjectively, it was in the interest of the Soviet bureaucracy, the stratum that controlled the means of production, to secure its domination by channeling the fruits of technological innovation to the Soviet consumer. Because of intensified international conflict with the West, Khrushchev's initial attempt to reform Stalinism was abandoned; technological development was once again concentrated on weaponry and space exploration. The second reform effort, Gorbachev's *glasnost* and *perestroika*, was pursued more thoroughly, but with unanticipated results. Lacking ownership of the means of production, the Soviet bureaucracy undermined the reform of Soviet socialism by switching its loyalty to the new "free market" system. "The bureaucracy quickly realized it could as easily exercise its power in the new system as in the old."

Peter Marcuse's essay has important implications for the current debate about the death of socialism. He admits that in a purely economic competition, capitalism has certain advantages over Soviet-style socialism. Capitalism has fewer restraints on the exploitation of workers, and it is also able to offer greater material incentives to its innovative managerial and technological elites. At the same time, the triumph of capitalism over Soviet socialism may enhance the prospects for qualitative change within capitalist countries. Whether the alternative is called socialism, the pacification of existence, or something else entirely, the failure to realize a qualitatively better mode of life in capitalist countries can no longer be blamed on the exigencies of the external Soviet threat.

Carver's "Marcuse and Analytic Marxism" examines a tendency within Marxism that has been remarkably immune—or is it only oblivious?—to contemporary theoretical challenges. Political or theoretical angst is not a characteristic of analytic Marxism, and its practitioners have pursued secure and successful academic careers. Since the midseventies, the analytic

Marxists have distinguished their work " 'from the increasingly discredited methods and presuppositions' " of other Marxisms. They combine the substantive themes of Marxism (e.g., class struggle, the transitions between historical stages, the nature of capitalism, etc.) with the methods of non-Marxist social science: analytical philosophy, empiricism, economic modeling. Their assumption is that a Marxism built on these methods will be more scientifically rigorous—if also devoid of the very emancipatory and critical intent that marked the work of both Marx and Marcuse.

The question is whether non-Marxist methods can simply be grafted onto Marxist themes. Returning to Marcuse's critique of non-Marxist social science in *One-Dimensional Man*, Carver shows how the fundamental principles of analytic Marxism are not neutral tools applicable to any subject. These principles—of the behavior of "individuals" abstracted from society, of the "free choices" of these individuals, of a world of scarcity and competition—are charged with a highly political and highly dubious content. With their non-Marxist methods, the analytic Marxists may be able to continue their stream of academic publications, but only by betraying the essence of Marxism. For Carver, the core of both Marx's and Marcuse's thought is not careerism but rather the demystifying critique of ideas and institutions which damage the lives of real people living in real societies. By their ahistorical presumption of freely choosing individuals operating in econometric models of scarcity, the analytic Marxists only *re*mystify these conditions.

Part II: Psychoanalysis and Feminism

In 1947, Horkheimer and Adorno's *Dialectic of Enlightenment* characterized Odysseus as the prototype of Western man. Domination was his essence. Odysseus used his reason to subdue his body and his sensuousness, to control his men and defeat his enemies, to conquer the mythologized forces of nature. Eight years later, in *Eros and Civilization*, Marcuse joined his former colleagues in the Freudian reinterpretation of Western culture. Marcuse's prototype was Prometheus, Marx's own culture hero. Prometheus was another rational achiever, but his story was even more telling as an allegory of the fate of Western civilization. The *Odyssey* concludes with the wily Odysseus reunited with his family and restored to his throne, but Prometheus the enlightener was bound and tortured, punished for his own achievements.

As always, Marcuse offered emancipatory alternatives. If Prometheus symbolized the fate of Western man, frustrated and unfulfilled because of his economic and technological achievements, there were other possible culture symbols. There was Narcissus, who was captivated by the contemplation of his own beauty. There was Orpheus, who sang so sweetly that he could charm nature itself. Narcissus and Orpheus were not symbols of reason and domination. Rather, they stood for the cultivation of erotic instinct, sexuality, and sensuousness, for new, nondominating relations between human beings and between human beings and nature. An aura of playfulness, receptivity, and passivity surrounded these models. In contrast to rational achievers like Odysseus and Prometheus, Narcissus and Orpheus represented an alternative set of values.

The reinterpretation of the classical culture symbols had immediate and long-term consequences. The images of Orpheus and Narcissus foretold Marcuse's later calls for a truly revolutionary political theory, one that combined reason with sensuality. His favorite noncanonical thinkers, Babeuf and especially Fourier, suggested an incipient feminism.[8] For the New Left, Marcuse's Freudianism raised the stakes of revolution. True emancipation was now more and other than the overthrow of the bourgeoisie and its state. True emancipation meant the elimination of the excessive, "surplus" repression of erotic instinct, which needlessly blocked the cultivation of sensuality and sexuality in an era of economic abundance.

Working in a more innocent age, Marcuse could still write about the Promethean dilemma and Orphic possibilities of *men* in the generic sense of humankind. With the eclipse of the New Left and the dispersal of its components into separate theoretical agendas and separate social movements, however, Marcuse's classical images were transvalued by a new "identity politics." Prometheus was now a *man* in the gendered sense of the term. Moreover, he was not just any member of the male persuasion but rather a particular kind of white, European, heterosexual man.

Marcuse used Prometheus, Orpheus, and Narcissus as suggestive *images* for the critique of Western philosophy and the formation of an emancipatory alternative. In fully developed identity politics, however, suggestive images became theoretical and practical *presuppositions*. If the legacy of Prometheus and his ilk was marked by a dominating conception of reason, then the politics of identity dictates censure: It is now time to renounce Prometheus and all his pomp and works. Likewise, the sheer non-Promethean identity of other groups—women, racial and ethnic minorities, homosexuals and lesbians—endowed them with at least a presumption of political virtue.

Steuernagel's "Marcuse, the Women's Movement, and Women's Studies" analyzes the relation of Marcuse's ideas to the various stages and tendencies within feminist theory. Abandoning hope in the revolutionary potential of the working class, Marcuse looked to outsiders, to those who were excluded from full participation in the system, as possible revolutionary agents. In the course of his supportive reflections on the revolutionary potential of the Women's Liberation Movement, Steuernagel suggests that he went too far, essentializing women as an inherent "other" to the patriarchal status quo. In this well-intentioned essentializing of women, Marcuse anticipates the theory and practice of feminism as identity politics, the latest and, in some respects, the most self-destructive and politically vulnerable stage of feminism. Separated from other elements of the Left, feminist identity politics becomes an end in itself, a substitute for truly radical politics that is all too prone to flights of rhetorical political correctness. Steuernagel does not address the dogmatic character of political correctness but concentrates instead on its political effects. For Steuernagel, the problem of a politically correct feminist identity politics is the backlash that it engenders. Political correctness makes the feminist movement vulnerable to conservative attack.

Although assigning Marcuse some responsibility for moving feminism to identity politics, Steuernagel turns to another Marcusean idea in her analysis of the current political plight of feminism. The rightist attacks on feminism constitute a "preventive counterrevolution." In practical terms, there has been no feminist revolution. Women have gained very little. The goal of antifeminist counterrevolutionaries is to roll back these few gains, including women's studies programs. Self-destructive bouts of rhetorical political correctness only give aid and comfort to the antifeminist enemy. In order to overcome the debilitating isolation of feminism, Steuernagel looks beyond the New Left coalition. She recommends a link between feminists and the working class.

Balbus's "Missing Dimension: Self-Reflexivity and the 'New Sensibility'" examines Marcuse's failure to formulate a new, genuinely revolutionary mode of social theory, one that combines Promethean reason with an Orphic concern for emotion, passion, and sensuousness. According to Balbus, Marcuse betrayed this goal by his insistence on the primacy of reason within the new combination of reason and emotion and by his continued demand for the primacy of the radical social theorist within radical social movements. The Orphic aspect of Marcuse cloaks his still-Promethean character.

For Balbus, Habermas and Foucault—the leading lights of contemporary, nonfeminist social theory—fare no better than Marcuse on this issue. Marcuse's goal of a theoretical synthesis of reason and emotion remains valid, but Balbus finds the means to achieve this goal in a psychoanalytically self-reflexive social theory. The new model for social theory is the therapy session. Here the dichotomy between reason and emotion dissolves in a loop, wherein reason elucidates emotion and emotion elucidates reason. Likewise, the pedagogical domination of the radical social theorist over the radical social actor is negated as theorists learn from the experiences of actors and actors are informed by the reflections of theorists.

Both Horowitz's "Psychoanalytic Feminism in the Wake of Marcuse" and Alford's "Marx, Marcuse, and Psychoanalysis: Do They Still Fit after All These Years?" address new developments in psychoanalytic object relations theory. Although object relations theory dates back to the 1930s, the new accounts of it have all been influenced by feminism. Horowitz questions these latest developments. He focuses his critique on Jessica Benjamin's influential *Bonds of Love*. Benjamin rejects Freud's and Marcuse's insistence on the primacy of sexual instinct as essentially monadological: a preoccupation with the sexual drives of individuals which ignores the fact that sexuality is intersubjective (that it is a relation) whose roots are embedded in child-rearing patterns. These patterns structure roles of patriarchy or gender equality and determine whether adult sexual relations will be based on domination and submission or mutual recognition.

Horowitz admits that Benjamin offers useful insights, but he defends the Freudian-Marcusean emphasis on the primacy of instinct. Gender roles and sexual relations may be intersubjective, but the component parts of these intersubjective relations are still embodied individuals driven by sexual instinct. More tellingly, Horowitz recruits Marcuse to expose the Achilles heel of object relations theory. This theory purports to be more social, relational, and intersubjective than instinct-oriented psychoanalysis, yet it lacks any concept of the larger social context of primal relations. Do capitalism or socialism or other social formations play no role in the patterns that determine gender roles and adult sexuality? Ultimately, the insights of object relations theory will only be fruitful when they are reintegrated with the two cornerstones of Freud's and Marcuse's metapsychology: a sexually instinctive individual within a sexually repressive social totality.

If Horowitz advocates the incorporation of elements of object relations theory within a still-Marcusean system, Alford proposes a more genuinely reciprocal synthesis. Alford concedes the central point made by Nancy Chodorow and other feminist object-relations theorists: The "key failure" of Marcuse's psychoanalytic theory is its neglect of human relationships. Yet Alford, like Horowitz, is unwilling to give up Marcuse's central point: his concept of an erotically instinctual individual.

Alford finds hints of a possible synthesis in the work of an earlier object relations theorist, D. W. Winnicott. Winnicott argues that the goal of human life was not sexual fulfillment but rather mutual recognition through relationships. The model of this mutual recognition is the relationship between mother and infant. Alford takes Winnicott's ideal relationship and fills it with Marcusean adult bodies driven by erotic instinct. Mutual relations are erotic relations, and societies are to be judged in terms of how they foster or deny these relations.

Part III: Artful Thinking

Eros and Civilization implicated the prevailing tradition of Western philosophy in a dominating concept of reason. Marcuse called for a new conception of philosophy that would synthesize reason and sensuousness. Marcuse also anticipated Balbus's suspicion that the very nature of philosophizing would guarantee the hegemony of reason within the new synthesis. The philosopher Marcuse thus questioned the value of the enterprise of philosophy itself. In his questioning of philosophy, Marcuse never worked himself into the paradoxes of Foucault. Nevertheless, his later works were increasingly preoccupied with the political implications of aesthetics.

In his later articulations of aesthetics as the "science of sensuousness," Marcuse reversed the Hegelian prioritization of absolute spirit. If the rational, truth-seeking activity of philosophy was inherently tainted by domination, then philosophy was demoted to the second rank, and its place was taken by art. Following Kant, Marcuse argued that art was the product of the imagination, of the synthesis of reason and sensuousness. The essence of art was beauty embodied in form. Broadly and politically conceived, aesthetics thus became the key to finding a genuinely liberating alternative to the prevailing one-dimensionality. Through the apperception of art, the imagination conjured images of a transcending other, more beautiful world. If, in his later works, reason became an uncertain ally on the path to emancipation, Marcuse was now a Schillerist: Beauty was the path to freedom.

The liberating value of an artwork did not lie in its overt political content. Politically tendentious art replicated rather than transcended the tawdriness of the real world. Nor did Marcuse value anti-art. In its assault on form, anti-art attacked the essence of art, which was beauty in form. Rather, Marcuse turned to the masterworks of the Western tradition. These masterworks were conservative in their own eras, glorifying and prettifying the status quo, and continued to play a conservative role in our era, as they provided moments of sheer escape and repose within an otherwise repressive and one-dimensional reality. But in their sensuous beauty and sheer alterity, great artworks also offered glimpses of utopia.

Needless to say, Marcuse's position was not the last word on the politics of art. Veterans of the New Left criticized Marcuse's aesthetics as a "flight into inwardness,"[9] a misdirected and escapist substitute for real politics and real political change. The postmodernist art of the eighties contradicted Marcuse's views on aesthetic form. With its genre mixtures and its blurred distinction between high and popular art, postmodernism eroded artistic form, the foundation of Marcuse's conception of aesthetic experience. Still later, and inevitably, art too entered the politics of identity. From this perspective, Marcuse's advocacy of the masterwork tradition was a defense of the hegemonic canon of Western art. In art as in philosophy, the canon ignored the achievements of the diverse outsiders.

Nicholsen's "Persistence of Passionate Subjectivity: Eros and Other in Marcuse, by Way of Adorno," offers an account of the fate of Marcuse's ideas. For Nicholsen, *The Aesthetic Dimension* is not merely the *last* book that Marcuse wrote before he died; it is his *ultimate* book. On the surface, *The Aesthetic Dimension* is only an extended essay on a limited subject: the critique of Marxist aesthetics. Nicholsen, however, invests this book with greater significance. In an era of conservative reaction, *The Aesthetic Dimension* represents Marcuse's deliberate subordination of his theoretical legacy to that of Adorno.

In terms of substance, the ideas of Marcuse and Adorno are congruent. The reason why Marcuse subordinated his project to Adorno's lies in the stylistic and formal differences in the presentation of their shared ideas. In comparison to Marcuse, Adorno's writing is more hermetic, more aphoristic, more reluctant to specify the empirical possibilities of liberation. During the period of New Left activism, Adorno was criticized for these very tendencies. But in a period of renewed conservative ascendancy, these same tendencies foster an interest in Adorno.[10] Adorno's hermeticism, aphoristicism, and reticence thrive "in a postmodern period that is fascinated with form but unable to critically conceive something other." Through Adorno, elements of Marcuse's ideas survive. Indeed, Nicholsen argues that it may be time for the reemergence of Marcuse himself. In her survey of contemporary work on human needs, environmental philosophy, agroecology, environmental ethics, and animal rights, Nicholsen sees empirical examples of the development of Marcuse's aesthetic sensibility, in which the relationship of human beings to internal, human nature and to external nature is no longer based on domination.

Nicholsen's essay focuses on aesthetics as a mode of consciousness. Becker's "Surveying *The Aesthetic Dimension* at the Death of Postmodernism" looks at the implications of Marcuse's last book for contemporary developments in art. The postmodernist eighties had a dual character. On the one hand, this was a time of "great aesthetic and political demoralization." Artists were confused "as to what to make work about." The ironical and form-bending experiments of postmodernist artists were, however, snapped up in the then-lucrative art market. On the other hand, the playful and profitable experimentation of the postmodernists engendered a reaction. With artistic post-postmodernism, art entered into the world of political correctness and identity politics. Once again art acquired a political seriousness, a didactic purpose: the critique of domination. An essential part of that critique was an emphasis on the works and themes of groups who were outside the prevailing patriarchal system.

Becker has reservations about Marcuse's romanticism and Eurocentrism. But she also sees the continuing usefulness of Marcuse's aesthetics as a corrective to the excesses of both postmodernism and post-postmodernism. If art is the embodiment of beauty in transcendent form, then the formal experiments of postmodernism jeopardize the beautiful essence of art. Likewise, postmodernist mixtures of high and pop culture lose that transcendent quality which can provide an image of a liberating alternative to the status quo. Although their motives are completely different, the politically correct works of post-postmodernist artists also risk the loss of transcendence. In their efforts to put art in the service of oppressed people, post-postmodernist artists simplify both the content and form of art to such a degree that it can be embraced as just another element in the prevailing one-dimensional order.

Part IV: Ecofascists and Cyberpunks

For Marcuse, technology meant more than tools and machines. It was a mode of life—the quintessentially Western mode of life. He revived the classical Greek notion of *techne* as the rational and purposive relation to the natural world. In this broader sense of the term, modern technology embodied the typical Marcusean duality. The material achievements of modern technology were the indispensable precondition for his vision of a pacified existence: for the significant reduction of the amount and types of onerous human labor; for the liberation of an external nature that no longer needed to be feared and conquered. In its present forms and uses, however, modern technology was the key factor in the perpetuation of the very unpacified forms of life in one-dimensional societies. Labor was tied to the production of weaponry and an endless stream of wasteful consumer gadgets. Nature was subjected to ever more efficient forms of depredation and destruction.

Marcuse's ideas helped to put technology on the theoretical and political agenda. Along with Heidegger, Ellul, and a few others, he was widely, though one-sidedly, characterized as one of the prophets of technological doom. And it was the dystopian aspects of Marcuse's ideas that captured the New Left. The New Left critique of a wasteful and destructive technology was an assault on the proudest achievement of advanced industrial society. Perhaps the development of a one-sided, antitechnological image of Marcuse was unavoidable. Once he had demystified technology, it was easy to *see* its destructive effects and much harder to *imagine* a pacified technological alternative.

With the defeat of the New Left, technology was no longer the central concept in a comprehensive vision of liberation. Its components were separated into distinct theoretical and practical tendencies. The purposive relation to nature became the province of ecological studies and the environmental movement, the context in which the old duality of technology persists. Since the task of ecologists and environmentalists was to arrest the damaging effects of modern technology on nature, these groups became the legatees of Marcuse's alleged pessimism about technology. But Nicholsen's remarks on agroecology point to a new direction. The solution to environmental problems may lie, not in the restraint of advanced technology, but rather in reconceived and redirected versions of the most advanced achievements in science and technology.

Technology in the narrow sense of tools and techniques became the domain of engineering and information science. Here once again the results were ambiguous. With regard to industrial production, advances in automation reduced the amount of needed labor power. But, as Marcuse observed, automation within a still-repressive social totality was no liberation from onerous labor. Rather than an enhancement of the sheer quantity of time available for pacified life, the automation of labor pushed increasing numbers of workers into the catastrophe of unemployment. Outside of industrial production, prospects in electronics and computers are a little brighter. Once the exclusive instruments of dominating elites, the most recent developments provide for greater control by individual users.

Luke's "Marcuse and Ecology" relates Marcuse's ideas about science, technology, and nature to contemporary ecology and environmentalism. To the extent that they acknowledge them at all, contemporary ecologists and environmentalists find Marcuse's ideas to be either too humanistic or too socialistic. Luke argues that Marcuse's original formulation of the ecological problem is superior to the later versions. Marcuse links nature to the project of human liberation. His new revolutionary sensibility is aimed at the elimination of the domination of reason over sense, man over man, man over nature. Disconnected from this comprehensive vision, the defenders of nature split into discrete and sometimes warring factions: deep ecology, ecofeminism, social ecology, soft-path technology, voluntary simplicity, bioregionalism. While Luke has reservations about Marcuse's ideas, he concludes that a linked conception of human and natural liberation is a sure antidote to the "dour green visions" of today's "penitential ecoauthoritarians" and "ecofascist rational choice" environmentalists.

Feenberg's "Critique of Technology: From Dystopia to Interaction" and Lukes's "Mechanical Reproduction in the Age of Art: Herbert Marcuse and the Aesthetic Reduction of Technology" suggest some hopeful, and still Marcusean, changes in the theory and practice of advanced technology. According to Feenberg, there are three stages in the evolution of the theoretical understanding of advanced technology. Instrumental theory followed Weber in viewing advanced technology as a purely neutral tool, amenable to any social purpose. Marcuse's work not only subjects instrumental theory to blistering criticism but also plays an important role in the formulation of the second, substantive stage of technology theory. Although Feenberg is well aware that Marcuse's entire revolutionary project is predicated on the capabilities of advanced technology, he also notes that Marcuse fosters a substantively dystopian vision in which advanced technology structures an entirely new and largely regrettable way of life.

Beyond the instrumental and substantive theories lies social constructivism. Constructivism is implied in Marcuse's call for an "aesthetic reduction" of technology, but its primary inspiration is Foucault. Constructivism breaks down the idea of a monolithic *technology* in order to focus on the multitude of microlevel interests and relationships that determine the ultimate form and function of new *technologies*. Feenberg maintains that constructivism is more than just a superior theory of technology. He notes how constructivism has sparked a new interactivist politics of technology, which has important consequences for the environmental movement, public access to information, and medical treatment, including the treatment of AIDS patients.

Lukes articulates the new developments in terms of Marcuse's aesthetic reduction of technology. Marcuse rightly condemns earlier stages of advanced technology for their narcotic, ascetic, and elitist effects. Pong, Nintendo, and the personal computer are every bit as numbing as the assembly line. The antiseptic world of cybernetics represents the most thorough conquest of sense and sensibility. Without an aesthetic reduction, the complexity of advanced technology provides the foundation for the claims to power of New Class technical experts.

The alternative appears in Marcuse's cryptic comments about the aesthetic reduction of technology. According to this idea, the internal imperative of advanced technology will reduce its dominating aspects and instead facilitate user control and communication. Fully reduced, technology reunites with art and thereby becomes a source for the new sensibility, the imaginative fusion of reason and sensuousness. The results are mixed, but Lukes outlines some promising developments. The isolated mesmerization of the PC is giving way to the use of computers as a means of communication. The "wilted libido" of the cybernerds, infatuated with computer war games, is replaced by the high-tech kinkiness of the cyberpunks: *Mondo 2000*, smart drugs, "Teledildonics," raves, *Cybergenics*. The alleged elitism of advanced technology is undermined by a new simplicity in use. Simulators, three-dimensional imagers, and acoustic scanners are leading to breakthroughs in environmental protection and medical research. Finally, and by way of confirmation of Marcuse's wildest speculation, technology reunites with art in the works of technoartists.

Contemporary work on ecology and technology has engendered a wealth of neologisms. That in itself may be a sign of a Marcusean sensibility, as it indicates a new playfulness with language.

Part V: Revisiting Marcuse

This book is just one of several revisits with Marcuse in the nineties. There is more Marcuse beyond the Marcuse we know. Kellner's "Marcuse Renaissance?" provides an overview of the unpublished materials in the Frankfurt Marcuse Archive. According to Kellner, these manuscripts offer a new view of the development of Marcuse's ideas, as well as a new interpretation of the intellectual relationship between Marcuse and his Frankfurt School colleagues. The archive materials reveal a Marcuse who was deeply politicized long before he became "ours." They also show how Marcuse and Neumann represented a political tendency within the Frankfurt School that coexisted with the more apolitical orientation of Horkheimer and Adorno.

Kellner maintains that there are pieces in the archive that shed new light on such contemporary political events as the ecocide and genocide of the Gulf War. However, the archive materials also confirm what Kellner considers to be the chief weakness in Marcuse's work: Marcuse's lack of interest in political democracy. Whatever their contents, the planned publication of the archive materials in a series of books will put Marcuse back on the agenda. In addition to his greater appeal to postmoderns, the continued interest in Adorno is partly due to the steady reissue of his works in new English translations.

In most respects, this particular revisit, this collection of scholarly essays on the history of ideas, is quite similar to other collections. Scholars cite ideas, essays, and books in the construction of their own particular perspective on a subject. And, like many collections of essays, the coverage of the subject is uneven. Despite the wide range of topics included in this book, gaps remain. There is an essay on Foucault and poststructuralism, but none on Derrida, Lacan, or deconstruction. Many of the essays mention Habermas, but there is no systematic treatment of the relation of Marcuse to this most prominent figure in the second generation of the Frankfurt School. Marcuse's wariness of popular culture is noted, but there is no confrontation with contemporary culture studies, which reject his cherished distinction between the historical transcendence of high art and the historical determination of pop art. There is a piece on Marcuse and environmentalism, but the relation of his ideas to the animal rights movement merits separate coverage.

In one important sense, however, this book is very different. It is not just a collection of scholarly essays with a purely intellectual interest; more is at stake here than the nuances of seventeenth-century social contract theories or the subtleties of eighteenth-century sonata form. It is also an exercise in memory: the remembrance of a thinker in his era of revolutionary hope.

In comparison to the nineties, this thinker and his era recall a time of unified political action and grand political goals. To revisit Marcuse is to remember a time when antiwar protesters, environmentalists, sexual liberationists, free speech advocates, racial and ethnic minorities, and feminists were confident in their common purpose, not paralyzed by their different identities. It is to remember a time when Monterey Pop, the Chicago Democratic Convention, and Earth Day were manifestations of the same struggle for a qualitatively new form of life, not the piecemeal resistance to this or that adversary. To revisit Marcuse is to remember the philosopher who assured the various segments of the New Left of the commonality of their purpose and who shared his vision of what the new life might be like. The remembrance of lost revolutionary hope gives this book a pathos that is lacking in most scholarly works.

But remembrance is not nostalgia. Marcuse revisited is not *Brideshead Revisited*, whatever the delights of the latter. The "remembered plenitude"[11] of the philosopher and the era is merely the point of departure for an assessment of the intellectual and political tasks of the present. In this respect, the book is not so much an account of ideas in two different eras as it is an account of the transition between these eras.

The New Left was defeated. This book provides a forum for the examination of the theoretical conditions and consequences of that defeat, which is generally interpreted in one of two ways. Some of the essays in this volume concur with the postmodern interpretation that this defeat was the outcome of the fundamentally flawed project of Marcuse and the New Left. The whole idea of the Great Refusal, of the erotic revolution led by students and the outsiders, was always just a fiction. In the still-conservative nineties, with the segments of the New Left riven by internal factionalism, the postmodern preference for microlevel moments of resistance appears to be sober political reasoning.

Many of the essays in this book also suggest a different interpretation. Marcuse and the New Left were *defeated*, not *refuted*. Marcuse's idea of a qualitatively new and pacified mode of life remains a possibility of advanced industrial societies. If the advocates of this new, pacified mode of life now find themselves divided and in disarray, this historical condition should not be raised to permanent status. Rather, it is necessary to assemble the components of the Next Left. Likewise, the project of the sixties and early seventies should not be abandoned, but it does need to be refined: to learn from its defeat, to correct its mistakes, to redefine itself in the new context of the nineties. The political experiences and theoretical insights of the postmoderns will be important parts of this process, but they will not define it. For in the last analysis, the modest resistance politics of the postmoderns is but another lingering symptom of defeat. Postmodern realism and sobriety is a political failure of nerve.

Is Marcuse a thinker for the nineties? For conservative culture warriors, he remains a vital theoretical adversary. For postmoderns, he epitomizes the illusions of the New Left. But for those who still believe in the possibility of a liberated existence, he continues to be what he was in life: a significant theoretical guide. More than this, in the fifteen years after his death he begins to take on a symbolic quality. Subjected to the unwarranted charge of pessimism during his lifetime, Marcuse now represents revolutionary optimism—a symbol of the waiting

> till Hope creates
> From its own wreck the thing it contemplates.[12]

Notes

1. Martin Jay, *Marxism and Totality: The Adventures of a Concept from Lukács to Habermas* (Berkeley: University of California Press, 1984), 223.

2. Herbert Marcuse, *One-Dimensional Man: Studies in the Ideology of Advanced Industrial Society*, 2d ed., with an introduction by Douglas Kellner (Boston: Beacon Press, 1991), 1.

3. See Herbert Marcuse, "The Obsolescence of Marxism," in *Marx and the Western World*, ed. Nikolaus Lobkowicz (Notre Dame, Ind.: University of Notre Dame Press, 1967), 409–17, and his "Obsolescence of the Freudian Concept of Man," in *Five Lectures: Psychoanalysis, Politics, and Utopia*, trans. Jeremy J. Shapiro and Shierry M. Weber (Boston: Beacon Press, 1970), 44–61.

4. Susan McClary, *Feminine Endings: Music, Gender, and Sexuality* (Minneapolis: University of Minnesota Press, 1991), 105.

5. For example, Allan Bloom, *The Closing of the American Mind*, with a foreword by Saul Bellow (New York: Simon and Schuster, 1987), and Roger Kimball, *Tenured Radicals: How Politics Has Corrupted Our Higher Education* (New York: Harper and Row, 1990), to cite only two of many works in this vein.

6. Peter Uwe Hohendahl, *Reappraisals: Shifting Alignments in Postwar Critical Theory* (Ithaca, N.Y.: Cornell University Press, 1991), 13.

7. Robert Hughes, "Art, Morals, and Politics," *New York Review of Books*, 23 April 1992, 26.

8. Candice E. Proctor, *Women, Equality, and the French Revolution*, Contri-

butions in Women's Studies, no. 115 (Westport, Conn.: Greenwood Press, 1990), 179–81.

9. Timothy J. Lukes, *The Flight into Inwardness: An Exposition and Critique of Herbert Marcuse's Theory of Liberative Aesthetics* (Selinsgrove, Pa.: Susquehanna University Press, 1985).

10. Indeed, a recent issue of *New German Critique*, no. 56 (Spring–Summer 1992), is devoted to the place of Adorno within postmodern theory.

11. Fredric Jameson, *Marxism and Form: Twentieth-Century Dialectical Theories of Literature* (Princeton, N.J.: Princeton University Press, 1971), 82.

12. Isaac Deutscher, *The Prophet Outcast: Trotsky: 1929–1940*, vol. 3 (New York: Vintage Books, 1963), 522.

Part I

From New to Post

Ben Agger

Marcuse in Postmodernity

Much has been written about the relationship between critical theory and postmodern theory.[1] My view is that the most critical elements of postmodern theory[2] both parallel and enrich themes from the Frankfurt School. A Left postmodern theory gives political form to many of the more abstract Frankfurt formulations of the critique of domination.[3] But the relationship between postmodern and critical theory is not reciprocal: Critical theory gives postmodern theory much more than postmodern theory affords critical theory, notably in the way in which critical theory politicizes and historicizes Foucault, Derrida, and Baudrillard. Postmodern theory typically positions itself against the transformational project of critical theory,[4] rejecting "metanarratives" of the Marxist philosophy of history out of hand. Here I suggest that Marcuse demonstrates the possibility of a postmodern version of critical theory as well as a critical theory of postmodernity. In particular, this postmodern version of critical theory issues in programs of critical cultural studies and a political sociology of new social movements. Although Marcuse certainly shared many aspects of Horkheimer and Adorno's critique of domination[5] and Adorno's aesthetic theory,[6] in crucial ways Marcuse anticipates certain postmodern themes that must be taken seriously by a third-generation critical theory seeking to rejoin issues of practice.[7] Marcuse anticipates postmodern theory's concerns with the lifeworld, discourse, and the body. He did not theorize postmodernity explicitly. But his differences with Adorno help illuminate shortcomings in Adorno's negative dialectics, which remains a suggestive treatment of late capitalism but not a nuanced empirical reading of transformational opportunities.

This is not to say that postmodern theory is somehow "more" political than Adorno. Baudrillard, Lyotard, Foucault, and Derrida provide no transformational philosophy of history, regressing behind the dialectical stance of critical theory. I am only suggesting that a Marcusean version of critical theory, learning from but transcending Adorno's negative dialectics, closely parallels a postmodern critical theory in terms of its attention to the politics of the lifeworld, discourse, and the body. In fact, I argue that greater attention to the texts and texture of Marcuse's critical theory obviates the labored engagement with postmodern theory so abundant today. Why Marcuse is neglected on the theoretical Left, thus forcing the engagement with postmodernism, remains an interesting question. I think the answer involves the periodization of Marcuse as a 1960s social and cultural critic, missing his more generic contributions to critical theory formulated in the turbulent context of the New Left.

My argument is that a Marcusean critical theory can shed light on postmodern capitalism.[8] Marcuse's concerns with the lifeworld,[9] discourse,[10] and the body[11] track the displacement of politics and power into heretofore nonpolitical venues in late capitalism. In my *Fast Capitalism*[12] I discuss these processes of displacement, suggesting a programmatic agenda for critical theory in postmodernity. My own postmodern version of critical theory stems in large measure from my own grounding in Marcuse, which animates my concerns with the lifeworld, discourse, and the body. In *The Discourse of Domination*[13] I reconstruct the genealogy of my argument for a Marcusean critical theory that closely parallels various postmodern themes.

Beyond the "End" of Ideology

A critical theory relevant to the 1990s needs to address the displacement and depoliticization of politics without sacrificing totalization and ideology critique. Contrary to the theories of Bell[14] and Lyotard,[15] ideology has not disappeared. Ideology still reinforces domination, although now its simulations are difficult to read as texts. Where Marx originally debunked religion and bourgeois economic theory as falsifying representations of the world, today the crisis of representation, well understood by many postmodernists, makes that ideology-critical debunking posture problematic. Indeed, the revival of a Marcusean critical theory issues in a version of cultural studies that seeks and destroys ideology in the variety of venues into which it has been displaced. Thus, critical theorists would apply Marcuse's programmatic critique of ideology developed in *One-Dimensional Man* in actual readings of ideologized quotidian discourses and practices that constitute one-dimensionality. For example, Miller's book on television represents this cultural critique at its best, moving back and forth between the theoretical apparatus of critical theory and its concrete deconstruction of a televisual "reality."[16]

Although, as I noted before, postmodern theory lacks a progressive philosophy of history, it usefully draws attention to lifeworld-grounded discourse and practices that both constitute and transact power through the various language games of the quotidian. Foucault and Baudrillard in particular suggest programs of critical cultural studies that fulfill the promise of the Frankfurt School's cultural theory, which, with a few exceptions, was never sufficiently rooted in everyday life. Books like Foucault's *Discipline and Punish* and Baudrillard's *Simulations*, although they lack a Leftist teleology, are better grounded than Adorno's *Aesthetic Theory* and his *Philosophy of Modern Music* and thus articulate strategies of critique and resistance arising from the lifeworld.

I have discussed the lifeworld grounding of critical theory elsewhere,[17] drawing on the legacies of phenomenological Marxism,[18] feminist theory, and Marcuse's critical theory. Postmodernists read the popular closely, identifying and deconstructing texts of power, which do not replace modernist ideologies but displace them into everyday life in ways that make them difficult to engage critically. Postmodern discourse and practice at their best afford critical theory a discourse-theoretic anchoring in the lifeworld. In his discussion of "the closing of the universe of discourse" in *One-Dimensional Man*, Marcuse comes very close to this discursive underpinning and the agenda of cultural studies that it supports.[19]

A discourse-theoretic version of critical theory helps debunk postmodern forms of ideology in late capitalism. Alone among the original Frankfurt theorists, Marcuse understood the need for such an underpinning in order to connect what he calls "sensibility" prefiguratively to new types of social and economic organization characteristic of a better society.[20] This attempt to bridge subjectivity and intersubjectivity originally flowed from his Freudian reconstruction of historical materialism in *Eros and Civilization*. The Freud book anchors *One-Dimensional Man* and *An Essay on Liberation*, both of which stress the politics of subjectivity.[21] *An Essay on Liberation* comes closest of all his works to an actual cultural-studies agenda, demonstrating ways in which cultural activities had clear political resonances during the 1960s.

By 1972, the year of publication of *Counterrevolution and Revolt*,

Marcuse had already put distance between himself and the student movement, which he deemed overly irrationalist and insufficiently theoretical. Nevertheless, his engagement with the New Left and counterculture in the 1969 book indicates his proximity to a postmodern cultural-studies agenda of the kind that follows consistently from a lifeworld-grounded version of critical theory emphasizing the displacement and depoliticization of politics in the society of the spectacle. Although the old and new Rights[22] savage Marcuse for the aid and comfort he gave the student movement, blaming him for extraparliamentary sins ranging from the Black Panthers to political correctness on college campuses, Marcuse *theorized* the cultural politics of the 1960s. Although this did not lead to a full-blown reformulation of critical theory, it is clear in hindsight that Marcuse matched Foucault's, Derrida's, and Baudrillard's acute understanding of the politics of discourse in an age of simulations, while improving on their postmodern aversion to politicizing and mobilizing narratives of radical social change. Marcuse was postmodern before his time in his attention to the lifeworld politics of discourse, culture, and sexuality. Unlike postmodernists and Adorno, he embraced the Great Refusal and thus preserved the possibility of societal transformation.

Although Marcuse's last book, *The Aesthetic Dimension*, closely resembled Adorno's own *Aesthetic Theory* in its apparent rejection of organized politics and new social movements, Marcuse deployed Freud to suggest the "promise of happiness" augured by art as a guide to social reconstruction.[23] Unlike Horkheimer and Adorno, who abandon politics, and better than Habermas, who endorses the politically vague notion of ideal speech, Marcuse suggests the concept of *the new sensibility*: a political, social, cultural, and sexual subject capable of transforming his or her lifeworld in the here and now.[24] The new sensibility refuses to postpone liberation to a distant future time, recognizing that the long road to socialism is inevitably littered with broken bodies.

This version of the new sensibility resembles feminist conceptions of the politics of the personal, albeit within the totalizing framework of historical materialism. Unlike Marcuse and his Frankfurt colleagues, many postmodern feminists reject the totalizing notion of grand narratives or philosophies of history. Indeed, postmodern and feminist theory combine to rebut "male Marxism."[25] To be sure, Marcuse's feminism was not explicit enough, requiring a fuller articulation of feminist theory with critical theory.[26] But I think it is clear that his concept of the new sensibility, arising from his Freudian-Marxist groundwork in *Eros and Civilization*, is highly compatible with the critique of male supremacy and heterosexism in its prefigurative transformation of the immediate social relations of one's lifeworld.

Perhaps the major difference between Marcuse and postmodernists lies in the very concept of subjectivity itself. Derrida and Foucault abandon the notion of the subject as an archaic residual from Western philosophical logocentrism, arguing that the subject is positioned by language and thus loses a great deal of transformational efficacy. Although Marcuse, like Adorno, recognizes that subjectivity has become politicized in an era of total administration, he holds out hope that the subject can liberate itself from what he calls "false needs" in *One-Dimensional Man*. This notion of false needs earns the wrath of postmodernists who insist on the relativity of needs as well as of language. But in fact Marcuse does not construct a definitive list of needs reflecting his own modernist-European cultural sensibility. He indicates that needs are false when they are imposed from above (and self-imposed unnecessarily). Needs dictated by reason, ever his Hegelian-Marxist standard of validity, are by definition true. Marcuse follows early Marx in making clear that he anticipates great diversity in the patterns of nonalienated needs (as Marcuse's student, William Leiss, elaborates in *The Limits to Satisfaction*).[27]

Marcuse holds onto the distinction between true and false needs, risking condemnation by postmodern relativists. He retains a regulative notion of the free and rational subject in order to suggest the possibility and necessity of lifeworld-grounded social change, rejecting both Adorno's unnuanced negative dialectics and totalizing eschatologies that leave no room for volition, hence liberty. One can retain a postmodern notion of subjectivity if one stresses the discursive capacities of the person who not only receives texts but, in the process of reading, strongly rewrites them; this provides a model for a normative notion of democratic public discourse.[28]

Marcuse, Nietzsche, Deconstruction

If postmodern capitalism is characterized by the dispersal of ideologizing texts directly into the sense and sentience of the quotidian lives people lead—e.g., via advertising—one needs to ground resistance in people's literary competencies. Derrida's central claim is that every reading is a writing, a version of the text that is inseparable from a noumenal notion of the "text itself." Indeed, there are no "texts themselves" for postmodernism but only versions, including readings. A postmodern version of critical theory, which addresses the narrativization of domination in late capitalism, is consistent with Marcuse's *Eros and Civilization, One-Dimensional Man*, and *An Essay on Liberation*. But Marcuse does not develop this version of critical theory explicitly. For his part, Habermas rejects the conservative tendencies of postmodernism in "Modernity versus Postmodernity"[29] and *The Philosophical Discourse of Modernity*.[30] And Habermas's own reconstruction of historical materialism in the two volumes of *The Theory of Communicative Action* restricts subjective agency to dialogue, failing to expand that category to include a variety of literary and discursive activities absolutely essential in order to transform late capitalism.[31] That is why Habermas's utopian concept of the ideal speech situation sounds like warmed-over John Stuart Mill and not a strong version of critical theory in its own right. Although I basically agree with Habermas's critique of postmodernism's frequent neoconservatism, I do not think that his communication-theoretic reformulation of critical theory goes far enough. Rather, it duplicates the reformism of his earlier *Knowledge and Human Interests* in which he introduces a neo-Kantian bifurcation of technical and self-reflective/communicative modes of action.[32]

I have already sided[33] with Marcuse's version of science and technology against Habermas's critique of his alleged "heritage of mysticism."[34] Central to Marcuse's *Essay on Liberation* is a vision of a new science and technology, which Marcuse derives from a Marxist reading of Nietzsche. This raises the Nietzsche question, as I called it in *Decline of Discourse*. Nietzsche is the basis for both Marcuse's version of critical theory and Derridean deconstruction, which suggests multiple Nietzschean personalities. Inasmuch as there is no singular Nietzsche but only versions, I would observe that individual stances on the Nietzsche question suggest quite different political inflections. The prophetic Nietzsche of gay science helps Marcuse articulate the new sensibility's emancipatory relationship to concepts and nature, whereas Nietzsche's notion of language as a prison house animates Derrida's postpolitical relativism.

I endorse the prophetic, emancipatory reading of Nietzsche begun by Marcuse in *Eros and Civilization*. There can be a radical Nietzsche, just as there can be a radical concept of postmodernity that stands not for disillusionment and venality but for the fulfillment of what Marx called prehistory in a regime of true needs, happy science, and democratic public discourse. Postmodernism can elaborate positive notions of needs, science, and discourse,[35] especially when it links a radicalizing reading of Nietzsche to the Marxist critique of domination—something utterly foreign to postmodernists who either condemn politics (Lyotard) or simply ignore it (Derrida's famous claim that "the text has no outside").

It is very important to understand that texts are nucleic communities through which power is transacted. Although the world is not all text, all texts are worlds, modes of social being. Nietzsche helps us seek out power in surprising places, which is precisely Foucault's important contribution to understanding criminality and sexuality as political and literary institutions. Unfortunately, unlike Marcuse, Foucault has no utopian concept of politics, even though his critique of the disciplinary society reads remarkably like Marcuse's analysis of total administration in *One-Dimensional Man*. Foucault is trendier than Marcuse these days for reasons that have more to do with cultural and intellectual real-estate value than with intrinsic theoretical merit. For that matter, the playful frissons of new French theory are much more fashionable than the architectonic constructions of German critical theory. Barthes and Baudrillard overtake Habermas in this context largely because they can be read casually, even cited authoritatively, without sustained analysis or exegesis. Critical theory declines when it exacts too high a price from readers, who are accustomed to facile engagements with texts. Hence, Foucault's excurses on discipline replace Marcuse's analysis of domination.

In the process, we lose Marcuse's vivid critique and utopian imagination. *One-Dimensional Man* echoes what Marcuse calls "the chance of the alternatives," leaving open the door of radical social change. Contemporary postmodernists cynically disdain the political, endorsing ironism as sufficient social theory. Even Jameson's *Postmodernism, or the Cultural Logic of Late Capitalism* eschews systematic social theory in favor of an immanent critique of postmodernism. But pastiches do not replace political and social theory, even if constructed with Jameson's considerable literary skill. Today "theory" is all the rage on university campuses, especially in the humanities. But what passes for critical theory is only an engagement with the possibilities of literary and cultural readings and not also a systematic approach to social theory, which is dismissed as naively modernist in its narrative pretensions. Where humanities people study Adorno and Marcuse, aesthetic and cultural readings are divorced from substantive analyses of domination and thus lose their critical edge.

Literary theory flourishes, but political critique declines. That is precisely what is wrong with postmodernism, for which Marcuse is a remedy of sorts. The revival here of Marcuse is not intended to relive the sixties, which have long since been commodified. But we could remember the sixties as the last, best time when personal and public transformations not only overlapped but fed into one another. For example, extremely interesting things happened in the year 1968, ranging from political assassinations and the May movement (which in a sense catalyzed poststructuralism and postmodernism) to the Tet Offensive, which might be seen as the dawn of postmodernity. I do not glorify those times, especially since the sixties are now a consumer durable, whether tie-dyed T-shirts worn to Grateful Dead concerts or the reissue of Beatles' music on compact disc. But some of us who came of age politically during the sixties did so in large measure through Marcuse, who introduced us to the Frankfurt School, from which we learned so much. Marcuse helped theorize the lives we led, which were genuinely "years of hope," as Gitlin described them.[36] Only in that context could Breines dedicate a Marcuse reader to both Adorno and Ho Chi Minh.[37]

In my *Cultural Studies as Critical Theory*, I trace the Frankfurt roots of cultural studies back to the 1960s, when the New Left realized that "the whole world was watching" and thus began to understand the screens of power[38] for what they are. This agenda of cultural studies is virtually impossible without Marcuse, who connected the analysis and critique of false needs to a critical theory of mass media and popular culture. In this regard he extended Horkheimer and Adorno's analysis of what they called the culture industry in *Dialectic of Enlightenment*. Although Horkheimer and Adorno recognized the tremendous import of the culture industry, they did not devote much attention to close analyses of cultural production and reception.[39] The Frankfurt theorists disdained the popular as a site of stupefaction in late capitalism.[40]

Marcuse's own *One-Dimensional Man* reiterates the section in *Dialectic of Enlightenment* on the culture industry. And yet Marcuse engaged the popular in more sympathetic terms because, I believe, he recognized that mass culture is not monolithic but heterogeneous. His *Essay on Liberation* amplifies the transformational potential of the counterculture, a force that was either ignored or condemned by Horkheimer and Adorno, both of whom felt threatened by the more extravagant expressions of youth culture. I am not saying that Marcuse celebrated drugs and rock music as politically authentic.[41] Rather, he recognized fissures in the edifice of mainstream mass culture which could be pried open still further. That the counterculture and New Left failed to presage serious transformations of American society, as Marcuse acknowledged in *Counterrevolution and Revolt*, does not discredit his openness to cultural counterhegemony.

Cultural studies is scarcely possible without some commitment to the heterogeneity and relative autonomy of culture (which Bakhtin calls polyvocality.) The Birmingham School emphasizes differences between class cultures in the United Kingdom.[42] Ryan and Kellner, in their important *Camera Politica*, an exemplary document of a Frankfurt-oriented cultural studies, suggest that mainstream Hollywood movies are not devoid of critical insights.[43] Feminist cultural studies emphasize the critical possibilities available to feminist cultural producers and consumers.[44] A Left cultural studies requires the assumption of autonomous or semiautonomous subjects capable of reading and writing strongly—exactly the same assumption animating Derridean deconstruction, albeit without deconstruction's aversion to political narratives.

Marcuse in America

Unlike almost all of his Frankfurt colleagues (Leo Lowenthal excepted), Marcuse remained in the United States after the Second World War ended, taking up teaching positions at Brandeis and then University of California–San Diego. Marcuse wrote for Americans, although he did not necessarily "write down." He was stylistically less dense than Adorno, and he engaged with the popular in ways that set him apart from his erstwhile Frankfurt colleagues. Moreover, Marcuse was politically active in the New Left, although the notion that he was somehow its "guru" is farfetched, especially inasmuch as few New Leftists yet comprehended *One-Dimensional Man* as a contribution to the corpus of Marcuse's critical theory. If there was a New Left guru, it was C. Wright Mills, whose work on power elites was central to the original Port Huron Statement of the Students for a Democratic Society (SDS).[45] Although Mills is claimed by American sociologists for his critique of Parsons[46] and in that context is even transmogrified into a neo-Weberian, Mills's *Marxists* indicates his affiliation to the tradition of Western Marxism. Mills described himself as a "plain Marxist." He also inaugurated the term *postmodernity*. Interesting work remains to be done on the complementarity between Mills and Marcuse.

Marcuse's engagement with America both reflected and produced his engagement with the transformational opportunities available in the lifeworld, including culture. Although I am not attempting a reductive sociology of knowledge, it is clear that Marcuse was less mandarin than Adorno, whom he otherwise closely resembled in his basic theoretical orientation. I would argue that Marcuse, in books such as *Reason and Revolution* and especially *One-Dimensional Man*, accepted Horkheimer and Adorno's basic critique of the Enlightenment, which grounded Adorno's later *Negative Dialectics*.[47] Marcuse broke away from Adorno in his involvement in 1960s new social movements, which had a valuable, if unfulfilled, prefigurative potential. Marcuse's sympathy with new social movements anticipates Habermas's later use of them as vehicles of his notion of communicative rationality and counterhegemonic consensus formation.[48]

As I said at the outset, a Marcusean theoretical agenda today would have two foci: critical cultural studies and work on social movements, largely from the perspective of political sociology. These research applications would embody Marcuse's perspective regarding, on the one hand, the relative autonomy of the lifeworld (through their concrete studies of cultural production, reception, and resistance), and, on the other, movement formation and mobilization. This sort of work is already under way, albeit frequently without a Marcusean imprimatur. The best antidote to Adorno's depressive negative dialectics and to postmodern theory's utter abandonment of the political is, as I have indicated, a differentiated concept of the lifeworld, from which all sorts of cultural and political projects spring. In many respects, this antidote retains and at the same time transcends Adorno's and Foucault's close attention to the micropolitics of discipline and domination. A Marcusean critical theory applied in the venues of mass culture and social movements analysis is less dogmatic than Adorno and Foucault were concerning the cooptability of critical and radical projects. This is not to say that Marcuse was blissfully unaware of the blockages to various radical projects. Even cursory readings of *One-Dimensional Man*, *Counterrevolution and Revolt*, and *The Aesthetic Dimension* indicate the extent of Marcuse's skepticism about heroic refusals or resistances in late capitalism.

We need to retrieve Marcuse's contribution to a critical theory with practical intent. Although I admire Habermas's reformulation of historical materialism for its ambitious scope, I have sided with Marcuse's utopianism about new science and technology. Today there is a minor Habermas industry, attesting to Habermas's skill at legitimating critical theory in the academy. But Habermas ignores the body, discourse, and gender, among other things. He has failed to learn from postmodernism and feminism. His neo-Kantianization of critical theory regresses behind Marcuse, Adorno, and Horkheimer, as I and others have duly noted. Indeed, in some respects, Habermas is closer to Weber than to Marx. And we are in the midst of a Weber renaissance, first in the personage of Giddens and now in Bourdieu, who is the latest Continental theoretical "find." The best medicine against Weber remains Marcuse's magisterial 1964 lecture on "Industrialization and Capitalism in the Work of Max Weber."[49] Weber's own ambivalence about rationalization resembles the postmodernist aversion to the philosophy of history, which attains global dimensions in the celebration of the putative end of communism.

Whether or not the Marcuseanization of critical theory's agenda of cultural studies and political sociology of new social movements requires fresh Marcuse scholarship is somewhat beside the point. This collection of essays aims to revitalize Marcuse, albeit without necessarily academicizing him. The challenge for Marcuseans is not to canonize him but to use his inspiration in order to explore questions of discourse and practice somehow off-limits to negative dialectics and communication theory, not to mention orthodox Marxism. Postmodernism asks important questions about the discursive nature of the disciplinary society, even if postmodernism cannot provide dynamic political answers, given its antipathy to politics and power.[50] I am simply suggesting that by returning to Marcuse, we can engage these postmodern problems of discourse and domination in non-cynical, mobilizing ways, thus diminishing the momentum of post-Marxism.[51] That is reason enough to reread Marcuse.

Notes

1. See, for instance, Peter Dews, "Power and Subjectivity in Foucault," *New Left Review* 144 (March-April 1984): 72–95, and *Logics of Disintegration: Post-Structuralist Thought and the Claims of Critical Theory* (London: Verso Books, 1987).

2. For example, Michel Foucault, *Discipline and Punish: The Birth of the Prison*, trans. Alan Sheridan (New York: Pantheon Books, 1977).

3. See Trent Schroyer, *The Critique of Domination* (New York: Braziller, 1973).

4. See, for example, Jean-Francois Lyotard, *The Postmodern Condition: A Report on Knowledge* (Minneapolis: University of Minnesota Press, 1984).

5. Max Horkheimer and Theodor Adorno, *Dialectic of Enlightenment*, trans. John Cumming (New York: Herder and Herder, 1972).

6. Theodor Adorno, *Aesthetic Theory* (London: Routledge and Kegan Paul, 1984).

7. See Herbert Marcuse, *The Aesthetic Dimension: Toward a Critique of Marxist Aesthetics* (Boston: Beacon Press, 1978).

8. See Fredric Jameson, "Postmodernism, or the Cultural Logic of Late Capitalism," *New Left Review* 146 (July-August 1984): 53–93, and Fredric Jameson, *Postmodernism, or the Cultural Logic of Late Capitalism* (Durham, N.C.: Duke University Press, 1991).

9. Herbert Marcuse, *An Essay on Liberation* (Boston: Beacon Press, 1969).

10. Herbert Marcuse, *One-Dimensional Man: Studies in the Ideology of Advanced Industrial Society* (Boston: Beacon Press, 1964).

11. Herbert Marcuse, *Eros and Civilization: A Philosophical Inquiry into Freud* (New York: Vintage Books, 1955).

12. Ben Agger, *Fast Capitalism: A Critical Theory of Significance* (Urbana: University of Illinois Press, 1989).

13. Ben Agger, *The Discourse of Domination: From the Frankfurt School to Postmodernism* (Evanston, Ill.: Northwestern University Press, 1992).

14. Daniel Bell, *The End of Ideology* (Glencoe, Ill.: Free Press, 1960).

15. Lyotard, *The Postmodern Condition*.

16. Mark Crispin Miller, *Boxed In: The Culture of TV* (Evanston, Ill.: Northwestern University Press, 1988).

17. Ben Agger, *A Critical Theory of Public Life* (London and New York: Falmer Press, 1991), *Cultural Studies as Critical Theory* (London and New York: Falmer Press, 1992), and *Discourse of Domination*.

18. Enzo Paci, *The Function of the Sciences and the Meaning of Man* (Evan-

ston, Ill.: Northwestern University Press, 1972), and Paul Piccone, "Phenomenological Marxism," *Telos* 9 (Fall 1971): 3–31.

19. Marcuse, *One-Dimensional Man*, 84–120.

20. Marcuse, *An Essay on Liberation*, 31–54.

21. See Russell Jacoby, *Social Amnesia: A Critique of Contemporary Psychology from Adler to Laing* (Boston: Beacon Press, 1975).

22. For example, Allan Bloom, *The Closing of the American Mind* (New York: Simon and Schuster, 1987).

23. Marcuse, *Eros and Civilization*, 157–79, and *The Aesthetic Dimension*, 69.

24. Marcuse, *An Essay on Liberation*.

25. See Chris Weedon, *Feminist Practice and Poststructuralist Theory* (Oxford: Basil Blackwell, 1987) and Jane Flax, *Thinking Fragments: Psychoanalysis, Feminism, and Postmodernism in the Contemporary West* (Berkeley: University of California Press, 1990).

26. See Jessica Benjamin, *The Bonds of Love: Psychoanalysis, Feminism, and the Problem of Domination* (New York: Pantheon Books, 1988), and Ben Agger, *Gender, Culture, and Power: Toward a Feminist Postmodern Critical Theory*, forthcoming.

27. William Leiss, *The Limits to Satisfaction: An Essay on the Problem of Needs and Commodities* (Toronto: University of Toronto Press, 1976).

28. Agger, *Decline of Discourse*.

29. Jürgen Habermas, "Modernity versus Postmodernity," *New German Critique* 22 (1981): 3–14.

30. Jürgen Habermas, *The Philosophical Discourse of Modernity* (Cambridge, Mass.: MIT Press, 1987).

31. Jürgen Habermas, *The Theory of Communicative Action*, vol. 1 (Boston: Beacon Press, 1984), and *The Theory of Communicative Action*, vol. 2 (Boston: Beacon Press, 1987).

32. Jürgen Habermas, *Knowledge and Human Interests* (Boston: Beacon Press, 1971).

33. Ben Agger, "Marcuse and Habermas on New Science," *Polity* 9, 2 (Winter 1976): 158–81.

34. Habermas, *Knowledge and Human Interests*, 32–33.

35. See Andreas Huyssen, *After the Great Divide: Modernism, Mass Culture, Postmodernism* (Bloomington: Indiana University Press, 1986), and David Harvey, *The Condition of Postmodernity* (Oxford: Basil Blackwell, 1989).

36. Todd Gitlin, *The Sixties: Years of Hope, Days of Rage* (New York: Bantam Books, 1987).

37. Paul Breines, ed., *Critical Interruptions: New Left Perspectives on Herbert Marcuse* (New York: Herder and Herder, 1970).

38. Timothy W. Luke, *Screens of Power: Ideology, Domination and Resistance in the Informational Society* (Urbana: University of Illinois Press, 1989).

39. Exceptions include Theodor Adorno, "A Social Critique of Radio Music," *Kenyon Review* 7, 2 (Spring 1945): 208–17; Theodor Adorno, "How to Look at Television," *Quarterly of Film, Radio, and Television* 3 (1954): 213–35; Theodor Adorno, "The Stars Come Down to Earth: The Los Angeles Times Astrology Column: A Study in Secondary Superstition," *Telos* 19 (Spring 1974): 13–90. For a discussion of the Frankfurt School's sociology of culture, see David Zaret,

"Critical Theory and the Sociology of Culture," *Current Perspectives in Social Theory* 12 (1992): 1–28.

40. See Martin Jay, *Adorno* (Cambridge, Mass.: Harvard University Press, 1984).

41. See Ben Agger, *The Discourse of Domination*, 219–38.

42. See Stuart Hall, ed., *Culture, Media, and Language: Working Papers in Cultural Studies, 1972–1979* (London: Hutchinson, 1980); Stuart Hall, "Cultural Studies: Two Paradigms," *Media, Culture, and Society* 2 (January 1980): 57–72; Stuart Hall, "Signification, Representation, Ideology: Althusser and the Post-Structuralist Debates," *Critical Studies in Mass Communication* 2 (June 1985): 91–114; Stuart Hall, "On Postmodernism and Articulation," *Journal of Communication Inquiry* (Summer 1986): 45–60; Stuart Hall, *The Hard Road to Renewal: Thatcherism and the Crisis of the Left* (London: Verso, 1988); Dick Hebdige, *Subculture: The Meaning of Style* (London: Methuen, 1979); Dick Hebdige, *Hiding in the Light: On Images and Things* (New York: Routledge, 1988); Paul Willis, *Learning to Labour* (Farnborough, Eng.: Saxon House, 1977); Paul Willis, *Profane Culture* (London: Routledge and Kegan Paul, 1978).

43. Michael Ryan and Doug Kellner, *Camera Politica: The Politics and Ideology of Contemporary Hollywood Film* (Bloomington: Indiana University Press, 1988).

44. See Teresa de Lauretis, *Alice Doesn't: Feminism, Semiotics, Cinema* (Bloomington: Indiana University Press, 1984); Teresa de Lauretis, *Technologies of Gender: Essays on Theory, Film and Fiction* (Bloomington: Indiana University Press, 1987); Laura Mulvey, *Visual and Other Pleasures* (Basingstoke, Eng.: Macmillan, 1988); Suzanna Danuta Walters, "Material Girls: Feminism and Cultural Studies," *Current Perspectives in Social Theory* 12 (1992): 59–96.

45. C. Wright Mills, *The Power Elite* (New York: Oxford University Press, 1959). See also Jacoby, *Social Amnesia*; Gitlin, *The Sixties*.

46. C. Wright Mills, *The Sociological Imagination* (New York: Oxford University Press, 1959).

47. Theodor Adorno, *Negative Dialectics* (New York: Seabury Press, 1973).

48. Jürgen Habermas, "New Social Movements," *Telos* 49 (Fall 1981): 33–37.

49. Herbert Marcuse, *Negations: Essays in Critical Theory*, trans. Jeremy Shapiro (Boston: Beacon Press, 1968): 201–26.

50. See John O'Neill, "The Disciplinary Society: From Weber to Foucault," *British Journal of Sociology* 37, 1 (March 1986): 42–60.

51. See Steven P. Dandaneau, "An Immanent Critique of Post-Marxism," *Current Perspectives in Social Theory* 12 (1992): 155–77.

Paul Breines

Revisiting Marcuse with Foucault: *An Essay on Liberation* Meets *The History of Sexuality*

While the rituals by which I affirm my links to the New Left of the 1960s have become fewer and further apart, one has remained constant. Every year since 1975, when I began teaching history at Boston College, I have assigned a book by Marcuse. In recent years, it has been exclusively *An Essay on Liberation*, which has the advantages of brevity, accessibility, and of being addressed to and about part of a college-age generation— mine—which is also that of many of my students' parents.

That I find myself in that sense *in* the book must have a lot to do with why I have fixed on it for use in a course. I probably like to teach it, in other words, because in vivid ways it reminds me who I am, or have been. Or better, it reminds me who I have aspired/desired/fancied myself to be: a certain sort of 1960s New Leftist student-then-academic visible through the cluster of forms and styles (personal, intellectual, social, sartorial, cultural, political) through which I have given meanings to my life for several decades. Actually, although *An Essay on Liberation* has been my choice, any of Marcuse's books would have worked, since what excited me so much about them is that each one made me want to *be like* its author: to think as wonderfully strangely as he could, to write such books, and to live, experience, and practice the ideals I found in them—the polymorphous perversity, the Great Refusal, the new sensibility, and the biological basis for socialism. It is no wonder that teaching *An Essay on Liberation* became so significant a ritual in my life.

But if annual reckoning with that text has been the most enduring sign of my ties to the New Left, Marcuse and his book have not gone unchallenged. For over the past four years, in my course on twentieth-century European intellectual history, I have assigned Michel Foucault's *History of Sexuality*, vol. 1, alongside Marcuse's *Essay on Liberation*, presenting them as counterpoised interpretations of the sexual politics of the sixties, specifically of 1968. Initially, I imagined this merely as pedagogically appealing: for my students, an interesting, potentially lively confrontation between a humanist Marxist and an antihumanist, a Freudian and an anti-Freudian, and so on.

It soon emerged, however, that more was involved. My ritual, I found, was being transformed from one primarily of keeping a faith to one of inner conflict. My students were soon stuck with a teacher suffering from vertigo brought on by the experience of being caught between conflicting, Marcusean versus Foucauldian, discourses. Never having been a structuralist, indeed, having been a foot soldier for the humanist (Lukács–Gramsci–Frankfurt School inspired) Marxist critique of structuralism and Althusser, I was belatedly discovering poststructuralism—and losing my immunity to it. As Marcuse had in the mid-1960s, so now Foucault, with his own dark, passionately critical, combative, sensual writing and his unerring capacity to disturb, was getting under my skin.

I have, in other words, been revisiting Marcuse with Foucault, specifically, revisiting *An Essay on Liberation* with *The History of Sexuality*. This essay is a report on some of what was found. Not the least important was a signifier, "myself." When I began to grapple with Marcuse and Foucault, my focus was on the differences between the two, the political-historical-epistemological ruptures—not least the fault-lines between modernism and postmodernism—that so sharply separate them. *An Essay on Liberation*, it should be noted, was published in 1969. It was promptly and widely recognized as the manifesto of the explosions of 1968, especially of the antirepressive, left-Freudian sexual politics that figured so largely in those explosions. Marcuse's smallest book, *An Essay on Liberation*, made its author's name big because of its links to a remarkable social upheaval. *The History of Sexuality* was published in 1976, by which time Marcuse's impact had waned while Foucault's had waxed. That shift had in turn been partly a result of the defeat and dissolution of the movements of the sixties. Foucault's *History* is indeed one of the great critiques, a kind of gay science, of the sexual politics of the New Left.

As the revisiting continued, however, I eventually found "myself" in the sense that I noticed how the differences between Marcuse's *Essay on Liberation* and Foucault's *History of Sexuality* also represent differences—New Left/post–New Left—within me, the commentator. The self I found when I found myself was a self divided. This was useful in turn, for it enabled me to notice that there are differences not only between the two texts but inside each of them as well. Marcuse's *Essay*, for example, has its Foucauldian possibilities while Foucault's *History* has its Marcusean, New Left markings. I want, then, to push, squeeze, and rub these two books against but also *into* each other because they are pushing, rubbing, and squeezing me into and against myself. This may be the case—I certainly hope it is—for others of you as well.

Preliminary Disclaimers

In what follows, I suggest that Foucault's *History of Sexuality* is a critical, and also a gay, dialogue with the New Left of the 1960s. I believe there is evidence in the text for thinking about it in these terms, but I do magnify the evidence with the tools of intuition and projection. I think this is a useful approach but definitely not the only one. I am also aware that in discussing Marcuse and Foucault as I do, I run the risk of flattening the differences between them.

More insistent and consistent followers of Foucault, for example, could argue that, far from being friendly to poststructuralism, I undercut it by normalizing it—that I erase what is really subversive and strange in Foucault by reducing his work to its alleged links to the familiar and more acceptable, that is, to the New Left. Similarly, one more loyal to Marcuse than I am might criticize me for diluting and denigrating Marcuse's position by tying it to the trendy and finally conformist poststructuralist bandwagon. Up to a point, I appreciate and accept both criticisms, although I would not agree that the New Left is simply familiar and acceptable or that poststructuralism is simply trendy and conformist. Beyond a certain point, though, it seems to me that the more strict Marcusean and the more strict Foucauldian positions slide into a place that is at least as odd as my own.

First, both criticisms fail to acknowledge the hybrid character of Marcuse's and Foucault's thinking. Second, both criticisms presuppose the very sort of essentialism—that, for example, Foucault's position finally has an essence, that essence being essentially different from the essence of

Marcuse's position—of which each theorist is quite critical. Finally, both criticisms seem to presuppose the purist's fear of miscegenation and hybridity—the fear that, in matters of theory, the mulatto, the "mixed" marriage, the bisexual, is contaminated. This is a fear worth overcoming. A postfinal caveat: My goal is not to generate a synthesis of Marcuse and Foucault but rather to deal with a midlife crisis, a symptom of which is the division between Marcuse and Foucault that is inside me, giving me both pain and pleasure.

One could also object that my approach compares a political, occasional, highly conjunctural Marcuse essay with a major Foucault work of theory. In this respect, it is Marcuse's *Eros and Civilization* (1955) that should be studied in relation to Foucault's *History of Sexuality*. The point is taken. My response is that Foucault's book is also very much an occasional text in the sense that it is *occasioned by* 1968, by the collapse of the hopes and expectations voiced in Marcuse's *Essay on Liberation* and shared in many ways by Foucault himself, at least by some of his selves or subject positions. And it is the relations between the texts and 1968 that interest me here.

Such an interest does not, I hope, entail a reduction of either text to its occasion, its situation. Indeed, being linked to a situation, a historical moment, is in any case not merely a limit. On the contrary, part of the greatness of *An Essay on Liberation* stems precisely from its immersion in the flow of 1968: from its attempt to link itself directly to the most utopian possibilities of a social movement, borrowing from it while offering it a language that, at the time, seemed adequate to its desires. And this from a thinker known and often reviled by Leftists and reformers for his pessimism.

Similarly, much of the greatness of *The History of Sexuality* stems from its position as an analysis of a defeat and a dissolution of that liberationist movement. In this sense, Foucault's book can be thought of in connection with such works as Marx's *Capital*, Antonio Gramsci's discussion of hegemony in the 1920s, Leon Trotsky's *Revolution Betrayed*, Wilhelm Reich's *Mass Psychology of Fascism* in the 1930s, Max Horkheimer and Theodor Adorno's *Dialectic of Enlightenment* in the 1940s, and even Marcuse's *One-Dimensional Man* in 1964. That is, Foucault's *History* is one of those rare and astonishing works that manages to push an account of a failure of a specific revolutionary project so intensively that it reaches the level of a radically new conception of past, present, and future. It embodies what Russell Jacoby has called the "dialectic of defeat": the radical possibilities of disillusionment. The sad point, which *The History of Sexuality* puts in bold relief, is that for great advances in critical social theory, nothing serves better than a revolution that failed or failed to occur.

Foucault's *Gauchisme*

It is time to turn to the two books themselves and to consider, first, the question of the New Left. From the opening pages to his book's end, Foucault makes clear that he is not only in a critical discussion with Reich and Marcuse—that is, with a certain tradition of Leftist sexual politics—but also through that tradition, in a critical exchange with 1968 and its legacies. As Foucault writes at the close of the next to last chapter, "This whole 'antirepressive' struggle [and he is referring to the left-Freudian theorists here] represented nothing more but nothing less—and its importance is undeniable—than a tactical shift and reversal in the great deployment of sexuality." But, he continues, one cannot "expect this critique [Reich's explicitly, Marcuse's implicitly] to be a grid for the history of that deployment." "Nor the basis," Foucault concludes—and here he extends his critique from the theorists of antirepressive sexual politics to the social movement that found its voice, and itself, in that theory—"for a movement to dismantle it."[1]

Yet Foucault's critique of the New Left version of the "repressive hypothesis" and his seemingly un-Foucauldian (because hopeful) suggestion of a movement to dismantle the deployment of sexuality are themselves more closely linked than is often noticed to the New Left, to 1968, and to a tradition of *gauchisme* that was revived in that year. Such critics as Alex Callinicos and Christopher Norris have not, for example, glimpsed the extent to which Foucault's work generally and his *History of Sexuality* in particular are not so much a departure from political engagement itself as a critique of the New Left, of 1968, from within.[2] For Foucault's perspective is linked to, even as it departs from, the New Left's own anticentralist Left rather than to the segment of its intellectuals who, in disillusion over dissolution, opted for either despair or the political right.

To borrow a phrase, if not quite the intended meaning, from David Halperin, Foucault's politics seem neither despairing nor disillusioned but, rather, queer.[3] That is, even as I want to link his political offerings to a Western *gauchiste* heritage and to the New Left of the 1960s, Foucault stretches, breaks with, and transforms those heritages. By *gauchisme* I mean the anticentralist outlook historically associated with anarchism and workers councils or soviets, that was revived and recast in the 1960s and was influenced in that period by, among other works, Marcuse's *Eros and Civilization* and his *One-Dimensional Man*. Foucault's critique of 1968 should be seen as *gauchiste*—and New Leftist—to the extent that it notices and highlights the presence of power in the liberationist movement itself and is a critique of that power's operations within the movement.

Especially pertinent here are the several pages in the chapter on "Method" in *The History of Sexuality* outlining a number of propositions regarding power. These pages offer some theses that are original and distinctively Foucault's *and* are extensions of impulses rooted in the New Left. "Relations of power," he writes, "are not in a position of exteriority with respect to other types of relationships (economic processes, knowledge relationships, sexual relations), but are immanent in the latter."[4] Power relations, in other words, are not outside anything.

This is, of course, now a somewhat familiar Foucauldian theme. As expressed in *The History of Sexuality*, the theses concerning power not being external to any relations can be read as having had as its most important addressee the New Left and 1968. In many respects, Foucault's book is a fairly direct rejoinder to Marcuse's *Essay on Liberation*. The second is that Foucault's book, like Marcuse's, was shaped by the political/cultural atmosphere of the movements of the sixties. In referring to that political/cultural atmosphere, I mean it to include the New Left movements' rejections of the preceding Stalinist atmosphere. Foucault had known both; so had Marcuse.

My final point is that Foucault's theses, coming as I suggest they do from the New Left, are also a break with it. That is not to say Foucault broke with critique and resistance to power. It is only to say that the division between Foucault and Marcuse, between Foucault and the New Left, is deep and not really bridgeable. Since that division is also "not in a position of exteriority with respect" to myself but is inside me, it is no wonder that I am having difficulties.

If this makes some sense, then the same may be true of the following. When Foucault stresses that power relations are not in positions external to other (apparently nonpower) relations, he is reminding the New—and old—Left of unsettling things. That, for example, power relations are as operative in the revolution and the revolutionaries as they are in the state and the police. And that power relations are not outside the bodies/minds of those who oppose power. And that when power is thought of as being located only "out there" in capital, bourgeois property, and the state, that very way of thinking is itself entwined in power relations; it is, indeed, a vital mechanism of sustaining the invisibility of power's position of interiority.

In the same section of *The History of Sexuality*, Foucault writes that "the representation of power has remained under the spell of monarchy. In political thought and analysis, we still have not cut off the head of the king."[5] In my view, this is addressed to the general reader and, with special emphasis, to the New Left. Part of the impulse for *The History of Sexuality* was its author's conviction that especially but not only in its sexual politics the New Left had fatally fancied itself outside power. This, I believe, is Foucault's *gauchisme en procès*, his Leftism in transformation. To see where he took it, the frame of discussion needs to be expanded.

Foucault, of course, sought to generate "a different theory of power" and of resistances to it.[6] It is in connection with the issue of resistances to power that Foucault specifically and critically invokes (and partially misreads) Marcuse. "Points of resistance are present everywhere in the power network. Hence there is no single locus of great Refusal [Marcuse's well-known term, which I think he uses first in *Eros and Civilization* in his discussion of Narcissus's refusal of the regime of instrumentalized sex], no soul of revolt, [no] source of all rebellions, or pure law of the revolutionary."[7] Here Foucault carries *gauchisme* and the New Left onto new terrain, where the historic idea of revolution itself is put into question. For the "plurality of resistances" he proposes as an alternative to the Great Refusal is the point at which his Leftism becomes "queer politics." Foucault's *History* discloses not only what is often called his "micropolitics" but also a kind of antipolitical politics of "mobile and transitory points of resistance." These points of resistance, he writes, "furrow across individuals themselves, cutting them up and remolding them, marking off irreducible regions in them, in their bodies and minds."[8]

Two observations are in order. One is that Foucault partly misrepresents Marcuse's notion of "Great Refusal." It is an ambivalent idea in Marcuse's work. On the one hand, his usages of the notion are not far from Foucault's supposedly contrasting idea of a plurality of resistances, since the Great Refusal actually refers to highly specific acts by individuals and small groups whom Marcuse views precisely as "mobile and transitory points of resistance." On the other hand, there is the Hegelian-Marxist implication of Marcuse's Great Refusal—the implication that already present within those microresistances is the jumbo synthesis of Great Refusal as "The Revolution." This latent part of Marcuse's Great Refusal is the part Foucault highlights. And as I read Foucault here, he is also attributing that master narrative of the revolution to 1968 as a whole.

The second observation regarding Foucault's critique is this: While I find it apt, I also find that it elides the indebtedness of his own critique to the sixties movements he criticizes. For it was those movements themselves that had already begun to generate in practice the idea of a "plurality of resistances." Again, although Foucault sets himself polemically apart from the New Left, he can also be seen as working through its contradictions from within.

Plural Resistances: Foucault and Marcuse

"It is doubtless," Foucault writes, "the strategic codification of these points of resistance that makes revolution possible." Then Foucault makes a striking statement but says it so quietly and matter-of-factly that one can easily miss the point. He initially appears to be on the verge of something uncharacteristic, namely, putting forward a vision of revolution. Instead, he does something characteristic. He proposes that the operation by which revolution emerges from a strategic codification of points of resistance is not liberation but something "somewhat similar to the way in which the state relies on the institutional integration of power relationships."[9] I take Foucault to mean that when the revolution comes into being by codifying mobile points of resistance to power, it carries out operations similar to those carried out by the state. A quiet but firm *adieu à la révolution, n'est-ce pas*? This is, fairly precisely, a New Left *and* a post–New Left critique of the New Left's drive toward revolution.

But it is also more than that. In this connection, I want to focus on a specific dimension of the notion of *The History of Sexuality* as the gay science of 1968 and the notion of his politics as being queer. Again, the publication date is significant. For 1976 situates the book not only in the wake of the defeat and break-up of the sixties movements but in the first waves of a birth. *The History of Sexuality* is not simply post–New Left; it is also post-Stonewall. In 1969, partly inspired by the models of black and New Left resistances swirling around them, gay men fought off a police raid on the Stonewall Inn, a well-known gay bar in lower Manhattan. Such raids had been regular. Only the resistance was new. The event has become a symbol of the emergence of gay liberation in this country and elsewhere in the West. I suggest that Foucault's book is part of this process.

More specifically, I propose that *The History of Sexuality* can be read as a gay critique of the historic heterosexism and homophobia of the Left, including that of both the New Left of the 1960s and the Reichean branch of the Freudian Left. I cannot fully prove this and am ready to accept the charge that my proposal reads into rather than from Foucault. Yet his book is certainly a critique of the widely presumed normalness and normativity of heterosexuality. What I read into this is that the critique is in part energized by its author's sense that heterosexuality was considered normative and obligatory also—even particularly—in the New Left, which thought of itself as subversive and liberatory in its sexual politics.

If one could accept this hypothesis, at least for exploratory purposes, then Marcuse, specifically his *Eros and Civilization*, becomes especially relevant. His 1955 "philosophical inquiry into Freud" was more than an exception to homophobia on the Left: During the late sixties and early seventies, Marcuse's *Eros* was retrieved and developed as a fertile and informing text of an emergent and sometimes hesitant gay liberation movement.

Paul Robinson's *Freudian Left*[10] of 1969 is one of several indications of how, in the years just before and after publication of Foucault's *History*,

Marcuse's version of the "whole antirepressive struggle" had special meanings for gays in a New Left that was not prone to let them speak. Although he was not yet writing as an openly gay historian, Robinson's account of the work of Geza Roheim, Wilhelm Reich, and Marcuse can now be seen as part of an effort by gay New Left intellectuals to theorize their sexuality. Signaling the important (and previously little regarded) place occupied by the figure of the homosexual in *Eros and Civilization*, Robinson stressed that Marcuse moved beyond liberal tolerance to an affirmation of homosexual persons. They are, in fact, the bearers of the repressed polymorphous perverse sexuality and natural bisexuality that haunts the dominant, genitally organized, patriarchal family, which reproduces heterosexuality. "In a certain sense," Robinson proposed, "the social function of the homosexual [in *Eros*] was analogous to that of the critical philosopher."[11]

The year 1971 saw the publication of Dennis Altman's *Homosexual: Oppression and Liberation*,[12] which made explicit the significance of Marcuse for gay liberation. Noting, in pre-Foucauldian fashion (in his subsequent work, Altman would go on to bring Marcuse and Foucault into connection with each other), that "Western societies are remarkable for their strong repression of sexuality," Altman indicated that his discussion of this matter was "particularly indebted to Marcuse for his exploration of the concepts of repression and liberation."[13] Along with Norman O. Brown, whose *Life against Death: The Psychoanalytical Meaning of History*[14] had also appeared in 1955, Marcuse, Altman writes, has "reminded us . . . that any real theory of sexual liberation must take into account the essentially polymorphous and bisexual needs of the human being."[15] Recently, Jonathan Dollimore's *Sexual Dissidence*[16] recalls the significance of Marcuse and Brown in the formation of gay liberation theorizing before Foucault.

Paul Robinson's desire-filled insight into connections between homosexuals and critical theorists is suggestive regarding another dimension of the Marcuse/Foucault relation. This dimension concerns the ground, if any, on which critical theory and its bearers, critical theorists, might be standing. For Marcuse, the Hegelian-Marxist critical theory itself is a historically *determinate negation* of late capitalist society, grounded in the dialectical unfolding of reason as reality. Even when, as in the recent era, critical theory no longer has its classical foundation in the proletariat, it is nevertheless still not based merely on an ethical, or subjective, postulate. It thus avoids the unfortunate fate of being, in Hegelian terms, a case of the "beautiful soul." This is evident in all of Marcuse's works, not least *An Essay on Liberation*. There, as elsewhere, critical theory, endangered and beleaguered as it may be due to the severing of its historic ties to a systemically revolutionary class, is nonetheless presented as being linked to History, to what poststructuralists call a master narrative.

Foucault's view is different, and in this regard, Judith Butler's *Gender Trouble: Feminism and the Subversion of Identity*[17] is very helpful. She suggests that Foucault's preface to the diaries of the hermaphrodite Herculine Barbin may contain a quite different approach to the origins and grounds of critical theorizing. The genealogical critique of the reified categories of sex, she writes, is, in Foucault, "the inadvertent consequence of sexual practices that cannot be accounted for within the medicolegal discourse of a naturalized heterosexuality." Herculine Barbin, Butler adds, "is not an 'identity,' but the sexual impossibility of an identity."[18]

These observations help illumine Foucault's approach to the question of the foundations of critical theory and its representatives. As I see it, for Foucault, the site from which critique is set in motion is not something big, such as the revolutionary class, nor something immanent in history. It is, rather, something small, marginal; precisely something that does not fit into the larger picture. Genealogical critique of normal sexuality is an "inadvertent consequence," an eccentricity. In Marcuse, critique is attached to the underlying mainstream; in Foucault, it is not a mainstream that is prized but a marginality.

Butler's *Gender Trouble* offers another suggestion that refers back to Robinson's linkage of the homosexual and the critical theorist. Foucault, she proposes, idealizes Herculine Barbin's "happy limbo of a non-identity"; indeed, he *identifies* with her/him. Butler proceeds perceptively to criticize Foucault for reproducing the lapse and erasure originally made by the doctors who had tried to explain Herculine Barbin. Like them, Foucault, according to Butler, fails to note the lesbian possibilities of the puzzling body and experience in question.[19]

Before concluding with several words on the presently almost unavoidable theme of identity, I have two related comments on the matter of the foundations of critical theory and theorists. The first concerns sexual difference and gender in Marcuse and Foucault, both of whose writings have been critically embraced (at different stages) by women for feminism. What Butler observes about Foucault can be transposed to Marcuse's enthusiasm, in *An Essay on Liberation*, for the expressions of androgyny and unmanly gentleness in the late 1960s counterculture, as well as to the delicate, almost effeminate sensuality of his pages on Narcissus in *Eros and Civilization*. Although I cannot yet fully develop the idea, I propose that there are affinities between the (admittedly small) gender-mixed aspects of Marcuse's and Foucault's work and the anti-authoritarian *gauchisme* of their respective politics. The related thought I do want to develop is that there is a proximity mediating the distance between Marcuse and Foucault on the issue of the grounds and bearers of critique. For in Marcuse, there is an interesting because quite un-Hegelian, un-Marxist, and fairly Foucauldian tendency to value the margins and the marginalities when speaking of the bearers of critique: homosexuals and other sexual nonconformists, avant-garde artists, racial minorities, youth revolters, bohemians, critical intellectuals without audiences, and the like. In this respect, too, he and Foucault are closer than first glance suggests.

But Marcuse was, after all, a Hegelian-Marxist, very much influenced by Lukács's *History and Class Consciousness*. Having noted this, it is worth adding that Marcuse and Foucault are both in important respects Heideggerians. Marcuse's Hegelian-Marxism was always somewhat at odds with itself. In *An Essay on Liberation*, for example, there is a lively battle between a kind of demasculinizing *gauchisme* and a kind of Lukácsian-Leninism, that is, a privileging of theory and theorists. Much less of the latter appears in Foucault, although parallel tendencies and tensions do arise in his work as well.

One also finds in Foucault—and rarely if at all in Marcuse—a hostility to intellect (and implicitly to intellectuals). This impulse in Foucault has connections both to a certain anti-intellectual tradition with a particular profile among French intellectuals going back to Proudhon and subsequently to Georges Sorel, Charles Maurras, and others, and to hostility to intellectuals in *gauchisme* from Roberto Michels early in this century through Daniel Cohn-Bendit in 1968. But in Foucault, anti-intellectual impulses—which I find in his disdain for the "immense verbosity" and "giant mill of speech" to which the medical intellectuals subject the body—seem to stem from a kind of naturalism of the body, as if it might have an integrity outside discourse and beyond the deforming reach of intellect.

I want to pursue this through its links to the matter of utopianism in Marcuse and Foucault. Marcuse, of course, is renowned as a utopian theorist. In *An Essay on Liberation* he calls for a move from Marx to Fourier, from realism to surrealism. On the other hand, it was Marcuse's consistent conviction that such a move was precisely not utopian. In his view, the "advanced industrial societies" had pushed material development to the point of having rendered obsolete (that is, having *made realizable*) the utopian (that is, the purportedly unrealizable) elements of utopian theories, including his own theorizing about the historical-erotic prospects of "nonrepressive desublimation."

As he is in his other works, so in *The History of Sexuality* Foucault is a critic of utopian theorizing generally and in particular of Marcuse's anti-repressive sexual utopianism. But as Judith Butler observes, in both his preface to *Herculine Barbin* and *The History of Sexuality*, one can glimpse a tendency toward what she calls a "sentimental indulgence in the very emancipatory discourse his analysis . . . was meant to replace."[20] That is, she discovers in Foucault "a kind of anti-emancipatory call for sexual freedom" and rightly terms this a "constitutive contradiction"[21] in and of his work.

This recalls my suggestion that an implicit metaphysics of the body can be gleaned from *The History of Sexuality*. Butler locates Foucault's almost hidden sexual utopianism in his idealization of Herculine Barbin's "intersexed body" and in the references in his *History* to the innocent and bucolic pleasures of intergenerational sexual relations between the mentally simple farmhand and the young girl in the village of Lapcourt in the 1860s. Foucault even speaks there in most un-Foucauldian terms of the "timeless gestures" and "barely furtive pleasures" as if they existed outside or before the onset of what he terms "a whole machinery for speechifying, analyzing, and investigating"; that is, before the onset of a regulative sexuality. Foucault, too, in other words, offers an emancipatory sexual politics and at least elements of a sexual utopianism. According to it, Butler suggests, the genealogical overthrow of "sex," as it has been discursively produced, results in "the release of a primary sexual multiplicity," a "happy limbo of [sexual] non-identity"—notions that are "not so far afield from the psychoanalytic postulation of primary polymorphousness or Marcuse's notion of an original and creative bisexual Eros subsequently repressed by an instrumentalist culture."[22]

Readers can also discern utopian moments in Foucault's occasional but each time pointed use of the phrase, "one day, perhaps." I have located only two such uses in *The History of Sexuality*, but one appears in the book's dramatic closing sentences. There Foucault writes that "we need to consider the possibility that one day, perhaps in a different economy of bodies and pleasures"—with the "one day, perhaps," containing the utopian longing—"people will no longer quite understand how the ruses of sexuality, and the power that sustains its organization, were able to subject us to that austere monarchy of sex, so that we became dedicated to the endless task of forcing its secret, of exacting the truest of confessions from a shadow."[23] But as if in hasty retreat from the territory he had just entered, Foucault reasserts the Foucault he wants us to see, closing the book (and the door on utopia he had just opened) with this emphatically post-1968 observation: "The irony of this deployment is in having us believe that our 'liberation' is in the balance."[24] The irony within the irony is that Foucault appears to be, along with Marcuse, one of the "us" who believed.

Conclusion

Having begun with Marcuse and Foucault, I hope to have reached Marcuses and Foucaults. If so, I am at the end but for the question of identity. On this matter, I will not try to explore their identities but will instead remark that Marcuse's *Essay* and Foucault's *History* are notable and notably linked in a genre. What I have in mind is not simply the genre of books from the Left dealing with sex and politics but a perhaps less familiar genre of handbooks of sexual-political identities for Left (and not only Left) intellectuals. In a certain but definite sense, these are all works dealing with, in Marcuse's phrase, "a new sensibility," with political questions being presented *as* questions of sensibility.

This class of books—and here Marcuse's *Eros and Civilization* must be included—contains the efforts of two men of the Left, one apparently straight, the other gay, both writing about relations among sex, knowledge, politics, power, and society, and about how and by *what sorts of people and practices, including the practices of their bodies*, those relations, which constitute us and our practices, might be transformed. In this respect, while they have roots in the projects of such varied predecessors as Oscar Wilde, Alexandra Kollontai, surrealists, dadaists, Mabel Dodge Luhan, Reicheans, and others, the books under discussion are part of a genre that has greatly expanded since 1968.

They entail, I am proposing, politics of identities in the specific sense that they embody the efforts and the desires of their authors to exceed themselves, to contend with themselves as if they were, in Nietzsche's remarkable closing words of *Ecce Homo*, "Dionysus versus the Crucified"—not as one or the other, but as the contention itself, as the "versus." *Gender Trouble*, too, is in this genre. In very different ways, these works are, in Butler's phrase, subversions of sexual-political identity as stable, essential, grounded in a natural sex, but they are also works *of* sexual-political identities and styles through which we, like those who wrote them, make ourselves up. I should, however, speak only for myselves.

Notes

1. Michel Foucault, *The History of Sexuality*, vol. 1, *An Introduction*, trans. Robert Hurley (New York: Random House, 1978), 131.
2. Alex Callinicos, *Against Postmodernism: A Marxist Critique* (New York: St. Martin's Press, 1990); Christopher Norris, *Uncritical Theory: Postmodernism, Intellectuals, and the Gulf War* (Amherst: University of Massachusetts Press, 1992).
3. David Halperin, "Bringing Out Michel Foucault," *Salmagundi*, forthcoming.
4. Foucault, *History of Sexuality*, 94.
5. Ibid., 88–89.
6. Ibid., 90–91.
7. Ibid., 95–96.
8. Ibid., 96.
9. Ibid.
10. Paul A. Robinson, *The Freudian Left: Wilhelm Reich, Geza Roheim, Herbert Marcuse* (New York: Harper and Row, 1969).
11. Ibid., 207–8.
12. Dennis Altman, *Homosexual: Oppression and Liberation* (New York: Outerbridge and Dienstfrey, 1971).
13. Ibid., 58.
14. Norman O. Brown, *Life against Death: The Psychoanalytical Meaning of History* (Middletown, Conn.: Wesleyan University Press, 1959).

15. Altman, *Homosexual*, 61.

16. Jonathan Dollimore, *Sexual Dissidence: Augustine to Wilde, Freud to Foucault* (Oxford: Clarendon Press, 1991).

17. Judith Butler, *Gender Trouble: Feminism and the Subversion of Identity* (New York: Routledge, 1990).

18. Ibid., 23.

19. Ibid., 95–96.

20. Ibid., 96.

21. Ibid., 97.

22. Ibid., 96.

23. Foucault, *History of Sexuality*, 159.

24. Ibid.

Peter Marcuse

Marcuse on Real Existing Socialism: A Hindsight Look at *Soviet Marxism*[1]

Herbert Marcuse's *Soviet Marxism*, published in 1958,[2] has, I believe, a great deal to contribute to an understanding of current developments in the Soviet Union and Eastern Europe. I admit that I am not unbiased in the matter,[3] but I hope the argument presented here will be examined on its own merits. It is derived from *Soviet Marxism* but also uses material from Herbert Marcuse's other major treatment of the topic (the last and, to my knowledge, the only other piece he wrote directly on Eastern Europe)—namely, the text of a talk given at the Bahro Congress in Berlin in 1978, "Protosocialism and Late Capitalism: Toward a Theoretical Synthesis Based on Bahro's Analysis."[4]

The recent events in the Soviet Union and its successor states have had a major impact on Marxism, both in theory and in practice, in the First World and in the Third World. It is easy to see in the Third World; in many countries national struggles took place in the space opened by the tensions between the great powers, and in others, such as Cuba, liberation movements had become largely dependent on the Soviet Union for their strength. In the First World, the impact has been stronger: Although the Left continues to adhere to the position that Soviet-style systems had nothing to do with Marxist goals, the collapse of the Soviet regimes has, perhaps unconsciously, been internalized as a defeat for the principles of socialism and the political parties that had espoused socialism. The collapse was certainly seen as a defeat for socialism by the Right, just as it was successfully sold as such in the popular media.

Marxist theoretical analysis has likewise had a strange aspect, strange in that it has largely shied away from analysis of what in the past produced the present. Rather, such analysis speaks only of the present and the future, predicting the disasters attendant on the forced introduction of a market system into hitherto centrally planned states. At best, Marxist theory has been applied to the present class structure of the successor states. The occasion has not as yet been used to reflect on whether the present events require a reexamination of the past and whether that reexamination would lead to a different analysis of the long-term processes of transformation and the "transition to socialism" with which Marxism has always been concerned. And yet, it seems to me, a reexamination is indicated, for, with very few exceptions, the course of recent history was hardly predicted by even the acutest analyses of the past. Granted, predictions of ultimate collapse abounded on both Left and Right. But it can hardly be said that the development of the reform movement within the Soviet Union, symbolized by *glasnost* and *perestroika*, was widely foreseen, or that the almost spontaneous melting away both of entrenched Stalinist regimes and of the efforts at their reform would occur as they did.

I will argue that Marxist theory does indeed suggest the likelihood of the trends that have led to the present results. I will further argue that both *Soviet Marxism* and "Protosocialism and Late Capitalism" can contribute significantly to an understanding of those trends and of their consequences today. Both pieces deduced the presence of trends toward change, toward reform, in the Soviet system. In *Soviet Marxism*, the analysis suggests an internal necessity of liberalization in the Soviet Union, although it is skeptical as to whether such "liberalization" will change the essentially nonsocialist character of the system. In the text on Bahro, Marcuse calls Bahro's book *The Alternative: A Contribution to the Critique of Actually Existing Socialism* "the most important contribution to Marxist theory and practice to appear in several decades," and Bahro in turn sees in internal developments in the German Democratic Republic (GDR) the hope of a fundamental change in the character of the Soviet-style society from within.

I want to focus here on the discussions of these liberalizing trends in the Soviet Union in these two works, although in each work that discussion is really secondary to the main analysis. In "Protosocialism," Marcuse's attention is devoted to the implications of Bahro's analysis of East European societies for the possibilities of change in the West, in particular the relationship of "base" and "superstructure" and the relationship of change in individuals and change in societal structures. Bahro finds agents of change present in Soviet-style systems while Marcuse explores the existence of analogous agents in the West. In the process, Marcuse does not explicitly critique Bahro's analysis of the situation in the GDR. Silence suggests consent, although perhaps criticism of Bahro's views of East German society was muted out of concern about solidarity, since Bahro was in jail at the time for espousing precisely those views.

The formulations of *Soviet Marxism* were more unambiguously influenced by the circumstances in which they were written. Alone among Marcuse's works written under contract, it was the product of stays at the Columbia and Harvard Russian research centers during the period of McCarthyism and at the height of the agitation justifying the Cold War. Outright defense of the Soviet Union was not in the cards at either institution, nor would Marcuse have wished to undertake such a defense; but an explicitly Marxist approach based on the validity of Marxist conceptions would not have been widely understood either. On the other hand, a wholesale attack on all aspects of Soviet society would have been easily misconstrued as an attack on socialism and a rejection of Marxism as a whole. Thus we encounter an "immanent critique" of Soviet Marxism, with which Marcuse begins the book and which he is at pains to justify theoretically in language that, today, seems forced and unnecessary to the main task.[5] But the circumspection served the purpose of permitting a Marxist critique of a pseudo-Marxist theory and a pseudosocialist (later "protosocialist") reality, which was the real aim of the book. The immanent critique is productive. Its discussions of the transformation of Marxian theory as it "ceases to be the organon of revolutionary consciousness and practice and enters the superstructure of an established system of domination" are fascinating. The detailed study of the dialectic as it is transformed from a critical tool of social analysis to an all-embracing philosophical system, for instance, is a model of clarification in the history of ideas.[6]

Marcuse's critique of Soviet Marxism as theory and ideology is not, however, my subject here. My concern is twofold: to examine the discussion of Soviet-style societies to gain a better understanding of the forces for change in that society, and to isolate important implications that analysis has for an assessment of the forces of change within our own society. A better understanding of the "base-superstructure" relationship is important for this process, since questions about the relative power of base and superstructure to produce fundamental changes in the social system as a whole remain central for both theoretical analysis and political practice.

Social Transformation in the Soviet Union

If the Soviet Union was not capitalist, it was not socialist either, "in the sense envisaged by Marx and Engels."[7] In classic Marxist terms, the difference lay in the ownership of the means of production: They were nationalized but not socialized, not put in the control of the "immediate producers." This was seen as an intermediate stage in the transition to socialism, in early Soviet Marxism.[8] The beginning question then is, what forces of change might be foreseen from the early and "transitional" revolutionary period? How might one, given a Marxist analysis, expect things to develop?

Understanding the early changes poses no particular problem; Marcuse spends little time on them and presents nothing that is radically different from previous accounts. The Bolshevik Revolution took place ("it is assumed that the initial intention and objective of the Bolshevik Revolution was to build a socialist society"[9]), not in an industrially advanced country, but in a backwards one. Without outside help (historically, it was the success of the German revolution that never came that Lenin had counted on), socialism was on weak footing. Add to the lack of positive help the presence of capitalist hostility and encirclement, and no normal development toward socialism, no smooth transition, could be expected. Marcuse places the turning point early, as far back as 1923, when it became clear that there would be no immediate revolution either in Germany or in any other advanced capitalist country. No "choice" was presented to the Soviet leadership under the circumstances; all energy had to be directed toward the building of the industrial base, leading to an ever-growing "priority of the Soviet state over Soviet Workers."[10] Whether the development was a result of internal weakness or the international context remains unclear. On the one hand, international events "defined" Soviet Marxism;[11] on the other hand, "there are no 'extraneous' causes . . . for all apparently outside factors and events will affect the social structure only if the ground is prepared to meet them, . . . if they 'meet' corresponding developments within."[12] In the end, one may argue that the distinction between internal and external is inapplicable in this situation in any event because "the class struggle is international by its very nature."[13] However that may be, "if the dialectical law of the turn from quantity into quality was ever applicable, it was in the transition from Leninism (after the October Revolution) to Stalinism. The 'retardation' of the revolution in the West and the stabilization of capitalism made for qualitative changes in the structure of Soviet society."[14]

But where do we go from there? Is the result, neither capitalist nor socialist, static? Or does "Soviet nationalization, under the historical condition of its progress, . . . possess an inner dynamic which may counteract the repressive tendencies and transform the structure of Soviet society"? Marcuse, writing in the first years of the Khrushchev regime but thirty years before Gorbachev, gives a clear yes. Why?

A number of threads come together to supply the answer. The first gives primacy to the external situation. It is worth quoting at length the key passage:

The "class interest" of the bureaucracy (that is, the common denominator of the special interests of the various branches of the bureaucracy) is linked to the intensified development of the productive forces, and administrative progress into a "higher stage of socialism" would most effectively secure the cohesion of Soviet society. On the other hand, the Soviet state has consistently diverted a very large sector of the productive forces (human and material) to the business of external and internal militarization. Does this policy forestall the transition to the "second phase"? The compatibility of an armament economy with a rising standard of living is more than a technical economic problem. The maintenance of a vast military establishment (armed forces and secret police) with its educational, political and psychological controls perpetuates authoritarian institutions, attitudes, and behavior patterns which counteract a qualitative change in the repressive production relations. Inasmuch as the bureaucracy is a separate class with special privileges and powers, it has an interest in self-perpetuation and, consequently, in perpetuating repressive production (and political) relations. However, the question is whether the repressive economic and political relations on which this bureaucracy was founded are not increasingly contradicting the more fundamental and general interests and objectives in the development of the Soviet state.

If our analysis of Soviet Marxism is correct, the answer must be affirmative. The fundamental Soviet objective in the present period is the breaking of the consolidation of the Western world which neutralizes the "interimperialist conflicts" on whose effectiveness the final victory of socialism depends. . . . In the Soviet Marxist analysis, Western consolidation is based on a "permanent war economy," which . . . sustains the rapid development of productivity in the capitalist countries and the integration of the majority of organized labor within the capitalist system. . . . The capitalist war economy is in turn sustained by the "hard" Soviet policy, which also stands in the way of Soviet progress to the second phase where it can effectively compete with capitalist capabilities. Consequently, the first step must be the relaxation of the "hard" policy. This, however, is a matter of internal as well as foreign reorientation, of shifting the emphasis from military and political to more effective economic competition, and of liberalizing the Stalinist bureaucracy.[15]

One might fantasize that Gorbachev had read these words, were it not that Marcuse was banned reading in the Soviet Union and, to my knowledge, no translation of *Soviet Marxism* was ever made there. It is certainly a quite precise description of the direction of the Soviet leadership's foreign and domestic policy after 1985.

But there are also more purely internal reasons to anticipate a liberalization in the Soviet Union. One goes back to the question of class structure. The bureaucracy dominates the decisions of the state, but its class base is uncertain. It does not "own" the means of production; it merely controls them. The distinction is important.[16] At bottom it means that the appropriation of the profits of production by the bureaucracy is not legitimized; its political and legal foundations are weak. If the bureaucracy is to consolidate its position, even in the short run, it must support the increase in production that can give rise to an increase in the standard of living as well as a general sense of progress.[17] Given such progress, the continuance of overt repression becomes not only unnecessary but counterproductive.

Technological progress itself requires liberalization, according to another strand in the argument supporting its likelihood. Technological rationality is inconsistent with a rigid, repressive, and command-centralized organization of economic activity; fully developed, it even "contains an element of playfulness."[18] While technological rationality and human freedom are hardly identical, the former is a means to the increased productivity that, today, any form of social organization must have if it is to be stable. The technological rationality that Marcuse foresaw as a necessity for the survival of the Soviet state did not of itself promise human freedom. And Marcuse is clear in his view that liberalization is not identical with socialism, that the necessity of technologically rational development does not imply the necessity of socialization of the means of production, of their control by their immediate producers. It is not socialism that Marcuse sees as the result of the internal dynamics of Soviet development, but a relaxation of overt repression.

An element of determinism creeps into the logic that links technological rationality with political liberalization. We know little of the social dynamics involved in the production of Sputnik and the Soviet Union's space program. Whatever it was, it produced highly advanced technology in a very repressive overall environment. And in just what sense can one speak, as Marcuse does at the end of the first paragraph in the long quotation above, of a "contradiction" between the interests of a bureaucracy in control of the state apparatus and the "more fundamental and general interests and objectives in the development of the Soviet state"? The movement toward increased productivity sometimes seems to take on a life of its own, a "law of history" governing the actions of men and women.[19] But the grounds for believing in a strong pressure for improved production in Soviet society are strong even without appeal to such laws.

Marxist theory itself provides a further impetus for liberalization in a state that historically takes such theory seriously, however it may distort, codify, or subvert its content. "The continued promulgation and indoctrination in Marxism may still turn out to be a dangerous weapon for the Soviet rulers."[20] For Marxist theory holds out the prospects of the free play of human faculties, the expression of creativity, liberation from repressive relationships in productive work and in play—concepts that can be tested against immediate experience and can raise problems if the gap is too large and too visible.[21]

Given the strength of these arguments, liberalization becomes merely a matter of time. Khrushchev's policies seemed to bear out the predictions of theory as Marcuse was writing; Gorbachev's policies, after Marcuse's death, seem to be incontrovertible confirmation. But then the question arises, why did liberalization fail and the entire Soviet system, not merely its most repressive elements, fall? Here we must go beyond *Soviet Marxism* for an answer and look at some of the more far-reaching implications of its analysis.

The Precipitous Decline

Marcuse clearly expected the Soviet economy to continue to grow, to increase both in productivity and output, and to produce more and more consumer goods at the same time as basic production advanced. He quotes Khrushchev's claim that the Soviet Union had, already in 1953, "the means for high-speed, simultaneous development of heavy industry, agriculture, and light industry."[22] Marcuse concludes that, "given conditions under which the growing production . . . is not . . . utilized for wasteful and destructive purposes, production is likely to generate the material and cultural wealth that would permit . . . the second phase."[23] Marcuse's use of the word "permit" rather than "produce" is not accidental. This is not technological determination, and Marcuse insists that radical social change must accompany technological progress for technology to be liberating. That technological progress would occur, however, Marcuse had no doubt.

Of course, events did not progress in a smooth or linear fashion in the Soviet Union or anywhere in Eastern Europe. The arms race in fact intensified, partially because of direct pressures from conservative administrations in the United States. The initial response in the Soviet Union was not liberalization but its opposite; Khrushchev's hold on power was broken by the mid-1960s. Thus when liberalization came, it may have come too late.

The arms race did not simply undercut the full use of the resources of the Soviet Union in developing its economy; because of the particular conditions of political repression, it actually undermined the advance of technical knowledge and the technical foundations for advancing productivity. Technological rationality, in Marcuse's exposition, is a necessary ingredient of advances in productivity and is itself a function of (made increasingly possible by) such advances. In a technologically underdeveloped society, a level of production must first be reached that makes technologically rational behavior both necessary and effective. But that rationality is itself a prerequisite of reaching the productivity level. Thus a vicious circle exists. It cannot be broken all at once; the areas in which technological thinking is most advanced slowly spill over into other areas, so that advances occur in different areas at different times and places. But precisely this process was aborted in the Soviet Union in the concentration and *isolation* of the best technical work in the space and armaments programs. Thus to the inherent chicken-and-egg dilemma were added blockages to "normal" processes. The failure to achieve balanced and wide-ranging technological progress was in part the foreseeable result of developments Marcuse's analysis did in fact explore.

Coupled with these externally rooted explanations for the decimated state of Soviet and most East European economies by the late 1980s were purely internal factors—economic problems inherent in any socialistically organized and Marxist-grounded society. Some economic problems, of course, had little to do with socialism but were simply decisions that could have gone either way under the control of the leadership: excessive centralization, distortions of investment policy, lack of responsiveness to technological changes and to changes in consumption desires, too rigid education policies, an inflexible command structure, failure to utilize markets at least as sources of information, and the clogging of other information flows.[24] A repressive political system and the absence of market indicators made errors in economic decisions more difficult to correct, but signs of problems existed; a "wiser" leadership might indeed have done much better, even within structures inherently required by Marxist theory in a socialist economy.

Socialism and Surplus Consciousness

Other aspects of the retarded progress of the Soviet economy, however, have more to do with its unambiguously socialist characteristics. The first involves the role of Marxist theory. No system that relies for its legitimacy, if not its direction, on Marxism, even in the form of Soviet Marxism, can afford to engage in activities absolutely counter to the fundamental principles of that theory. Thus, for instance, the exploitation of workers needs to be ameliorated, not exacerbated, over time. Except in conditions of wartime or other dire emergency, the living and working conditions of industrial workers must be improved. In the Third World, likewise, a political system basing itself on the concepts of Soviet Marxism cannot exploit workers as imperialist countries would. Unemployment cannot be tolerated on any broad basis; consequently, the simple layoff of workers whose jobs become obsolete is a difficult matter. In these and other ways, a Soviet Marxist system suffers from competitive disadvantages compared to a system without such inhibitions. It might be expected, therefore, that a Soviet-style system would lag behind in the competition with advanced capitalist economies, even under the best of circumstances.

The second socialist-grounded factor in the impeded progress of the Soviet economy has to do with the role of the bureaucracy and the intelligentsia. Technical advance comes from a technical intelligentsia. However recruited, however organized, whatever their ideology, a level of education and training and ability is necessary to produce innovation, and those possessing these levels are among the critical components of the intelligentsia. Bahro speaks of them as developing a level of "surplus consciousness" under real existing socialism: "free human capacity that is no longer absorbed by the struggle for existence." More specifically, "The industrial, technological-scientific mode of production, in which intellectual labor becomes an essential factor, engenders in the producers . . . qualities, skills, forms of imagination . . . that are stifled or perverted in capitalist and repressive noncapitalist societies."[25]

Both Bahro and Marcuse saw such surplus consciousness as a factor, perhaps *the* factor, that would permit a break in the "chains of domination, the subjugation of human beings to labor."[26] Marcuse, in his discussion in 1978, was not concerned to look at the impact of the increase in such surplus consciousness on technological progress, but the exploration is potentially fruitful. For the specific forms by which "skills, forms of imagination . . . are . . . perverted" are quite different in capitalist and repressive noncapitalist societies. Capitalism provides rewards for the application of these forms of imagination to inherently unrewarding tasks, real existing socialism did not. Marcuse (and Bahro) saw surplus consciousness as leading to the end of the domination of compensatory inter-ests[27] over emancipatory interests. Real existing socialism did not permit the full expression of emancipatory interests, and therein lay the potential for an explosive rupture of its system of domination. This was the main point of Bahro's analysis,[28] and Marcuse applied it, *mutatis mutandis*, to capitalism.

But within capitalism, compensatory interests are much more fully ad-dressed than within real existing socialist societies. That was not an issue that either Bahro or Marcuse, in his essay on Bahro, explored, although clearly, from extensive discussions in *One-Dimensional Man* and later works, it was an essential part of Marcuse's overall assessment of the strengths and weaknesses of capitalism. The consequence is that surplus consciousness can be better harnessed to the interests of technological ra-tionality in a capitalist than in a repressive socialist society. Even at the level of observation of everyday life, the result is evident. The dynamism, the energy, the search for innovation that is found in the leading advanced industrial societies, however distorted and unproductive in a human sense it may be, seems altogether absent under real existing socialism, appear-ing, if at all, in artistic work but certainly not in industrial production or the commercial service sector. Put crudely, the Soviet-style systems gave up one set of incentives for technological progress and increasing produc-tivity without substituting any equally effective alternative.

Thus, Marcuse's analysis would suggest that, even apart from "exter-nal" pressures and even apart from the particular mistakes of particular leaders or particular organizational strategies, it is unlikely that repressive Soviet-style socialism could satisfy its promise of increased productivity and a steadily increasing quality of life for its populations. Whether un-der the best of circumstances (i.e., no "external" problems and a "wise" leadership) a socialist economy might be expected to perform as or more efficiently than a capitalist one, we cannot tell from the historical record, but there is certainly some theoretical reason to doubt it. At least in the short or intermediate range, heightened productivity is not able to give the goal of socialism its appeal, its promise for the future. That conclu-sion, which is implicit in all of critical theory, emerges concretely from Marcuse's analysis of Soviet Marxism.

The bureaucracy itself could have attempted to overcome these inher-ent difficulties in advancing productivity, either through measures designed to increase the allocation of resources to consumption (and thus to enhance the satisfaction of compensatory interests for the intelligentsia) or through reforms in the organizational hindrances to progress (the over-centralization, etc.). There is some evidence that, at least in the GDR, the bureaucracy tried such reforms, such as the shift of industrial capacity to the production of consumer goods in 1971. But in the Soviet Union, contrary to Marcuse's expectations that the bureaucracy would seek minimal reform in the quest for self-preservation, the bureaucracy abandoned Gorbachev and moderation, preferring to endorse a snowballing surrender of the existing bases for their power and prestige to hostile forces of change. Why did this unexpected surrender of the system by the bureaucracy it had produced take place? If the "class interest" of the bureaucracy lay in the reform of the system, as Marcuse states at the beginning of the long quotation cited previously, why did it so quickly abandon that reform?

The answer is that the bureaucracy was not, indeed, a "class" whose ownership of the means of production provided a basis of power and privilege. The bureaucracy did control the productive processes, but control and ownership are not the same thing, as I have already argued. Its class base was uncertain. "Bureaucracy by itself, no matter how huge it is, does not generate self-perpetuating power unless it has an economic base of its own from which its position is derived, or unless it is allied with other social groups which possess such a power base."[29] When "free market" pressures appeared and received powerful support from the outside, when internal political division gave the upper hand to market-oriented forces of change, the bureaucracy quickly realized it could as easily exercise its power in the new system as in the old. Not being dependent on relations of ownership, it had little to lose by a change in those relations and possibly even something to gain. History, with hindsight, vindicates the "nonclass" analysis.

Marcuse recognized from the outset that internal reform was only a possibility in the Soviet Union and that the likelihood that such reform would break through the bounds of real existing socialism to some form more akin to what Marx and Engels had envisaged was an even slimmer possibility. History remains inconclusive as to whether that possibility ever existed. If it did, it probably came closest to manifesting itself in the GDR during the brief period of the *Wende* or in Czechoslovakia at the very beginning of the velvet revolution.[30] In the first case, German unification quickly wiped out whatever possibilities existed; in the latter case, neither the ideological nor the practical political support for a real reform of socialism was ever substantial. In both cases, the external context sealed the fate of whatever possibility for a reform socialism might have developed.

The Ramifications of the Demise

Thus the Soviet Marxist chapter of the narrative of socialism seems closed. Does Marcuse's analysis lead us to any insights into the future? Marcuse's Bahro review, although it abjures any convergence theory,[31] points out strong parallels between real existing socialist and real existing capitalist societies. He finds a drive toward technological rationality in each, although with different motors and different effects. He finds disparate forces for change in each, but none that comes close to an assurance of progress toward a radically different social order—no "revolutionary subject" on either side. Rather, he finds an internalization of subordination, a "transformation of freedom into security,"[32] in both social orders; but he also finds, in both, serious sources of instability, principal among them the existence of a surplus consciousness, of unsatisfied human drives, aspirations, and desires hitherto incapable of fulfillment but now visibly within the range of the possible.[33]

What inhibits the realization of that possibility, what prevents instability from maturing into fundamental change? Here the answer is quite different in the two systems. In the one, the Soviet, it is the combination of internal repression and the external "threat" that justifies it. Liberalization, he foresaw, might be one step in the direction of stability, whether or not of further change. In the capitalist world the situation is rather the opposite. The external threat serves both to justify an internal economic policy, sometimes called the "permanent war economy," and to provide legitimacy to a liberal regime even though that regime falls far short of fulfilling the potential of the technical progress it has made possible. Externally, Soviet Marxist theory had always counted on conflicts among the capitalist powers to provide it with a respite within which to solidify its position internationally; the reality had proved otherwise, ironically, in that the very existence of the Soviet Union and its allies had furnished a basis on which the Western powers have been able to come together and bury their own conflicts. That analysis is not one with which Marcuse significantly disagreed,[34] although he saw many more forces for stability and potentials for progress in the West than the theorists of Soviet Marxism ever saw or acknowledged.

The disappearance of the Soviet Union changes this picture dramatically in the capitalist countries. The threat from outside, which so long justified massive military expenditures and investment in wasteful technology, is harder and harder to find. It is harder and harder to explain the reasons for the continued existence of poverty, repression, injustice, racism, and xenophobia in a world in which the possibility of plenty for all is more and more apparent and its postponement less and less able to be justified by the threat of an outside menace. If worldwide competitiveness increases to the point where economic crises follow each other in an accelerating tempo, the original "anomalous" position in which the Soviet Union found itself at its birth might not confront another protest from below: The revolt this time might come from the most developed countries. If, on the other hand, that competitiveness is brought under control and progress does indeed continue more or less smoothly, the means for capturing surplus consciousness within the confines of compensatory interests may become slimmer and slimmer. Environmental constraints and their human meaning, to which Marcuse was increasingly turning his attention at the time of his death, suggest other limits on the extent to which compensatory interests can forever be at the same time stimulated and satisfied. So the "surplus consciousness" of those doing well, coupled with the discontent of the excluded, under the constraints of a finite natural environment, may yet open the door to a form of liberation that neither Soviet-style socialism nor anti-Soviet-style capitalism has yet made possible.

Notes

1. This essay was first commissioned by Marx Wartofsky and will appear in his edited Festschrift to Robert Cohen, to be published by Kluwer Academic Publishers.

2. Herbert Marcuse, *Soviet Marxism: A Critical Analysis* (New York: Colum-

bia University Press, 1958; new paperback edition with introduction by Douglas Kellner). A Vintage Press edition was published in 1961 with a new preface, and the subsequent French edition likewise has a new preface. See Douglas Kellner, *Herbert Marcuse and the Crisis of Marxism* (Berkeley: University of California Press, 1984), 197–228, both for bibliographic information and a substantive critique. All page references, unless otherwise noted, are to the 1958 edition.

3. Apart from filial affection, those of my own experiences that may color this discussion are described in Peter Marcuse, *Missing Marx: A Personal and Political Journal of a Year in East Germany, 1989–1990* (N.Y.: Monthly Review Press, 1991).

4. It is reprinted in Ulf Wolter, ed., *Rudolf Bahro: Critical Responses* (White Plains, New York: M. E. Sharpe, 1980).

5. "This study attempts to evaluate some main trends of Soviet Marxism in terms of an 'immanent critique,' that is to say, it starts from the theoretical premises of Soviet Marxism. . . . The critique employs the conceptual instruments of its object, namely, Marxism, in order to clarify the actual function of Marxism in Soviet society. . . . [It assumes] that Soviet Marxism (i.e., Leninism, Stalinism, and post-Stalin trends) is not merely an ideology promulgated by the Kremlin in order to rationalize and justify its policies but expresses in various forms the realities of Soviet developments." Marcuse, *Soviet Marxism*, 1. If one accepts that "the theoretical premises of Soviet Marxism" are indeed the theory developed by Marx and Engels and that theory, in Marxist understanding, plays a historical role going beyond ideology, one might as easily have said, "this study is a Marxist critique of Soviet Marxism."

6. Marcuse, *Soviet Marxism*, chapter 7: "Dialectic and its Vicissitudes," 136–59.

7. Ibid., 8, n. 1.

8. Marcuse, agreeing, says that "the abolition of private property in the means of production does not, by itself, constitute an essential distinction as long as production is centralized and controlled over and above the population." Marcuse, *Soviet Marxism*, 81. In "Protosocialism and Late Capitalism," he speaks of "the abolition of private ownership of the means of production" as the "indispensable precondition of socialism . . . [the real difference lies] in the way in which the material and intellectual forces of production are used." Herbert Marcuse, "Protosocialism and Late Capitalism: Toward a Theoretical Synthesis Based on Bahro's Analysis," in Wolter, ed., *Rudolph Bahro*, 24–48.

9. Marcuse, *Soviet Marxism*, 8, n. 1.

10. Ibid., 74.

11. Ibid., 6.

12. Ibid., 3.

13. Ibid., 96.

14. Ibid., 74.

15. Ibid., 171–72.

16. I have explored it in legal terms in "Law, Land, and Property Rights in Eastern Europe," in *The Post-Socialist City*, ed. Michael Harloe et al. (London: Blackwell, forthcoming).

17. Marcuse, *Soviet Marxism*, 118.

18. Ibid., 257. See, in general, chapter 12, "Ethics and Productivity."

19. In a brief discussion of the concept of historical laws in Marxism, Marcuse refers to the "irreversibility" of historical processes determined by the "basic form of societal reproduction," but the example he gives is of the emergence of the feudal system out of the agricultural economy of the late Roman empire! Ibid., 3–4.

20. Ibid., 265.

21. Ibid., 267.

22. Quoted in *Current Digest of the Soviet Press* 39 (7 November 1953): 177.

23. Marcuse, *Soviet Marxism*, 170.

24. Innumerable Western texts expand on these and other issues. One of the less ideological is Janos Kornai, *Economics of Shortage*, 2 vols. (Amsterdam and New York: North-Holland Publishing Company, 1980).

25. Marcuse, "Protosocialism and Late Capitalism," 27.

26. Ibid., 28.

27. ". . . not through a policy of reducing consumption but through a 'genuine equalization in the distribution of those consumer goods which determine the standard of living.'" Marcuse (quoting Bahro), ibid., 35.

28. Based on it, Bahro believed an overthrow of the existing regime in the GDR from the inside was possible. Marcuse did not take a position on Bahro's belief. Marcuse, "Protosocialism and Late Capitalism," 36.

29. Marcuse, *Soviet Marxism*, 109.

30. For more detailed discussion, see my *Missing Marx*.

31. In *Soviet Marxism*, he already spoke of the "fundamental difference . . . paralleled by a strong trend toward assimilation." Marcuse, *Soviet Marxism*, 81. Elsewhere, he speaks of "an essential link between the two conflicting systems . . . in the technical-economic basis common to both systems, i.e., mechanized . . . industry as the mainspring of societal organization in all spheres of life." Marcuse, "Protosocialism and Late Capitalism," 6.

32. Marcuse, *Soviet Marxism*, 191.

33. Marcuse emphasized that the "turn to subjectivity," in Bahro's formulation, was ambivalent. Marcuse "Protosocialism and Late Capitalism," 46. Although Marcuse was also much concerned with what Bahro called the "essentially aesthetic motivation" of socialism, I would suspect he would not have followed Bahro on the road Bahro subsequently took on the relationship of the subjective to the political.

34. See, for instance, Marcuse, *Soviet Marxism*, 99.

Terrell Carver

Marcuse and Analytical Marxism

In this chapter I shall be reviewing the claims of "analytical" or "rational-choice" Marxism and using Marcuse's work to put criticisms of it into better words than mine. This project entails a good deal of stipulative argument to identify the school and its tenets and a certain amount of imaginative reconstruction to put Marcuse into a dialogue with them and their views. As a manipulative narrator I intrude to make this possible, and the reader is further burdened with an introspective account of why it was exciting for me to read Marcuse in the 1960s.

My justification for this exercise is the claim that practicalities in politics can turn on abstract issues in philosophy; specifically, that a fictive encounter between "my Marcuse" and the analytical school will dramatize the political timidity that analytical or rational-choice theory instantiates. It is an interesting question why this encounter has to be fictive. The answer is that the analytical school signally fails to engage on its own behalf with the issues that Marcuse handled so well. I hope that this essay will stimulate analytical Marxists to recognize that their presuppositions must be defended, not just stated, and that they must engage with their critics, not just dismiss them.

Analytical or Rational-Choice Marxism

Much of Marcuse's work reads well now, and it also read well in the 1960s. Or so it seems to me. It also seems that the reasons why this is so in both time frames are similar but not identical. As context changes, so do readings, and so do judgments.

In particular since the mid-1970s, analytical or rational-choice Marxism has come on the scene, beginning (for me) in the very early 1970s with G. A. Cohen's occasional conference and seminar papers given at Oxford and no doubt at numerous other venues.[1] The magnum opus that appeared in the late 1970s had been, so I understood then, some ten or fifteen years in the making.[2] At first glance British analytical philosophy, as done by Cohen, seems to have little in common with the "empirical" social science of Jon Elster and the economic model-building of John Roemer, the two other leading lights of the school.[3] Indeed there are very significant differences in general methodology and particular views. But all three of these writers followed a methodology presumed to be subsequent to, even unconnected with, the approach followed by Marx.[4] The self-characterization of the analytical axis deserves quotation and comment:

> The books in the series [Studies in Marxism and Social Theory] are intended to exemplify a new paradigm in the study of Marxist social theory. They will not be dogmatic or purely exegetical in approach. Rather, they will examine and develop the theory pioneered by Marx, in the light of the intervening history, and with the tools of non-Marxist social science and philosophy. It is hoped that Marxist thought will thereby be freed from the increasingly discredited methods and presuppositions which are still widely regarded as essential to it, and that what is true and important in Marxism will be more firmly established.[5]

I recall finding this advertisement arrogant and ungenerous at the time it was published—indeed, when the publishers were circulating it for comments on the idea of doing the series—and it still strikes me that way. What price methodological pluralism after those snidely coded messages? What is this methodology that is "dogmatic or purely exegetical"? What are the methods and assumptions that are "increasingly discredited"? And what exactly are the "tools of non-Marxist social science and philosophy"? It seemed to me then, and it seems so now, that there are certainly competing accounts of these "tools" based on competing accounts of social science and of science as such, not to mention more specific controversies. Moreover, it is a large presumption that there is some alternative "Marxist" social science and philosophy, when in fact there are dialectical-materialist, Lukácsian, Althusserian, Gramscian, and numerous other variants, even empiricist ones. What is going on when so much that is unspecified is treated so dismissively? This is exclusionary language and does not count for much, so I think, in describing and justifying the analytical or rational-choice approach to the noninitiate.

But since the 1980s the situation has changed for the better, as analytical or rational-choice Marxism has a defender, Alan Carling. Carling is willing to argue the case without the intellectual arrogance and imperialism displayed by the founders, but with an ability to assess what he sees as the strengths and at least certain sorts of weaknesses.[6] He rightly points to the use of what amounts to rational-choice models in Marx's own work, as does Elster: "Rational action is, essentially, action that optimizes in the light of incentives and constraints."[7] He admits the tendency of rational-choice "explanations" to collapse into rationalizations and the failure of rational-choice theory to explain exploitation based on differences of gender.[8] Yet even his work does not confront the so-called grand issues that must necessarily arise, although some are touched on in the critical essays collected by Ware and Nielsen.[9] But Marcuse could be usefully revisited as a way of highlighting these issues, and I propose here to reread him to develop a number of criticisms of analytical or rational-choice Marxism.

Grand Theory

Marcuse's work now looks prophetic. Analytical or rational-choice social theory, including the "Marxist" school, appears to be a manifestation of a good many things he rejected and an inversion of what he recommended. Marcuse questioned the terms of this type of political theory, namely, that theorizing begins with an assumption that individuals may be conceptualized quite apart from and in necessary opposition to "society"; that in their activity as human agents they are "free to choose"; and that their world is one of scarcity and competition. The theoretical terms that analytical or rational-choice theorists promote, however abstractly, presume that material consumption is the sum and limit of life, that collective action is alien and difficult for human individuals, and that a balance of supply and demand represents such harmony as can be achieved in society.[10] Whatever Marxism there is in the analytical or rational-choice school, it is not in their assumptions, which are rather those of theorists taking the "economic approach."

Unlike analytical or rational-choice theory, in which theorists (with their facts or factual assumptions) and politicians (with their values or goals) pursue separate careers (or at least separated functions), Marcuse's work presents the theorist as a political agent in the very act of theorizing. It is clear for Marcuse that theory is aimed at the polity, not at disengaged specialists; and science itself, whether "social" or otherwise, is conceptualized as a political activity: "No matter how one defines truth and objectivity, they remain related to the human agents of theory and practice, and to their ability to comprehend and change their world."[11] Puzzles and paradoxes are not his starting point, as they frequently are for analytical and rational-choice theorists; indeed, he forswears any "escape into . . . that which is only academically controversial."[12]

Marcuse's notion of a scientific problem is really a large-scale political critique—specifically, waste and maldistribution in the contemporary economy and elitism and mystification in contemporary politics. His proof that these are problems is ostensive rather than deductive; the reader is encouraged through example to begin to assess the world differently. Perception for Marcuse is contextual, and his discursive accounts promote a reconceptualization of politics, society, and economy, such that the reader begins to perceive anew. Moreover, it is clear what the result of theorization is supposed to be: judgment and action. Humans do not merely live for themselves in the present and attend to the future as more of the same. They explore self-development and engage in reinvention of the collective context. They are capable of creative thought and social innovation, and that is what theory is intended to encourage.

In theorizing, Marcuse is above all attentive to language, to the way it is used, or could be used, to structure experience, to reveal possibilities, to exercise power, to manipulate, and to mystify. His approach to political discourse is hermeneutic, historical, critical, and creative. In particular he is excellent in his description of the way that elites can maintain power by defining or redefining terms, by divorcing "present" from "past" experience, by pretense and inversion: most notably, his allegations that a "false neutrality" has infected our moral vocabulary and that Orwellian language has become commonplace.[13]

It was easy for some Marxist critics to connect Marcuse with the idealist tradition in German philosophy and to wonder what kind of Marxism he was using—whether in fact his work did not represent in method and substance just what Marx had rejected when he and Engels settled "accounts with our erstwhile philosophical conscience."[14] Was not his work emotional, unrigorous, nonmaterialist, unscientific? Where were the abstract theorizations of Marx's economics and the empirical propositions of his theory of history?

Reading Marx

Marcuse's work made it possible to read Marx differently: The "philosophical," interpretive, exploratory Marx was not just the early Marx. The Marx of the *1844 Manuscripts* had only recently come into English in the early 1960s; this was the "humanist" Marx, who philosophized about life, labor, history, and the human condition. The "determinist," "scientific" Marx was presumed to be the later Marx, though how much later was a matter of debate. Humanists, structuralists, and anticommunists were all agreed on two Marxes, one philosophical and one scientific, though there were opposing views on which was the more significant or interesting.

Marcuse's own views were certainly different, and they certainly influenced me. He linked the early to the late Marx in a very balanced and straightforward way, seeing the propositions concerning commodities and labor in *Capital* as developmental specifications of the theory of alienation in the *1844 Manuscripts*. He put a sharp boundary between Marx's work and nineteenth-century positivism; I note now that Engels did not appear in the index to *Reason and Revolution* at all! Marcuse's approach made it possible for me to see a continuity in Marx's thought, between the substance and the method. The *Grundrisse* and *Capital* were for me just as philosophical, just as exploratory, and just as sensitive to the power of linguistic representation in society as anything done by the early Marx, in fact, more so. Rather than read Marcuse as an idealist who Hegelianized Marx, I read them both as linguistic philosophers of power, as hermeneutic social scientists, as politically committed theorists, and as historical researchers, well aware that whatever "present" we have is necessarily an interpretation of the past. Indeed, all social phenomena are historical, and all investigation is interpretation:

Analysis uncovers the history in everyday speech as a hidden dimension of meaning—the rule of society over its language. And this discovery shatters the natural and reified form in which the given universe of discourse first appears. The words reveal themselves as . . . the terms which society imposes on discourse, and on behavior. This historical dimension of meaning can no longer be elucidated by examples such as "my broom is in the corner" or "there is cheese on the table."[15]

In my view the famous "guiding thread" in Marx's 1859 "Preface to a Contribution to a Critique of Political Economy" is not the centerpiece of Marxism, as Cohen presumes at the outset of his less than "purely exegetical" book;[16] nor can the best of Marx's work be captured in terms of "causal-cum-intentional" explanations from whatever text, as Elster argues.[17] This is not to say that the 1859 "Preface" is meaningless, or that there are no propositions in Marx, falsifiable, false, or otherwise, or that nowhere in his work does he isolate problems and produce explanations. Rather, I am saying that by example as much as in substance, Marx's work represents a critical view on commercial society, a powerful method of discursive analysis, and a source of inspiration for a social science that delves beneath the surface of commonplace presumptions concerning what a problem is and what an explanation might look like: "For the scientific subversion of the immediate experience which establishes the truth of science as against that of immediate experience does not develop the concepts which carry in themselves the [political] protest and the [ethical] refusal. The new scientific truth which they oppose to the accepted one does not contain in itself the judgment that condemns the established reality."[18]

In short, after reading Marx in the light of Marcuse, I found that Marx was not as he seemed, that conventional social science was dully narrow, and that politics was not what people said it was. Moreover, why had Marx for so long been presented as an "empirical" social scientist (but not a very good one), why would the social science of the 1960s, and even now, not let go of this perception, and why was it that empirical social science attracted the funding?

Reading Marcuse

Because of his background in philosophical idealism, which after all Marx praised for "developing the active side," the connections between

Marcuse and the "linguistic turn" in philosophy—and ultimately some aspects of poststructuralist and postmodern strategies in political theory—should not be difficult to make. This is true despite Marcuse's stringent criticism of "ordinary language" philosophy. His complaint was not that attention was focused on language but that what counted as problematic language and, even more, what counted as the language of philosophical enlightenment about a problem were drawn too narrowly and unimaginatively around the doings of "Joe Doe," "Richard Roe," and other hypothetical and wholly uncritical characters.[19] The conjuncture of linguistic turn (in its Germanic manifestations) with Kuhn's revisionist view of science was foreshadowed in Marcuse's discussion of "one-dimensional thought": "This real context in which the particular subjects obtain their real significance is definable only with a theory of society. For the factors in the facts are not immediate data of observation, measurement, and interrogation. They become data only in an analysis which is capable of identifying the structure that holds together the parts and processes of society and that determines their interrelation."[20]

But perhaps surprisingly, there are even more precise moments of prescience from Marcuse. He made human nature a historical phenomenon and human biology a cultural one. This seems remarkably close to postmodern theorizations of social science and Foucauldian theorizations of the body. Marcuse noted the intimate connection between our very being and the technological apparatus that surrounds us; we cannot live without our machines or our activity of machine making and artifact consumption. Donna Haraway's theory of the cyborg seems to say much the same thing.[21] Similarly, Marcuse's analysis of the cultural power of concepts, particularly concepts of the body, is informed by a sense of the way that social power has worked to change our bodily "biology" in the history of civilization.[22] His view that exploitation in advanced capitalist societies is not only hidden but "transfigured," in particular that "happiness and fun" are manufactured commodities, prefigures the validatory fantasies that Baudrillard observed in the United States—Disneyland is there to make the rest of the social environment seem real.[23]

I hope the reader does not begin to think that Marcuse can now be made to say anything whatsoever. Despite his politics of the oppressed, of dialogue, and of coalition, I do not, for example, see him as a significant contributor to feminist thought or to the politics of gender and sexuality—not that he was especially insensitive or unaware but rather that the issues are not impressively explored, so it seems to me. Perhaps others have read him as inspirational in that context; I did not.

Reading Marxism

Analytical or rational-choice Marxists, though advertising themselves as a school, are not themselves unified by interest, method, or politics; in fact, as with many intellectual schools, there are famous disputations, most notably Elster and Cohen on "functional explanation."[24] But the similarities in their work, both methodological and substantial, raise the obvious issue: Given their overwhelming continuities with the assumptions of analytical philosophy and rational-choice theory, in what sense are they Marxists? After all, even Marxism as a concept is not limitlessly flexible; no concept is, otherwise it would be useless. And what is it that separates writers in the school, at least in their eyes, from non-Marxist analytical philosophers, empirical social scientists, formal modelers, game theorists, strategic analysts, and economists with a sociological perspective?

Methodologically, I think there are certain continuities with Marxism, that is, with Marx's writings as interpreted by Engels when he attempted to assimilate Marx's work to empirical science, physical and social. In that view, "ideal" concepts reflect "material" facts in a causal model confirmed by observation, or, more weakly, intentional explanations of human behavior may be conceptualized without a full account of the causal mechanisms presumed to be involved. Having attempted to distinguish Engels's reading of Marx, and Engels's interpretive framework for reading Marx, from alternative readings, especially the traditional Marxist one, I feel entitled to make this connection.[25] Marx's own practice, as I explain later, was somewhat different.

In terms of the agenda of problems in which the analytical and rational-choice school is interested, however, there is considerable continuity with Marx and a break with conventional analytical philosophy and rational-choice theory, insofar as these problems are approached in a more open-minded and sympathetic way. A list of issues explored would include class formation, class struggle, exploitation, historical transitions in economic activity and political structures, typical and even individual responses to economic constraints among political agents, class consciousness, the defining features of capitalism, the development of a socialist critique of commercial society, medium- and long-term alternatives to contemporary social organization, national and international perspectives on political change, and no doubt numerous others.[26] In terms of an agenda, the school is Marxist, and so was Marx. Methodologically, though, Marx is not a Marxist—in my view. And neither was Marcuse. But analytical or rational-choice Marxists are methodologically close to Engels, when he fancied himself a scientist.

One clue as to why this should be so is that analytical and rational-choice theorists generally are not particularly interested in ideology, that is, how concepts are formed and used to mislead, constrain, exclude, discourage, cut off inquiry, make possibilities invisible, and render potentialities nonexistent. Exposing what it is to be ideological, unmasking specific configurations of ideological thinking, was the driving force of Marx's critical social science; that ideology was an important weapon in the class war was for him a major hypothesis.[27] An empiricist epistemology, according to which thought is always a reflection of something, negates the investigative and hermeneutic qualities in Marx's theorizing. Marx's contribution to the theory of ideology was not to have one in the sense that some thought is or is not "ideological," as if that were interesting in itself, but rather to use the insight that concepts construct and constrain our activities in society. An unmasking or unveiling analysis, conducted in theoretical form, could reveal the way that power is instantiated and operates through, for example, religious, economic, or political discourse. For Marx, concepts were themselves essential to the human social world, not merely a way of referring to some presumed extraconceptual reality.

Reading Theories

Analytical and rational-choice theorists are representative of an empiricist understanding of social science, in that they take and construct concepts as if language were transparent to "reality." Thus they see ideology as a category, if they see it at all, rather than as a strategy to unmask, to unveil, to "show that which this reality prevents from being."[28] In the empiricist view, as I see it, observation has an epistemological priority over generalities and abstractions, and social theory is reduced to propositions that are supposedly testable against "experience." Marcuse's characterization of "positivism" poses similar criticisms and points to the political sterility that it enforces. He states that positivism is "(1) the validation of cognitive thought by experience of facts; (2) the orientation of cognitive thought to the physical sciences as a model of certainty and exactness; (3) the belief that progress in knowledge depends on this orientation. . . . Philosophic thought thus turns into affirmative thought; the philosophic critique criticizes within the societal framework and stigmatizes non-positive notions as mere speculation, dreams or fantasies."[29]

Discursive theorizing—in which concepts are analyzed as at least potentially suspect and then probed for their potential relationship to structures of power—is thus rejected by analytical or rational-choice theorists in favor of "explanation." These explanations are atomistic and history-less in analytical and rational-choice theory, even when the evidence is supposedly historical, as the transmission of knowledge among social agents over time never features in their frameworks. By contrast, Marcuse wrote, "historical concreteness militates against quantification and mathematization on the one hand, and against positivism and empiricism on the other."[30]

Analytical and rational-choice Marxism fails to locate the theorist and audience in a political context; moreover, the model of the human being that is employed is essentially a mechanistic one, and the operative notion of explanation is deterministic.[31] Are these the appropriate models to apply to human action? Do analytical and rational-choice Marxists apply these models to themselves and their own actions? What is the political role of their theorizations? I think we should be told.

The use of economic models merely distances the problem. Are the assumptions of empirical "rational utility maximization" hypotheses about all individuals, typical individuals, probable actions in statistical numbers, ideal-typical representations, or what?[32] They certainly do not represent anything exploratory—hence the reference to "assumptions." Nor do they represent concepts used by human agents in any important sense; they seem more like programming than thoughts. Marcuse complained of a "false neutrality" in politics; I would complain of a "false clarity" in social theory. Marcuse characteristically wondered, "Are exactness and clarity ends in themselves, or are they committed to other ends?"[33] Logical rigor, mathematical modeling, and propositional reductionism merely disguise the emptiness of the analytical or rational-choice exercise. What is the substance of this work? How can there be explanation without the transmission of ideas through history? What model of psychology or agency is actually doing the explaining? What is supposed to happen when analytical or rational-choice explanations are actually produced? What is the purpose of rational-choice theory and analytical philosophy? Marcuse stood for communication and action in society in order to identify and produce a future that was at least potentially different from the present in significant ways. Social science as contextless "knowledge" was definitely not his desideratum.

Conclusion

Science exists in the human context, and the human context is political. Otherwise what purports to be science is ideological, in the sense that it masks or veils the potentialities of human existence in a politically complicit way. In analytical and rational-choice Marxism, a whole realm of analysis is rendered invisible. It is still hard work demystifying the familiar, deriving knowledge from concepts, and connecting the scientific with the political. But reading Marcuse is a good way into the struggle: "The desideratum is rather to make the established language itself speak what it conceals or excludes."[34]

Notes

1. G. A. Cohen, *History, Labour, and Freedom: Themes from Marx* (Oxford: Oxford University Press, 1988).
2. G. A. Cohen, *Karl Marx's Theory of History: A Defence* (Oxford: Oxford University Press, 1978).
3. Jon Elster, *Making Sense of Marx* (Cambridge: Cambridge University Press; Paris: Éditions de la Maison des Sciences de l'Homme, 1985); John Roemer, *A General Theory of Exploitation and Class* (Cambridge, Mass.: Harvard University Press, 1982).
4. John Roemer, ed., *Analytical Marxism* (Cambridge: Cambridge University Press; Paris: Éditions de la Maison des Sciences de l'Homme, 1986), 102–3.

5. Elster, *Making Sense of Marx*, ii, and similarly in other books in the series.

6. Alan Carling, "Rational Choice Marxism," *New Left Review* 160 (1986): 24–62.

7. Alan Carling, "In Defence of Rational Choice: A Reply to Ellen Meiksins Wood," *New Left Review* 184 (1990): 108.

8. Carling, "Rational Choice Marxism," 55–58.

9. Robert Ware and Kai Nielsen, eds., *Analyzing Marxism: New Essays on Analytical Marxism* (Calgary, Alta.: University of Calgary Press/Canadian Journal of Philosophy, 1989).

10. Jon Elster, *Nuts and Bolts for the Social Sciences* (Cambridge: Cambridge University Press, 1989).

11. Herbert Marcuse, *One-Dimensional Man: Studies in the Ideology of Advanced Industrial Society* (London: Routledge and Kegan Paul, 1964), 166.

12. Ibid., 199.

13. Herbert Marcuse, *An Essay on Liberation* (London: Allen Lane, Penguin Press, 1969), 8.

14. Karl Marx, "Preface to a Contribution to a Critique of Political Economy [1859]," in Karl Marx and Friedrich Engels, *Selected Works in One Volume* (London: Lawrence and Wishart, 1980), 182.

15. Marcuse, *One-Dimensional Man*, 181.

16. Cohen, *Karl Marx's Theory of History*.

17. Elster, *Making Sense of Marx*, 3.

18. Marcuse, *One-Dimensional Man*, 140.

19. Ibid., 186–89.

20. Ibid., 190.

21. Donna J. Haraway, *Simians, Cyborgs, and Women* (London: Allan Lane, Penguin Press, 1991).

22. Marcuse makes a point which is similar to Foucault's. See Michel Foucault, *History of Sexuality*, vol. 1, trans. Robert Hurley (London: Allan Lane, Penguin Press, 1979).

23. Jean Baudrillard, *Selected Writings*, ed. Mark Poster (Cambridge: Polity Press, 1988).

24. Alan Carling, *Social Division* (London: Verso, 1991).

25. Terrell Carver, *Marx and Engels: The Intellectual Relationship* (Brighton, Eng.: Harvester Press/Wheatsheaf Books, 1983).

26. See, among others, Robert Brenner, *Merchants and Revolution* (Princeton, N.J.: Princeton University Press, 1992); Adam Przeworski, *Capitalism and Social Democracy* (Cambridge: Cambridge University Press, 1985); Roemer, *Analytical Marxism*.

27. Karl Marx, *The Eighteenth Brumaire of Louis Bonaparte*, in Marx and Engels, *Selected Works in One Volume*, 96–179.

28. Marcuse, *One-Dimensional Man*, 199.

29. Ibid., 172.

30. Ibid., 142–43.

31. Jeffrey Alexander, "The Centrality of the Classics," in *Social Theory Today*, ed. Anthony Giddens and Jonathan Turner (Cambridge: Polity Press, 1987), 11–57.

32. Peter T. Manicas, *A History and Philosophy of the Social Sciences* (Oxford: Basil Blackwell, 1989).

33. Marcuse, *One-Dimensional Man*, 176.

34. Ibid., 195.

Part II
Psychoanalysis and Feminism

Trudy Steuernagel

Marcuse, the Women's Movement, and Women's Studies

The United States is on the verge of a counterrevolution, and the women's movement and women's studies are two of its prime targets. Herbert Marcuse's writings in *An Essay on Liberation* and *Counterrevolution and Revolt*[1] are particularly useful in understanding this impending counterrevolution and also in developing an effective theory and practice to combat it. Although Marcuse made few direct comments about feminism, his writings provide important insight into the forces behind a counterrevolution directed at women. Equally important, and perhaps less obviously, Marcuse's movement in *Essay on Liberation* and *Counterrevolution and Revolt* from a traditional, objective, class-based analysis of revolution to a privileging of subjective factors leads him to articulate an identity politics that closely resembles the orientation of much of contemporary American feminism.[2]

Identity politics, for Marcuse, was meant to supplement rather than replace class struggle. For feminism, however, identity politics has become an end in itself, and has, in effect, turned in against itself, making the women's movement and its academic arm, women's studies, particularly vulnerable to the counterrevolution. The radical possibilities of the women's movement and women's studies can be retained, however, if identity politics is reconnected to class struggle and feminism directs its attention to issues confronting women as workers.[3] Marcuse's thoughts on the relationship between identity politics and class struggle are important for reconnecting feminism to class-based politics and helping the women's movement and women's studies to respond to the threat of the counterrevolution.

According to Marcuse, the counterrevolution in the West is based on fear and is "altogether preventive," since there is no revolution to be undone and none imminent.[4] Susan Faludi's *Backlash*, a richly detailed account of "the undeclared war against American women," illuminates the kind of threat that feminism poses to American life. For Faludi, like Marcuse, the backlash of the 1980s is "a preemptive strike," linked not to the achievement of women's full equality "but [to] the increased possibility that they might win it."[5] According to Faludi, gender increases in meaning for individuals as class decreases. In a country such as the United States, where class often has little meaning for individuals, gender becomes more status-laden. "If the American man can claim no ancestral coat of arms on which to elevate himself from the masses," Faludi writes, "perhaps he can fashion his sex into a sort of pedigree."[6] There are class differences among men who create the backlash[7] and women who accept it.[8]

For Faludi, several key myths, including the "man shortage," the "infertility epidemic," the "divorce revolution," "cocooning," and professional women's "burnout," have been promulgated by a hostile or lazy media and supported by those threatened by women's drive for equality. Faludi details the incredible power of a system to mobilize the forces of science, politics, language, philosophy, and religion on the side of oppression. The real problem, according to Faludi, is not women's demand for equality but the continued inequality that taxes women's emotional, physical, and financial resources. Unfortunately, the system uses the tools of mass media and mass marketing to seduce women into believing that feminism is the enemy.

Faludi argues that the backlash has always been a part of women's history in the United States. But the contemporary version is based on mass marketing and mass media, "two institutions that have since proved more effective devices for constraining women's aspirations than coercive laws and punishments,"[9] and is ominous because it is not nearly as recognizable. The "repulsive unity of opposites,"[10] to use Marcuse's term, camouflages the backlash. Women are led to believe they have it all and are unhappy because of it when in reality they have very little. The backlash is not organized, nor is there a "single string-puller."[11] But this is one of the reasons for its power. "A backlash against women's rights succeeds to the degree that it appears *not* to be political, that it appears not to be a struggle at all. It is most powerful when it goes private, when it lodges inside a woman's mind and turns her vision inward, until she imagines the pressure is all in her head, until she begins to enforce the backlash too—on herself."[12]

Clearly, oppression organized around gender cannot be overcome solely through class struggle. Historically, a women's movement independent of the Left was necessary to address the specifics of women's oppression and to give women a voice in constructing their own identity.[13] Likewise, it is important to remember that the declining significance of class in American culture has shaped American feminism and led to an emphasis on identity politics disconnected from class. An examination of *An Essay on Liberation* and *Counterrevolution and Revolt*, with their shift from class analysis to identity politics, provides a context for a more detailed examination of the consequences of this emphasis. Although Marcuse never developed a full theory of identity politics, his ideas parallel many of those involved in the formation of the contemporary women's movement.

Marcuse's flirtation with identity politics came as a result of his pessimism concerning the working class. Although the latter would remain for Marcuse the objective agent of revolution, its lack of revolutionary consciousness and imagination disqualified it as the subjective agent.[14] In fact, Marcuse argued that the working class was now a "conservative, even counterrevolutionary force."[15] Indeed, if the laboring class were to achieve control of society's wealth-producing resources without a transformation in its consciousness, the results would perpetuate rather than eliminate domination and exploitation.[16] Marcuse, moreover, had few illusions that the working class could become the subjective agent of revolution, since it was so tightly integrated into society. This integration, for Marcuse, was as much psychological as it was economic and political. Advanced capitalism, he argued, had engendered among the workers a set of needs the satisfaction of which could only occur within the context of the historical circumstances that created them.[17] The workers believe themselves happy with the "Establishment" because it delivers the goods.[18]

As a consequence of his rejection of the working class, Marcuse turned to those who were not or should not be as satisfied with the existing state of affairs, individuals he referred to collectively as the "Great Refusal." The Great Refusal had two main components. The first comprised those who rejected the way of life promoted by the Establishment. Students, for Marcuse, constituted a significant faction of this group. They were part of the Great Refusal by dint of their revolutionary political consciousness and their identity based on a "radical transvaluation of values."[19] Because of structural changes within capitalism, he argues, this group poses a unique threat. Although they are potential members of the working class, they will be selling their mental rather than their physical labor.[20] Ironically, the space created for them to develop as mental workers, the universities, actually served to distance them from integration into the Establishment. Students, he contends, have developed a "new sensibility" that signals a break in the domination of advanced capitalism, a domination that has created a "second nature of man which ties him libidinally and aggressively to the commodity form."[21] Those who possess this new sensibility have reached down into their second nature and have discovered new needs for freedom. Unlike the traditional working class, whose domination extends to their "instinctual structure,"[22] the students have free instincts that cause them to react differently than those who give the system their peaceful and willing cooperation. In Marcuse's words, these rebels "want to see, hear, feel new things in a new way: they link liberation with the dissolution of ordinary and orderly perception."[23] It is their desire to take the humanist values of the universities and transform them into humane living conditions for all, thereby fulfilling the promise of their education.[24] They have rejected the roles society has planned for them and have embarked on the task of defining themselves and creating their own understanding of who they are and what their role will be in a liberated society. The fact that they take this emerging identity and connect it to the need for radical political change gives them a revolutionary consciousness.

The second component of the Great Refusal included those whose marginalization by the Establishment prevented their integration; and it is here that Marcuse makes the move to identity politics. These individuals have revolutionary potential as a result of their race and sex and not as a result of revolutionary political consciousness. Marcuse, in effect, assumes that their politics are radical because they are blacks or women. Marcuse was attracted, for example, to the revolutionary potential of black ghetto-dwellers. The black population, for Marcuse, is more "expendable" to capitalist society than the white population because it is not as tied into the production process.[25] But this expendability contributes to its revolutionary potential. Marcuse did not believe, however, that the black ghetto population in the United States had a revolutionary political consciousness. "Cruel and indifferent privation," according to Marcuse, "is now met with increasing resistance, but its still largely unpolitical character facilitates suppression and diversion."[26] What is more, class and racial differences separate the ghetto population from the mainly white, middle-class students who do have revolutionary political consciousness. The black ghetto population, therefore, shares with the students a rejection of the system, but not the consciousness of how and in what direction to change it.

Women, he argues, as a consequence of their marginalization, were free from much of the destructive repression experienced by males. For Marcuse, two processes affecting women occur simultaneously: their marginalization and their identity formation. Although women are more oppressed by men, they are less brutalized and remain "more human than men."[27] Again, as in the case of blacks in the United States, women's revolutionary potential is linked primarily to their marginalization in the production process and the reduced levels of integration: "This isolation (separation) from the alienated work world of capitalism enabled the woman to remain less brutalized by the Performance Principle, to remain closer to her sensibility: more human than men."[28] A free society, the definite negation of the male principle, would be a female society, involving the "femalization" of the male.[29]

It is in his discussion of the radical potential of the Women's Liberation Movement, however, that Marcuse's turn to identity politics becomes problematic. Marcuse, in effect, essentializes women, accepting and advocating an identity for women that was formed, not through a series of autonomous choices, but in opposition to the identity created by the Establishment for men.[30] "That this image (and reality) of the woman has been determined by an aggressive, male-dominated society does not mean that this determination must be rejected, that the liberation of women must overcome the female 'nature.'"[31] Women, then, are radical only to the extent they accept the definition of other. Marcuse, moreover, fails to see the problem that arises when, based on their personal experiences, women hold a different understanding of the effect of their gender on their lives. He does not discuss how class and racial differences would affect this definition of the other. The political practice was to be founded on a single identity. "The Women's Liberation Movement," he writes, "becomes a radical force to the degree it transcends the entire sphere of aggressive needs and performances, the entire social organization and division of functions."[32] Patriarchy has created an image of women, a "female counter-force," which "may still become one of the gravediggers of patriarchal society."[33]

Identity Politics

The problematic aspects of his identity politics were unaddressed by Marcuse but were central to the theory and practice of feminism. As noted, Marcuse turned to identity politics because of his rejection of the working class as the subjective agent of revolution. He also believed that historical circumstances dictated a concentration on the development of a new subjective agent. The identity politics he advocated was not intended to replace either the development of revolutionary political consciousness or class analysis. It was intended to complement both and to bring the marginalized groups into the ranks of those who did have the needed consciousness, such as the student segment of the Great Refusal. It was his belief that the members of the Great Refusal had to engage in political education to foster the new sensibility and consciousness among all people, including the working class. In the case of the women's movement, however, the focus has been on an identity politics[34] that separates it from the Left and makes it an easy target for the counterrevolution.

Why and how did this happen? Marcuse's thoughts on women are similar to those that appeared among feminists at the time of the emergence of radical feminism. A comprehensive discussion is provided by Alice Echols in *Daring to Be Bad*.[35] Echols's account of the disputes between the "politicos" and the "radical feminists"[36] illuminates the historical roots of the women's movement and its emphasis on identity politics. During the period covered by her study, 1967 through 1975,[37] debate between the politicos and the radical feminists involved, among other issues, the relationship between the women's movement and the Left. Was women's liberation a wing of the Left, as thought by the politicos, or an independent movement neither counterrevolutionary nor peripheral to the Left?[38] Radical feminism was a reaction to the "anti-feminism of the left and the reluctant feminism of the politicos."[39] As a response to what they perceived as the Left's "dismissal of gender as a 'secondary contradiction,'" radical feminists had a tendency "to privilege gender over race and class, and to treat women as a homogenized unity."[40] It was radical feminism, according to Echols, that was the "hegemonic tendency" within women's liberation until 1973. Beginning that year, cultural feminism challenged radical feminism, and after 1975 it dominated the women's movement. As a result of the ascendancy of cultural feminism, Echols suggests, "liberal feminism became the recognized voice of the women's movement."[41] Cultural feminism focused on personal rather than social transformation,[42] and, with the eclipse of radical feminist activism in a political sense, it became the province of liberal feminists interested in obtaining equality for women within the system.

There are a number of similarities between Marcuse and the cultural feminists. Both see women as essentially similar to one another, and both valorize traditional female culture, believing it to be a product of women's marginalization and oppression.[43] Marcuse and the cultural feminists regard a change in consciousness as preceding economic and political change.[44] In addition, Marcuse's writings on women, the Women's Liberation Movement, and cultural feminism all emerged during a period of backlash.[45] By focusing on creating a women's culture and developing alternative institutions and lifestyles, women could survive the onslaught of the New Right.

But much of Marcuse's work is more sympathetic to radical feminism than cultural feminism. The latter, for example, believes motherhood can empower women and eliminate differences of class, race, and sexual preference.[46] Marcuse, on the contrary, is critical of the linkage between women and mothering. For Marcuse, "the image of the woman as mother is itself repressive; it transforms a biological fact into an ethical and cultural value and thus it supports and justifies her social repression."[47] Like the radical feminists, Marcuse rejects lifestyle politics as an alternative to political activism.[48] Although he does not discuss the subordination of women's liberation to the Left, he is more comfortable with the radical feminist position of transforming the relationship than with the cultural feminist advocacy of severing it.[49] For Echols, both cultural and liberal feminists share the belief that change is a product of individual effort rather than collective struggle and that it is possible to disregard the "material barriers to women's liberation."[50] Marcuse, despite his misgivings concerning the future of class struggle, remained committed to collective action and did not consider lifestyle politics a viable substitute.

The ascendancy of cultural feminism and the resulting increase in the influence of liberal feminism in the contemporary women's movement created the conditions for the dominance of an identity politics divorced from class analysis. The sexism of the Left and its unwillingness to acknowledge gender as a primary source of oppression led to a women's movement reluctant to reconcile with its former radical partner. As noted, Marcuse intended identity politics to supplement class struggle, but this was not the direction taken by the women's movement. Liberal feminism was still committed to the system under fire from radicals. Identity politics, although important in empowering and legitimating an oppressed group, became enmeshed in constructing the meanings of identity for the members of the group. Marcuse did not fall prey to this particular difficulty because he accepted the image of women developed by advanced capitalism. His hope was that women would embrace and then act on this identity of "other." When feminist identity politics attempted to reach out to other women, however, it became engrossed by what is involved in living a woman's life and being seen by society as a woman. In the case of the women's movement, outsider status became valuable less for its potential for revolutionary consciousness than for the fact of its existence: rebel in itself but not for itself.

Political Correctness

Within the women's movement and women's studies, identity politics has become an end in itself. Too often the discourse is dominated by charges and countercharges of oppression and exploitation, a direct and often necessary result of the use of politics to form identity. The outsider status, consistent with Marcuse's belief, is assumed to confer a special type of wisdom on the oppressed. Unfortunately, this makes both the women's movement and women's studies vulnerable to one of the main weapons of the counterrevolution—the "political correctness" debate[51]—and, without a solid connection to the Left, vulnerable to their own self-destructiveness.

Political correctness, according to Barbara Epstein, "comes out of a movement, or a political atmosphere, that is dominated by identity politics."[52] With identity politics there is more orientation "toward moral than strategic thinking; it often seems more concerned with what language is used than with what changes are made in the social structure."[53] If, as Marcuse argued, outsider status conferred a moral status on women elevating them above men, then the door was opened for those who were even more marginalized to claim higher status. Because of this reasoning, the women's movement and women's studies came under attack in the political correctness controversy.

Political correctness has become a substitute for radical politics. For Epstein, identity politics, with its emphasis on what separates one identity from another, makes it difficult to speak and act across the boundaries that identify the identities.[54] Furthermore, people are confronted with the task of trying to make their experience fit into the categories of their identity. Identity, as Epstein notes, "can take on different meanings at different times or can be more or less important at different points in people's lives."[55] Self-consciousness about language and behavior, sensitivity to diverse backgrounds, and concerns about continually redefining identity become ends in themselves, and their reasons for being become lost and disconnected from a radical political agenda.

The counterrevolution's use of political correctness to turn feminists against one another and to discredit them by trivializing the accomplishments of the women's movement and women's studies is apparent in some recent writing in the *Chronicle of Higher Education*. An account of the 1992 meeting of the National Women's Studies Association, for example, displays the traps identity politics is likely to encounter as well as the manner in which legitimate discussions of oppression can be trivialized by the counterrevolution. The headline of the story, "Women's-Studies Group, Hoping to Heal Wounds, Finds More Conflict,"[56] does little to alert the reader to the scholarly contributions of feminism. The following paragraphs opened the story:

> This year's annual meeting of the National Women's Studies Association was supposed to heal fractures that crippled the organization after a large group of minority women staged an angry walkout at the 1990 conference.
>
> The 1992 meeting, whose theme was "Enlarging the Circle: The

Power of Feminist Education," started on a promising note: the screening of "I Am Your Sister," a video depicting a successful multicultural conference. In opening remarks, Deborah Louis, the association's leader, then urged members to find common ground despite their different backgrounds and agendas.

It soon became clear how difficult that would be. Within half an hour, the keynote speaker, Annette Kolodny, dean of the University of Arizona's Faculty of Humanities, had offended lesbian women by making what were described as "heterosexist" remarks. Other women complained that a white woman should not have been selected to start a conference aimed at opening the association up to minority women.

Then, meeting organizers apologized to Jewish conferees who had been inconvenienced by the scheduling of the Friday-night session, which interrupted Shabbat.

Complaints about Meals

Later that evening, some "eco-feminists"—scholars who believe in a feminist approach to environmental issues—complained that every meal served at the conference included meat.

Finally, one conferee complained that participants should be asked in the future to forgo hair spray and perfume, which allergy sufferers might find irritating.

And so it went at the 15th annual meeting of the NWSA, an academic meeting unlike most others.[57]

For those in and out of academia, the image of women and women's studies promoted by this story supports rather than confronts the stereotype. If, for example, individuals who had little direct contact with women's studies were to gain most of their information from the *Chronicle*, a major source in the field of higher education, what would be their impression? Women's studies scholars are unable to overcome women's innate pettiness; they are bitches first and foremost, and no amount of education can change them. Certainly people attending the conference operated with a heightened awareness of oppression. Those who turn to women's studies and feminism to seek their identity and to create an environment compatible with that identity discover other aspects of their lives—their racial or ethnic heritage, for example—that are also involved in their sense of who they are. Charges of oppression are not uncommon in a sympathetic environment because they have a good chance of being heard and because, in the act of speaking the charge, the accuser experiences a sense of power. Obviously, these kinds of controversies do exist and should not be dismissed, but neither should they dominate the work, or the image, of the conference. The vulnerability of the women's movement, however, opens it to attacks by counterrevolutionary forces.

Another example of how identity politics feeds into the political correctness distraction appears in the pages of the *Chronicle*. In the January 15, 1992, issue, philosopher Christina Hoff Sommers[58] writes critically of many academic feminists. In her words, "These women think of themselves as victims, yet they have huge salaries, they run programs and departments."[59] Sommers, who identifies herself as a "liberal feminist" in the tradition of John Stuart Mill and Mary Wollstonecraft, distances herself from the majority of feminist philosophers, whom she terms "gender feminists." This group "want[s] to eradicate wherever possible the differences between men and women and to abolish the traditional family."[60] It is the gender feminists, she goes on to argue, who dominate women's studies departments, academia, and feminist scholarship.

Not surprisingly, the profile of Sommers in conjunction with an ongoing discussion of political correctness[61] resulted in a torrent of commentary. The debate escalated with the publication in the February 5, 1992, issue of an opinion piece by Daphne Patai, a professor of women's studies and Portuguese.[62] Patai, writing as one "exercised over ideological policing within feminism,"[63] is critical of identity politics and its assumption that "a person's racial or ethnic identity and views are one and the same."[64] Although Patai urges that her comments not be used to attack feminism or women's studies, she is clearly alert to the possibility. "I began to realize that we were confronting a new dogma sanctifying a reversal of privilege: Instead of the old privileges accompanying the status of 'white,' truth, righteousness, and automatic justification in the world of women's studies now reside with 'women of color.' "[65] Patai argues that this is a duplication of an old injustice and cannot be a way of creating a more just world. Feminism, she contends, has run rampant and has attacked knowledge, standards, and qualifications. "The intellectual and political questions posed by feminism were developed to challenge unfair stereotyping and exclusion of women, not to exempt them from evaluation."[66] She is afraid that feminists who criticize these kinds of actions are seen as hostile to feminism and marginalized. "Feminism is hurting itself with identity politics."[67]

Clearly, there is a place for identity politics on the Left, but not as a replacement for a radical vision. What is a more useful relationship between identity politics and radical politics? As Marcuse indicates, identity politics is crucial to the formation of revolutionary consciousness. Feminism, for Marcuse, was a sign that a counterrevolution was imminent even if there were no immediate signs of revolutionary consciousness, much less action. In this respect, it was a symptom, albeit an important one, of a broader malaise. When proposed as a substitute for a radical political agenda, identity politics can play into the hands of the counterrevolution.[68] The interests of feminism and the Left would be best served by reestablishing their alliance[69] and pursuing an agenda focused on issues of women, family, and work. These issues have historically divided feminists[70] and have muted the feminist voice in policy debate.

This strategy has much to recommend it. It would reconnect identity politics to a radical political agenda without diminishing the feminist voice, and it would reestablish the link between subjective and objective factors, a point on which Marcuse offered little guidance. It would also do much for children, the group forgotten by both pursuers of identity politics and the Left. Such tactics would push the Left to address the isolation Marcuse saw as a threat to its effectiveness. "Allergic to its factual separation from the masses, not ready to admit that it is expressive of the social structure of advanced capitalism and that its separate character can be overcome only in the long struggle to change this structure," he wrote, "the movement displays inferiority complexes, defeatism, or apathy."[71]

The involvement of women in the workplace is a part of changes in the structure of capitalism, part of what Marcuse refers to as the "qualitative rupture."[72] No one is immune from the consequences of the twentieth century's major social revolution, the changes in women's social roles. The Left, guided by a feminist consciousness, can lead the way. The material conditions are right for the development of a revolutionary political consciousness among men and women that originates in feminism. The details of such a process are discussed by Ethel Klein in *Gender Politics*.[73]

Klein links the development of feminist consciousness to the completion of a three-stage process: affiliation with the group, rejection of the traditional definition of the group's status, and acceptance of the idea that discrimination against the group rather than individual failure is responsible for the status of the individual and other members of the group.[74] Women, according to Klein, come to feminism through the experience of nontraditional roles arising from work, divorce, and reduced childbearing. Men, in contrast, develop feminist sympathy rather than feminist consciousness. This appears as "an abstract, ideological commitment to equality" rather than the "internalized political perspective derived from personal experience"[75] that characterizes feminist consciousness.

Women's changing social roles have spurred changes in the lives of men and women. Boys and girls may well spend some portion of their childhood in single parent homes.[76] In all probability, their mothers will be in the workforce at some point in their childhood, and this could occur before their first birthday.[77] What will this mean? As more males experience nontraditional roles, will they develop a feminist consciousness? For Klein, the different paths of childhood produced men with a lessened commitment to feminism.[78] With more and more children involved in nontraditional experiences, however, the paths might converge, fostering feminist consciousness in both men and women. This could be the basis of a newly invigorated radical politics.

The women's movement and women's studies are threatened by a counterrevolution. To stave off the assault, they need to reconnect to radical politics. Much has transpired since Marcuse wrote *An Essay on Liberation* and *Counterrevolution and Revolt*. The women's movement has accomplished much, and women's studies have had an impact on scholarship and academic life. Although the working class remains committed to the Establishment, there are signs that this integration is disintegrating. However, the students whom Marcuse embraced so passionately are now some twenty years older, and there are few indications that the current generation of students see themselves as part of the Great Refusal. Even Marcuse was unable in 1972 to sustain his 1969 optimism. His work does remind us, however, of the need to think in terms of the potential inherent in historical circumstances. It also causes us to revisit the specter of a counterrevolution. The ability of the women's movement and women's studies to construct a strategy to combat the counterrevolution in all its facets, including political correctness, will depend on the ability to reconnect with the Left. Feminism has the potential to reinvigorate the Left.

Trudy Steuernagel

What were once thought of as "women's issues" are now the potential basis for the development of a radical political consciousness. Marcuse lives!

Notes

1. Herbert Marcuse, *An Essay on Liberation* (Boston: Beacon Press, 1969), and *Counterrevolution and Revolt* (Boston: Beacon Press, 1972). These works represent an extension of ideas developed in *Eros and Civilization: A Philosophical Inquiry into Freud* (New York: Random House, 1955) and *One-Dimensional Man: Studies in the Ideology of Advanced Industrial Society* (Boston: Beacon Press, 1964).

2. I use "identity politics" in a fashion similar to that employed by Shane Phelan in her *Identity Politics* (Philadelphia, Pa.: Temple University Press, 1989). The "agenda" of identity politics is dominated by claims of individuals to construct meaning(s) for themselves in a free and autonomous fashion. Identity politics assumes a commonality among those who share a trait, i.e., ethnicity, gender, sexual orientation.

3. This is similar to a point made by Barbara Epstein concerning progressive academic culture. She argues—and this is a point that will be addressed in more detail in the discussion of women's studies—that political correctness is a substitute for radical politics. Barbara Epstein, " 'Political Correctness' and Identity Politics," *In These Times* 16 (26 February–10 March 1992): 16–17.

4. Marcuse, *Counterrevolution*, 2.

5. Susan Faludi, *Backlash* (New York: Crown Publishers, 1991), xx.

6. Ibid., 47.

7. Ibid., 66.

8. Ibid., xx.

9. Ibid., 48.

10. Marcuse, *Counterrevolution*, 129.

11. Faludi, *Backlash*, xxii.

12. Ibid.

13. Although it is difficult to make generalizations about the women's movement and feminist theory on identity construction (since clearly there is no single agreed-upon understanding of the term), it appears the problems of personal identity discussed by William Connolly are all involved. In this respect, identity politics, drawing from Connolly, involves problems of individuation, species identity, the unity of the person, and the sense of the term from social theory, that is, the problem of identity and the individual's relationship to roles and norms. See William E. Connolly, *Appearance and Reality* (Cambridge: Cambridge University Press, 1981), 151–72.

14. According to Marcuse, not since the First International has there been an effort to combine the subjective and objective factors in revolution. *An Essay on Liberation*, 14.

15. Ibid., 16.

16. Ibid., 4.
17. Ibid., 16.
18. Ibid., 13.
19. Ibid., 6.
20. Ibid., 59.
21. Ibid., 11.
22. Ibid.
23. Ibid., 37.
24. Ibid., 61.
25. Ibid., 58.
26. Ibid., 57.
27. Marcuse, *Counterrevolution*, 77.
28. Ibid.
29. Ibid., 75.
30. For a discussion of the status of identity in modernist critical theory, see Stephen T. Leonard, *Critical Theory in Political Practice* (Princeton, N.J.: Princeton University Press, 1990). On p. 52, Leonard notes that Adorno cautioned against a " 'logic of identity' which assumes that a universal interest can be readily vested in any particular interest."
31. Ibid., 77-78. See the similarity between Marcuse's argument and Temma Kaplan's discussion of "female consciousness." Temma Kaplan, "Female Consciousness and Collective Action: The Case of Barcelona, 1910-1918," in *Feminist Theory*, ed. Nannerl O. Keohane, Michelle Z. Rosaldo, and Barbara C. Gelpi (Chicago: University of Chicago Press, 1982), 55-76.
32. Marcuse, *Counterrevolution*, 75.
33. Ibid., 78.
34. To a large extent, the problem of identity within feminism was ignored initially because so many of the women involved in the contemporary movement were white and middle class. As the women's movement attempted to address the needs of all women, the differences in needs and interests became more apparent and the commonality less so.
35. Cultural feminism, seen by Echols as evolving from radical feminism, "was a countercultural movement aimed at reversing the cultural valuation of the male and the devaluation of the female." In contrast, radical feminism was "a political movement dedicated to eliminating the sex-class system." Alice Echols, *Daring to Be Bad* (Minneapolis: University of Minnesota Press, 1989), 6.
36. Following Echols, "radical feminists," unlike "politicos," do not attribute women's oppression to capitalism and do not believe a socialist revolution would liberate women. Echols portrays neither radical feminists nor politicos as monolithic.
37. Note that this period encompasses the publication of *An Essay on Liberation* and *Counterrevolution and Revolt*.
38. Echols, *Daring*, 52.
39. Ibid., 101.
40. Ibid.
41. Ibid., 243. Liberal feminists wanted to integrate women into the public sphere.
42. Ibid., 5.

43. Ibid., 247.

44. Ibid., 251.

45. Ibid., 245.

46. Ibid., 251.

47. Marcuse, *Counterrevolution*, 74.

48. Echols, *Daring*, 251.

49. Ibid., 252.

50. Ibid., 279.

51. See, for example, Allan Bloom's discussion of feminism in *The Closing of the American Mind* (New York: Simon and Schuster, 1987) as well as Faludi's critique, *Backlash*, 290ff. Obviously, political correctness is not the worst thing that can happen to women, but it is one of the early signs of the counterrevolution and cannot be ignored.

52. Epstein, "'Political Correctness,'" 17.

53. Ibid.

54. Ibid.

55. Ibid.

56. Courtney Leathererman, "Women's Studies Group, Hoping to Heal Wounds, Finds More Conflict," *Chronicle of Higher Education*, 1 July 1992, A13–14.

57. Ibid., A13.

58. According to the account of the 1992 NWSA conference, Sommers was present but her sister wore her name tag. "'Christina had said some women might be hostile to her being here.'" Ibid., A14. For Sommers's account of the same conference, see Christina Hoff Sommers, "Sister Soldiers," *New Republic*, 5 October 1992, 29–33.

59. Scott Jaschik, "Philosophy Professor Portrays Her Feminist Colleagues as Out of Touch and 'Relentlessly Hostile to the Family,'" *Chronicle of Higher Education*, 15 January 1992, A1, A16, A18. For this quote, see A18.

60. Ibid.

61. See 15 January 1992 edition, for example, as well as the letters in the editions of 5 February 1992; 12 February 1992; and 19 February 1992.

62. Daphne Patai, "The Struggle for Feminist Purity Threatens the Goals of Feminism," *Chronicle of Higher Education*, 5 February 1992, B1–2.

63. Ibid., B1.

64. Ibid.

65. Ibid., B2.

66. Ibid.

67. Ibid.

68. For Marcuse, the counterrevolution falls particularly heavily on colleges and brown and black militants. *Counterrevolution*, 24. Cutbacks in funding for higher education and the Los Angeles riots do little to discredit his judgment.

69. This is a point made by Vicky Randall, *Women and Politics* (Chicago: University of Chicago Press, 1987), 323. Randall cautions against "dissolving autonomous feminist organizations or relinquishing separate feminist identity."

70. In particular, issues of equality versus difference and of special treatment versus gender neutrality have been divisive. See Dorothy McBride Stetson, *Women's Rights in the U.S.A.* (Pacific Grove, Calif.: Brooks/Cole Publishing Com-

pany, 1991), 182, 200. Stetson is an advocate of this women, work, family approach.

71. Marcuse, *Counterrevolution*, 33.

72. Ibid.

73. Ethel Klein, *Gender Politics* (Cambridge, Mass.: Harvard University Press, 1984).

74. Ibid., 2–3.

75. Ibid., 7.

76. According to the U.S. Census Bureau, as of 1991, 72 percent of children lived with two parents. This represents a decrease from the 1970 figure of 85 percent. Among African-Americans, 57.5 percent of children live in single-family homes. Most of these reside with their mothers. Children living in single-parent homes are six times more likely than children from two-parent homes to live in poverty. *Akron Beacon Journal*, 17 July 1992, A4.

77. As of 1988, 52.5 percent of children younger than age three had mothers in the work force. Sara E. Rix, ed., *The American Woman 1990–1991* (New York: W. W. Norton and Company, 1990), 379.

78. Klein, *Gender Politics*, 122.

Isaac D. Balbus

The Missing Dimension: Self-Reflexivity and the "New Sensibility"

> For the real subject matter is not exhausted by its purpose, but in working the matter out; nor is the mere result attained the concrete whole itself, but the result along with the process of arriving at it.
>
> —*G. W. F. Hegel*

An Essay on Liberation culminates in the claim that "the radical transformation of society implies [a] union of [a] new sensibility with a new rationality."[1] In any socialist society worth living in, we would not only work but also *feel* and *think* in a fundamentally different way than we do under capitalism. We will never live in the new society, moreover, unless this different sensibility and different rationality somehow already inform the struggle against the old society. This insistence on both the scope and urgency of liberation remains, for me, Marcuse's most memorable message.

Marcuse also insisted that critical theory was an essential ingredient in the "radical transformation of society." But if radical transformation implies the union of a new sensibility and a new rationality, and if critical theory is a necessary part of radical transformation, then an authentically radical critical theory would itself have to be informed by, and contribute to, the union of a new sensibility and a new rationality. Yet Marcuse never drew the proper conclusion from his own premises. Thus he failed to ask the question: What *kind* of critical theory would be consistent with the union of the new sensibility and the new rationality?

Nor is this metatheoretical problem posed within contemporary (non-feminist) critical social theory. Since Marcuse's death in 1979, critical reflection on the role of the critical theorist has been largely dominated by the debate between Jürgen Habermas and Michel Foucault over the possibility of an emancipatory reason that is based on a common neglect of the possibility of emancipatory emotions. Yet this debate points beyond itself to the very possibility of a marriage of emancipatory reason and emancipatory passion that it would preclude. I suggest that Marcuse's vision of a union of a new sensibility and a new rationality implies a standard for emancipatory communication between critical social theorists and critical social actors[2] that is, however, betrayed by Marcuse's explicit position on the role of the radical intellectual. By contrast, psychoanalytically self-reflexive social theory encourages a relationship between social theorists and social actors that *would* satisfy that implicitly Marcusean standard.

Emotional Neglect: Neither Habermas nor Foucault

Habermas's conception of an " 'ideal speech situation' " in which there is " 'symmetry among participants' " and " 'interchangeability among dialogue roles,' "[3] together with his conviction that communication between social theorists and social actors is emancipatory to the extent that it approximates the conditions of ideal speech, leads him to the conclusion that the distinction between social theorist and social actor is merely an unavoidable fiction that the communication between them is designed to overcome. "In a process of enlightenment," he tells us, "there can only be [equal] participants."[4] Thus Habermas demands a democratic dialogue between the educators and the educated.

At the same time Habermas denudes this dialogue of any emotional content. The discourse designed to "enlighten" both social theorist and social actor is defined as a special form of communication that "excludes . . . all motives except the cooperative search for the truth." Only this exclusion of all noncognitive components from the communication ensures that the consensus in which it culminates is the result of no force other than the "force of the better argument."[5] To put this the other way around, any intrusion of the emotions into the communication bespeaks the presence of power and thus necessarily invalidates the consensus in which it issues. Habermas's implicit equation of "power" and "passion" necessarily leads to the conclusion that emancipatory communication must be as *dispassionate* as it is democratic.

For Foucault, Habermas's discourse is no more democratic and no more dispassionate than any other discourse that purports to disclose a universal human truth. All "true discourses" function as "regimes of truth" that "induce regular effects of power" by virtue of the self-sacrifices they demand in the name of "Truth" and the "status [they grant to] those who are charged" with enunciating it.[6] The will to knowledge betrays a will to power that is masked—and therefore maintained—by the very opposition between knowledge and power on which all true discourses are based.[7] In the case of Habermas, Foucault would say, the assumption of a universally human communicative competence gives rise to the norm of an ideal speech situation founded on the opposition between "force" (power) and the "force of the better argument" (knowledge) that effectively ensures the domination of those who have been trained to make "better arguments" over those who have not. Consequently, Habermas's true discourse incites social actors to play by the rules of a game that is rigged in favor of the social theorist.

Foucault's deconstruction of true discourse is vulnerable, of course, to the familiar objection that *his* discourse claims to speak the truth about the complicity between the will to knowledge and the will to power and that it is therefore founded on the very opposition between truth and power that it purports to deconstruct. Hence his critique of the authoritarian effects of all true discourse either cancels itself out or must be modified in order to distinguish between true discourses that express, and true discourses that contest, the will to power.[8] Either Foucault's true discourse is as authoritarian as any other, or his discourse must be a member of a set of emancipatory discourses. But Foucault cannot distinguish between authoritarian and emancipatory discourses because he simultaneously denies Habermas's claim that discourses can be free from desire and affirms Habermas's equation of desire and power.

Thus the deconstruction of the Foucauldian deconstruction of Habermas's discourse culminates in the conclusion that their common equation of desire and power must be annulled in favor of the distinction between authoritarian and emancipatory desire. Emancipatory discourses are discourses that are animated by emancipatory desires. This brings us back—

or rather forward—to Marcuse's vision of a union of a new rationality and a new sensibility.

The New Sensibility but the Old Rationality

Marcuse's synthesis of Marx and Freud in *Eros and Civilization* enabled him to claim that the alienated labor endemic to capitalist societies demands a "de-sexualization of the body" that unleashes the destructive manifestations of the death instinct, and that a resexualization of the body and a concomitant "weakening of primary aggressiveness" would be thus necessary in the disalienated socialist society of the future.[9] And in *One-Dimensional Man*, his critique of scientific rationality as *Herrschaftswissen*—knowledge for the sake of domination—implied that a new form of reason would necessarily accompany this eventual ascendance of the life instincts over the death instinct.[10] But it was not until the emergence of the counterculture and the publication of *An Essay on Liberation* in 1969 that he argued that this simultaneously instinctual and cognitive transformation is necessary *now*, that it is a prerequisite of socialist construction: "[The] causes [of domination] are economic-political, but since they have shaped the very instincts and needs, no economic and political changes will bring this historic continuum to a stop unless they are carried through by men [*sic*] who are physiologically and psychologically able to experience things, and each other, outside the context of violence and exploitation."[11] Thus any liberation struggle worthy of that name must be "carried through" by individuals whose "nonaggressive, erotic, receptive faculties" have supplanted their "aggressiveness and guilt," individuals who are "tender, sensuous, [and] no longer ashamed of themselves" or their bodies. Revolution presupposes a "type of man [*sic*] who would speak a different language, have different gestures," a person who "want[s] to see, hear, feel new things in a new way."[12]

However necessary, the new sensibility is not sufficient for human liberation. Although the senses "have a share in producing the images of freedom . . . the most daring images of a new world, of new ways of life, are still guided by concepts, and by a logic elaborated in the development of thought."[13] Reason retains an essential revolutionary role. But this will be a new form of reason that does not dominate but is "receptive" to, and harmonizes with, the sensuous nature within us and without us. In *An Essay on Liberation*, the emphasis is on a new relationship between reason and *internal* nature that would make it possible for work to become play and thus for the opposition between technique and art to be overcome.[14] Three years later in *Counterrevolution and Revolt*, Marcuse realizes that this new reality principle, this "aesthetic ethos," also implies a new relationship between reason and *external* nature, in which the recognition of nature "as a *subject* in its own right" would ground "the development of the scientific concepts."[15] But in both works the only offspring of the marriage of sensibility and rationality is a new science and technology, understood as a force of production.[16]

Marcuse does recognize, first in *An Essay on Liberation*, that "the new sensibility and the new consciousness . . . demand a new *language* to define and communicate the new 'values,'" and, in *Counterrevolution and Revolt*, that "communication of the radically nonconformist, new historical goals of the revolution requires an equally nonconformist language (in the widest sense)."[17] But the only "nonconformist" language he considers is the "living art" of the counterculture that purports to transcend the "divorce of the arts from reality" inherent in the traditional "aesthetic form." This consideration culminates in a defense of this traditional form and a repudiation of the "false and oppressive notion . . . that art could become a component part of revolutionary (and prerevolutionary) *praxis*."[18] And so Marcuse never even poses the problem: What does the union of the new sensibility and the new rationality imply for the kind of communication that *would* become a "component part" of that praxis?

This gap is particularly glaring in light of Marcuse's own insistence in *An Essay on Liberation* on the indispensable role of political education in the struggle for socialism. Without "critical theory" as a "guide [to] political practice," the new sensibility can easily degenerate into a mere "withdrawal [that] creates its artificial paradises within the society from which it withdrew." Thus by itself the new sensibility "cannot possibly be a radical and revolutionary force. It can become such a force only as the result of enlightenment, education."[19]

In *Counterrevolution and Revolt* it becomes clear that the "enlightenment" he has in mind is not a union of sensibility and rationality but rather the *subordination* of the former to the latter. He tells us that socialist transformation is only possible "if the rebels succeed in subjecting the new sensibility . . . to the rigorous discipline of the mind."[20] The subjection of the new sensibility to the "rigorous discipline of the mind" scarcely suggests a form of reason that "does not dominate, but is receptive to and harmonizes with, the sensuous nature within us." It betrays instead a commitment to the very *Herrschaftswissen* that Marcuse contests.

The subjection of the rebel's sensibility to the discipline of the mind requires, in turn and in the first instance, the subordination of her sensibility to the discipline of *other* minds: "Self-liberation is self-education but as such it *pre*supposes education by others. . . . All authentic education is political education, and in a class society, political education is unthinkable without leadership. . . . The function of this leadership is to 'translate' spontaneous protest into organized action which has the chance to develop and transcend immediate needs and aspirations toward the radical reconstruction of society."[21] The task of the radical intellectual, in short, is to "translate" what the rebel *feels* into what the intellectual already *knows*, to teach her that capitalism necessarily cripples her sensibilities and that the "complete emancipation" of these sensibilities therefore requires the "radical reconstruction of society."[22] Thus for Marcuse political education is the enlightenment of sensuous social actors by rational social theorists. Social actors are not recognized as rational "subjects in [their] own right" but merely as objects of a process of translation in which they do not participate and over which they exercise no control. The theorist is the teacher and the actor is the student. Same as it ever was.

And it is not clear why this student would come to class. Why should the social actor "listen to reason" if she doesn't already possess it? Unless the social actor has already begun to reflect on the question of the social origins of, and obstacles to, her new sensibility, why should she even be interested in the social theorist's answer to this question? But if she has already begun her reflections, then any answer she may arrive at has as legitimate a claim to be heard as the answer of the theorist. Thus the voluntary nature of the participation of the social actor in the process of political education presupposes that she be recognized as an active participant in—a subject, not an object of—this process. It presupposes, in other words, that the sensuous social actor be recognized as a rational social theorist.

Isaac D. Balbus

It also presumes that the rational social theorist has become a sensuous social actor. Recall that the individual with the new sensibility "would speak a different language" and wants to hear "new things in a new way." We should expect, then, that even the most intellectually motivated social actor will turn a deaf ear to any intellectual discourse that is not spoken in this—in *her*—new and different language. This means that the critical theorist will only be able to fulfill the task of "guiding" political practice in the direction of "radical reconstruction" if his guiding language is itself infused with the new sensibility. Successful political education presupposes that the educator has learned to be as "nonaggressive, erotic, and receptive" as those whom he would educate.

Thus any political education that was consistent with the commitment to the union of the new sensibility and the new rationality would have to be predicated on the mutual recognition of the sensuality of the social theorist and the rationality of the social actor.

Marcuse's failure to recognize the necessity for what might be called this new theoretical sensibility is revealed in an account of the prospects for successful political education that is at once overly idealistic and overly skeptical. He tells us, on the one hand, that "those who are educated have a commitment to use their knowledge to help men and women realize and enjoy their truly human capabilities," but, on the other, that "in a society where the unequal access to knowledge and information is part of the social structure, the distinction and the *antagonism* between the educators and the educated are inevitable."[23] The lofty moralism of his appeal to the commitment of the educators to the educated is undermined by the sober realism of his insistence on the inevitable enmity between them. And so his account reaches an impasse. The only way to avoid this impasse would be to explore what Marcuse ignores: the possibility of a new theoretical sensibility. This is the problem to which I now turn.

Psychoanalytically Self-Reflexive Social Theory

My argument is that political education informed by psychoanalytically self-reflexive social theory would both embody and contribute to the union of the new sensibility and the new rationality. All self-reflexive theory is based on the assumption that social theory is social action and that a satisfactory theory of social action must therefore clarify the conditions of its own possibility.[24] What is specific to *psychoanalytically* self-reflexive social theory is that the theorist sees social action as a struggle either to defend against or to mitigate emotional suffering and thus she understands her theory to be an intellectual expression of her own participation in that psychological struggle. Psychoanalytically self-reflexive theory is a "receptive" form of reason that seeks, not to dominate, but rather to affirm its dependence on the sensibilities of the social theorist.

This effort to find the sensuous social actor in the rational social theorist is bound to be a painful process. Transgressing the standard methodological boundary that safely separates the observer from those whom she observes inevitably evokes the very anxiety that, according to George Devereux, this boundary is designed to dispel.[25] But this is the only way to avoid the implication that the social theorist is ruled by reason while the social actor is imprisoned by passion and hence that there "are two distinct breeds of men [*sic*]." By cultivating "the ingrained *habit* of viewing [his] own beliefs as [he] view[s] those held by others," the self-reflexive theorist not only learns more about himself but also deepens his sense of "kinship with those whom [he] stud[ies]."[26] In clarifying the connection between his intellect and his emotions, he simultaneously contributes to the development of his emotions.

The development continues when the self-reflexive social theorist communicates this connection to (other) social actors. In speaking publicly of his personal struggle to become "tender, sensuous [and] no longer ashamed," the theorist at once carries on his struggle and seeks support for it from people who are also committed to it and therefore know just how difficult it can be. He also learns more about this struggle from those fellow sufferers who may be currently negotiating it more successfully than he. The sensibilities of the psychoanalytically self-reflexive theorist are educated by the very social actors he would educate. Thus he is in a stronger position after the public dialogue than before to renew his painful personal struggle.

In speaking publicly about her emotional development, the psychoanalytically self-reflexive social theorist also facilitates her theoretical development. The correction or modification of her hypotheses on the social origins of, and obstacles to, the new sensibilities of her interlocutors depends on their willingness to help test these hypotheses in the light of their own experience. In welcoming their participation in this process, the social theorist recognizes that the sensuous social actors are also rational social theorists. In effect she invites them to evaluate her hypotheses in view of what they already know about the roots of, and roadblocks to, their own emotional development and thus to publicly renew a process of self-reflection that they are assumed to have already begun. Only the willingness of the social theorist to share the results of *her* self-reflection justifies the confidence that this invitation to self-revelation will be accepted. Unless the social theorist has disclosed her suffering (as the source of her theory), there is no reason to expect that the social actor will disclose his own. And without the disclosure of his suffering, there is no way to evaluate the hypotheses about its social origins. *A public discourse on the (personal) context of the discovery of the theory is therefore essential to the (personally informed) public discourse that becomes the context of its justification.*

This context of justification becomes, in turn, the context for the next theoretical discovery. If the dialogue reveals that some of the social actors have experienced a certain kind of suffering (e.g., narcissism) but not the conditions that have been hypothesized as its social origins (e.g., overprotective mothering), or that some have experienced these conditions but not that suffering, then the theorist may modify his theory of the social origins of, and obstacles to, the new sensibility.[27] Any modification of a theory will of course entail a modification of its self-reflexive application, that is, of the theorist's account of the emotional origins of his own theory. The public dialogue serves to deepen both his understanding of others and his understanding of himself.

Everything that happens to the social theorist as a result of his participation in this dialogue also happens to the social actor. His personal-theoretical encounter with the social theorist (as well as the other social actors) simultaneously strengthens his struggle against his suffering and heightens his awareness of the social obstacles with which any such struggle must ultimately contend. Thus the social theorist makes an essential contribution to the personal and political education of the social actor. If I have emphasized here what the social theorist learns from the social actor rather more than what the social actor learns from the social theorist, it is only because the more familiar emphasis on the importance of the latter typically neglects the necessity of the former. The point I wish to underscore is that *the successful (personal and) political education of the social actor depends on the successful (personal and) political education of the social theorist*. The only realistic response to the venerable political question, Who shall educate the educators?, is "the educated."

Conclusion

Everything I have argued about the relationship between the context for the justification and the context for the discovery of a psychoanalytically informed theoretical argument applies, of course, to my own psychoanalytically informed (metatheoretical) argument. If the disclosure of the personal context for the discovery of a psychoanalytic theory is essential to its public justification, my effort to justify my own metatheory demands that I reveal its emotional origins. This is a long story, all of which I hope to be able to tell at another time. Here I have space for only a small, but I believe important, part.

My case for psychoanalytically self-reflexive theory is, in effect, an argument for the political importance of the struggle to be a deeply feeling person and a deeply thinking intellectual at the same time. I do not think I would have had any reason—intellectual or emotional—to make that political argument if this struggle had not been so central to the last ten years or so of my personal life. In the course of my psychoanalytically informed psychotherapy, I learned just how much—and how well—my commitment to impersonal theoretical discourse served to defend against early and persistent emotional pain, which I needed to feel more fully in order to live with more pleasure; had I not made this discovery, I doubt that I would have been moved to make the case for overcoming the opposition between personal and theoretical communication. And now that I have learned to feel that pain more fully, I find that I have very little need—frankly, very little *patience*—for the impersonal theoretical discourse to which I was once so committed. What I need instead is to communicate with people who share my need for communication that is at once intimate and intellectual.

My metatheoretical argument could therefore be dismissed as a hopelessly parochial projection were it not for the fact—or at least what I take to be the fact—that so many people in our (American) society have come to feel exactly the same need. As Anthony Giddens has recently argued, "high

115

modernity" is increasingly a condition of generalized self-reflexivity.[28] There are literally tens of millions of Americans in psychotherapies, psychological workshops, and self-help groups who do emotional work on themselves that is as deep as it is difficult. For these people—people who are on the road to the recovery of their early pain and the abandonment of their destructive defenses against it—the new sensibility is no abstraction but something on which they have staked their very lives. If critical theory does not speak to *them*, then perhaps it has nothing important to say. That, at any rate, is my interpretation of the contemporary meaning of the enduring metatheoretical message of Herbert Marcuse.

Notes

1. Herbert Marcuse, *An Essay on Liberation* (Boston: Beacon Press, 1969), 37.
2. This distinction should not imply that social actors are not in some important sense already social theorists and that social theorists are not in an equally important sense already social actors. Of course they are. The distinction is merely drawn between those who are, and those who are not, theorists by profession. This will later become clear.
3. Jürgen Habermas, cited in Isaac D. Balbus, *Marxism and Domination* (Princeton, N.J.: Princeton University Press, 1982), 223.
4. Jürgen Habermas, *Theory and Practice* (Boston: Beacon Press, 1973), 40.
5. Jürgen Habermas, *The Theory of Communicative Action*, vol. 1 (Boston: Beacon Press, 1984), 25.
6. Michel Foucault, *Power/Knowledge* (New York: Pantheon, 1980), 131.
7. Michel Foucault, "The Discourse on Language," in *The Archeology of Knowledge* (New York: Harper and Row, 1972), 215-37.
8. Isaac D. Balbus, "Disciplining Women: Michel Foucault and the Power of Feminist Discourse," in *After Foucault*, ed. Jonathan Arac (New Brunswick, N.J.: Rutgers University Press, 1988), 138-60. See also Herbert Dreyfus and Paul Rabinow, *Michel Foucault: Beyond Structuralism and Hermeneutics* (Chicago: University of Chicago Press, 1983), 132.
9. Herbert Marcuse, *Eros and Civilization: A Philosophical Inquiry into Freud* (New York: Vintage Books, 1962), 44, and *Counterrevolution and Revolt* (Boston: Beacon Press, 1972), 75.
10. Herbert Marcuse, *One-Dimensional Man: Studies in the Ideology of Advanced Industrial Society* (Boston: Beacon Press, 1964).
11. Marcuse, *An Essay on Liberation*, 25.
12. Ibid., 31, 23, 21, 37.
13. Ibid., 29.
14. Ibid., 24, 30-31.
15. Marcuse, *Counterrevolution and Revolt*, 60-61. Emphasis in the original.
16. For a consideration of the way in which Marcuse's Marxist productivism lim-

its even his most advanced positions, see Balbus, *Marxism and Domination*, chapter 7.

17. Marcuse, *An Essay on Liberation*, 32–33, *Counterrevolution and Revolt*, 79–80.

18. Marcuse, *Counterrevolution and Revolt*, 81, 85, 107 (emphasis in the original).

19. Marcuse, *An Essay on Liberation*, 5, 37, 89.

20. Marcuse, *Counterrevolution and Revolt*, 131.

21. Ibid., 47 (emphasis in the original).

22. Karl Marx, "Private Property and Communism," in *The Marx-Engels Reader*, ed. Robert C. Tucker (New York: Norton, 1978), 87.

23. Marcuse, *Counterrevolution and Revolt*, 47 (emphasis added).

24. Alvin Gouldner, *The Coming Crisis of Western Sociology* (New York: Basic Books, 1970), chapters 1 and 13. See also Theodor W. Adorno, "Subject and Object," in *The Essential Frankfurt School Reader*, ed. Andrew Arato and Eike Gebhart (New York: Urizen Books, 1978), 497–511, as well as Arato and Gebhardt's introduction to part 3 of that work, 371–406.

25. George Devereux, *From Anxiety to Method in the Behavioral Sciences* (The Hague: Mouton and Co., 1967).

26. Gouldner, *The Coming Crisis of Western Sociology*, 490 (emphasis in the original).

27. I say "may modify" because limitations in the actors' (as well as the theorists') understanding of their own experience obviously complicate the problem of determining whether that experience verifies or falsifies the hypotheses of the theorist. Additional communication—both explicit and implicit—concerning that experience can help overcome these limits, but some ambiguity will inevitably persist. Thus the theorist's decision on the fate of his hypotheses is always based on an interpretation that is open to further evaluation. This is true of any process of theoretical verification. One advantage of a specifically psychoanalytically self-reflexive process of theoretical verification, however, is that it becomes possible to challenge the *emotional* stake that both theorists and actors have in hanging on to their hypotheses. Thus it is far more likely than any other process to encourage theoretical innovation.

28. Anthony Giddens, *Modernity and Self-Identity* (Stanford, Calif.: Stanford University Press), 1991.

Gad Horowitz

Psychoanalytic Feminism in the Wake of Marcuse

Sexual Pleasure or Mutual Recognition?

The left-Freudian voices of the 1960s are now silenced. Their successors, psychoanalytic feminists of the school of Nancy Chodorow and Jessica Benjamin, want to theorize domination no longer in the language of sexuality but in the language of "object relations" and "the intersubjective view." For Marcuse, the source of domination and alienated labor is repression of bodily desire; for Benjamin, the source of domination is the denial of the subjectivity of women by men, the construction of a psychic structure in which "one person must play subject and the other must serve as his object."[1] Polarization of subjectivity and objectivity, masculinity and femininity, is the fundamental structure of domination.

According to object relations theory, Freud mistakenly founded the edifice of psychoanalysis on the concept of sexual drive, located inside the person and inherently independent of any relationship with other persons. This conception gives way to the view that sexuality is inherently relational. There is no desire for bodily pleasure per se; pleasure itself must be "redefined," says Benjamin, as "pleasure in being with the other."[2] Object relations theory has seen the primary relation with the mother as a "symbiotic" merger. Benjamin, speaking for the new intersubjective view, argues that "the infant is never totally undifferentiated from the mother but is primed from the beginning to be interested in and to distinguish itself from the world of others."[3] Therefore, a reframed psychoanalysis is called for, one that emphasizes reciprocity as opposed to either instinctual gratification[4] (as in Freud, Reich, Marcuse, Norman O. Brown) or separation-individuation (as in ego psychology and object relations theory).

The notion that only the mother is active, that the baby is passive or merged with an omnipotent mother, and that the baby internalizes images

118

of the other to develop the self is not false, according to Benjamin; it refers to "one of the structures of the psyche." But "it's not the only one."[5] There is also a structure of intersubjective mutuality in which both partners are active and each wants to be recognized as subject, as the author of action, and to recognize the other as subject. Here there is a differentiation and "mutual attunement" of mother and child as subject relating to subject, a pleasurable affective interchange in which each makes itself known to the other and each becomes not only more separate over time but also more capable of "sharing with and appreciating the other."[6] Thus separateness is not forced on a narcissistic child; rather, separateness is there with narcissism from the beginning. The sense of oneness can "coexist with (enhance and be enhanced by)" rather than conflict with "the sense of separateness."[7]

The mutual attunement of mother and child is never perfect; its inevitable failures intensify the child's tendency to escape from the tensions of intersubjectivity to fantasies of absolute domination, absolute submission, total independence of the other, perfect union with the other. Domination/submission is "a peculiar transposition of the desire for recognition."[8] Hence it is the intersubjective dimension of the mother-child relationship—not infantile sexuality—that succumbs to domination.

According to Benjamin, Herbert Marcuse was able to see the possibility of a fundamentally different relationship between humanity and nature in which nature is not dominated. It is "objectified and instrumentalized but known as an independent subjective other." However, "his adherence to drive theory made him unable to ground it psychoanalytically, because he lacked a model of the psyche in which the self truly seeks to know the outside world and longs for contact with the other." He "could only envision connection as a return to oneness, a dedifferentiation and irrationality, a romantic . . . reunion with nature."[9] Marcuse "affirms the 'limitless narcissism' of the babe at the breast who does not recognize the mother's, or anyone else's, equal subjectivity. A deeper critique is necessary, one which rejects the terms of sexual polarity, of subject and object, and so rejects any revolt that merely reverses these terms."[10]

It is true that Marcuse's *Eros and Civilization* has been misinterpreted constantly for the past thirty years as a call for the abolition of all repression, for regression to primary narcissism. In fact Marcuse distinguished *basic* from *surplus* repression, and he advocated a regression to primary narcissism that would coincide with the maintenance of "divisions and boundaries that are real." He criticized Norman O. Brown's "mystical" appeal "for the restoration of original and total unity."[11] Marcuse argued that unnecessary surplus repression of narcissistic infantile sexuality gives rise to a rigid, superindividuated ego capable of experiencing only separateness, never "regressing" to oneness. Abolition of surplus repression would permit the evolution of a new kind of ego, able to experience oneness and separateness simultaneously. Narcissism is, as Marcuse put it, "the *germ* of a different *reality* principle," in accordance with which "the opposition between . . . subject and object is overcome"[12] and yet will simultaneously "continue to exist."[13]

Benjamin speaks of a "flexible ego" for whom "the experience of union is simply an excursion. The feeling of losing oneself . . . does not obliterate the self . . . one does not really lose oneself."[14] In mutual recognition, separateness is not experienced as the antithesis of oneness; oneness "could coexist with (enhance and be enhanced by) separateness."[15] The experience of "losing the self in the other and the sense of being truly known for oneself . . . coalesce."[16] This is not very different from the dialectical regression to primary narcissism called for by Marcuse. It is not the case that *only* an intersubjective theory can give us access to the simultaneity and mutual enhancement of oneness and separateness beyond the polarization of subject and object.

At the same time, it is true that the language of intersubjectivity has a great deal to contribute to the psychoanalytic grounding of Marcuse's new erotic reality principle. We can see that dialectical regression is not simply a *return* to an infantile oneness that *retains* adult separateness but a return to infantile intersubjectivity from a more highly differentiated adult intersubjectivity. The ego returns to its origins not only because it is "strong" enough to be flexible, to "tolerate" the regression, but because flexibility belongs to its infantile nature.

The language of intersubjectivity also helps make sense of Marcuse's concept (borrowed from Charles Odier) of a "maternal superid" reconciling rational conscience, compassion, and instinctual pleasure and displacing the punitive paternal superego in a nonrepressive civilization. Benjamin shows that we can find in the intersubjective dimension of the pregenital object relation the sources of an erotic conscience, which, unlike the classical Freudian superego, does not depend on the internalization of the authority of the father. "Mutual recognition cannot be achieved through obedience, through identification with the other's power, or through repression. It requires, finally, contact with the other."[17] Polymorphous perverse sexuality is not only that which is contained by conscience—it is also that which informs conscience. As Marcuse himself puts it in *An Essay on Liberation*, "prior to all ethical behavior in accordance with specific social standards . . . morality is a 'disposition' of the organism . . . rooted in the erotic drive."[18]

If it is difficult to conceptualize and spell out the implications of a new reality principle in the language of sexuality exclusively, it is equally difficult to conceptualize *nature* in the language of intersubjectivity exclusively. The mutual recognition of consciousnesses is in danger of forgetting that drive for bodily pleasure, that *jouissance* which is not simply between persons but precedes and transcends all subjectivity and intersubjectivity and hence cannot be located simply in the relationality of subjects. Deprivation is more than deprivation of mutual recognition, and satisfaction is more than the satisfaction of the delineated and interrelated person. The spontaneity and sensuality of a living, embodied being is larger than self-and-other.

If it is true that there is in reality no such phenomenon as sexuality without an object, perhaps it is equally true that there is no object relation without the sexual body. Each side of this equation needs to be conceptualized in distinction from the other at some point in theory. Sexuality has to be seen in relational context, and relationality has to be seen in sexual context. There is no inherently sexless desire for recognition. "Self" and "other" and "intersubjectivity" are no more immune to reification than "instinctual drive."

The danger is too great that ideologists of surplus repression will assimilate Benjamin's position to that of the neo-Freudian revisionists criticized by Marcuse for their "defamation of the pleasure principle" in his epilogue to *Eros and Civilization*. Stephen Mitchell, for example, has recently declared that Freud's view of sexuality "as existing apart from and prior to socialization" represents a defensive maneuver, a neurotic escape from "our relational responsibilities."[19] Mitchell agrees with the revisionist Erich Fromm that sexuality is merely "the expression of an attitude toward the world in the language of the body," that bodily pleasure is merely a means of establishing contact with another person. "Sexuality is not a powerful, dangerous . . . push from within but . . . a function, an expression of the relational matrix."[20] It is just a language that provides "metaphors for expressing different types of relationships"[21]—just a "metaphor which serves important functions in terms of self-organization."

Mitchell rejects Freud's "romanticization of animals and early man as somehow closer to pleasure." Freud was wrong when he conceptualized "a realm of unfettered pleasure, free of the tyranny of the object and social necessities."[22] There is no such realm. Human beings are only subjects. Sexuality is just a language. There is nothing animal about human beings, only a "metaphor of the beast,"[23] a fantasy of boundless pleasure that falsely represents our sexuality as something not entirely subsumed within relationships. Civilization is not based on a breaking of the instinctual life of human beings, for there is no such instinctual life. The discontents of civilization can be fully comprehended in terms of the escape of lazy subjects from the demands of mutuality.

That Benjamin might regret such utilization of the concept of relationality is indicated in a few sentences in which she restates—without acknowledgement—Marcuse's call for regression to polymorphously perverse infantile sexuality: "When the sexual self is represented by the sensual capacities of the whole body, when the totality of space between, outside, and within our bodies becomes the site of pleasure, then desire escapes the borders of the imperial phallus and resides on the shores of endless worlds." But she attributes the loss of these capacities not to repression of pregenital sexuality but to the loss of the "early attunement and mutual play of infancy."[24] As if "drive theory" and the language of sexuality could lead only to the "imperial phallus."

Can the language of sexuality be entirely subsumed within the language of mutual recognition? Can the pleasure of the whole body be derived theoretically from intersubjectivity only? Does the body itself not demand recognition by theory? And what of the *energy* of desire—the "drive"—not as a reified metapsychological concept but as real intensity, as lived quantity? Is there only quality? Benjamin would like to theorize polymorphous sexuality, but without the language of sexuality, she is unable to ground it psychoanalytically. Like the other object relations theorists, she lacks a model of the psyche as embodied. It is as if the subjects in attunement were inevitably, but only empirically, incidentally, accidentally, embodied.

Repression of Bisexuality or Gender Polarization?

Freud dealt with the polarization of subjectivity and objectivity as a concomitant of the repression of infantile bisexuality. Benjamin follows Chodorow in dismissing the language of sexuality and bisexuality, focusing exclusively on the formation of gender identity as determined by the cultural institution of mother-monopolized child rearing.

Because children must become individuals by distinguishing their identities from that of the parent, and because the primary parent is always the mother, children turn to the father, the man. They strive to identify with him, the bearer of the idealized phallus, symbol of difference and separation from the mother. Only in boys is this identification with father encouraged by both parents. Because boys' first identification is with a member of the opposite sex—that is, because father does not mother—they must repudiate that identification completely in order to achieve a precarious masculine gender identity. In order to be men, they must not be like mother in any way. They must renounce nurturance and acquire icy autonomy, becoming—as Benjamin puts it in taking up this approach—nothing *but* subject, knower and master of the objective external world. Here is the polarization of activity and passivity: The wholeness of recognition, of doing and being done to, succumbs to splitting. The "two sides are represented as opposite and distinct tendencies, available only as alternatives. The subject can play only one side at a time, projecting the opposite side onto the other."[25] Domination/submission displaces mutual recognition and emotional attunement. "Rationality" (Marcuse's "repressive reality principle" or "performance principle") forbids "affective exchange" with the other. "Independence from the mother as object rather than recognition of her as subject constitutes the essence of individuation. . . . The image of the other . . . is not that of a vitally real presence but a cognitively perceived object."[26] "She is in control of" the all-powerful father, "whom one takes as one's ideal."[27] All emotional attunement, empathy, vulnerability, dependence, all feelings of continuity with the other are "now experienced as dangerously close to losing oneself in the other . . . the devaluation of the need for the other becomes a touchstone of adult masculinity." Here is the origin of the "ideal of a self-sufficient individual," the "ideal of individuality and rationality" that is now the chief manifestation of male hegemony, having survived "even the waning of paternal authority" in the modern family.[28]

The girl, since she belongs to the same sex as the mother, has no need to establish radical separateness from her in order to establish her gender identity; indeed, continuity with the mother (lack of individuation) is equated with being a woman. Mother encourages daughter to maintain continuity, to reproduce her lack of subjectivity, to become a subordinated mother object like her mother before her. The girl is not allowed to identify with father, to separate herself, like the boy, from mother and from helplessness, because of father's need "to assert difference from women." The father will not recognize his daughter as he does his son as a subject like himself. He sees her as "a sweet adorable thing, a nascent sex-object." He "offers seduction rather than identification."[29]

"What Freud called penis envy, the little girl's masculine" sexuality, says Benjamin, is really her desire to identify with the father as subject, to be recognized as "one who can will things and make them happen."[30] However, for Benjamin there is nothing particularly relevant to sexuality and sexual repression in the girl's surrender of her desire to identify with her father and her assumption of the identity of woman—the one who idealizes and submits to the domination of the man, who has what she can never possess, the phallus, symbol of subjectivity split from and mastering objectivity. Benjamin does discuss woman's lack of "sexual agency"[31] as an *effect* of woman's loss of recognition as a subject, but not as *repression* of the active sexuality of women.

Instead of calling, as Marcuse does, for the abolition of surplus repression of bisexuality, Benjamin calls for a dissolution of gender polarity—for "different gender arrangements" in which mother and father no longer represent objectivity as opposed to subjectivity: "Both parents can be figures of separation *and* attachment, both boys *and* girls can make use of identifications with both parents without being confused about their gender identity."[32] Mothers and daughters would reclaim their subjectivity; fathers and sons would rediscover the capacity to experience dependence and emotional attunement without anxiety.

I believe that the intersubjective view of gender polarization loses an essential strength of the Freudian-Marcusean approach: its grasp of the sexual character of polarization and its consequent explicit challenge to heterosexism. If the child were no longer compelled to identify exclusively with the parent of the same sex, women would become subjects, men would become empathic and nurturant—*and* the normalcy of gender identity would no longer entail exclusive heterosexuality. Queer behavior would become normal. Freedom of the child to identify with each parent—and freedom of each parent to manifest characteristics previously assigned exclusively to the opposite sex—would mean that human qualities presently denigrated as belonging to the "butch" woman, the "dyke," the "sissy," and the "faggot" would pervade the private and public spheres of life. Benjamin's repression of the language of bisexuality makes it easy for her to avoid any hint of challenge to heterosexism.[33] The end of patriarchy is not just a new experience of intersubjectivity. Yet the language of intersubjectivity makes it easy to underestimate the magnitude of the changes in sexuality that would follow the abolition of domination.

Benjamin's account of patriarchal domination is an advance on Marcuse's work,[34] not only in its comprehension of the importance of mother-monopolized child rearing but in an additional, very significant respect: She deconstructs the polarity of activity and passivity, whereas Marcuse accepted it, subjecting to radical criticism only the phallocentric assumption that men must repudiate passivity and women must repress activity. Marcuse did not challenge Freud's assumption that passivity and activity are opposites, and thus are alternatives, and that sexual life must first be experienced in terms of the polarity or antithesis of activity and passivity.[35] It therefore seemed "obvious" that lifting the surplus repression of bisexuality would result in something like androgyny, men and women capable of *both* activity and passivity, with both still imagined as alternatives, as distinct tendencies that can be realized only one at a time. Benjamin's account makes it clear that the notion of bisexuality suffers from the tendency of psychoanalysis to stress "complementarity in interaction over mutuality. The other is represented as the answer, and the self as the need; the other is the breast, and the self is the hunger. . . . This complementarity of activity and passivity forms a dual unity which can be internalized and reversed ('now I'm the Mommy and you're the baby'). The dual unity form has within it this tendency to remain constant even in reversal, never to equalize but simply invert itself within relationships of dependency . . . the complementary dual unity is the basic structure of domination."[36]

It becomes clear that the salience of the issue of activity-passivity in the psychic life of the preoedipal child is itself a product of surplus repression; and that "bisexuality," if read as two souls (masculine and feminine) in one body, is itself a product of the repression of infantile polymorphous, multivalent sexuality: multisexuality.

Class Domination or Mother-Monopolized Child Rearing?

Very near to the beginning of her book, *Bonds of Love*, Benjamin states that the psychoanalytic inquiry into domination takes "woman's subordination . . . for granted. Even the most radical of Freudians left strangely untouched psychoanalysis's most profound and unexamined assumption about domination: the subordination of women to men."[37] This is not altogether true, and Benjamin herself provides a qualification. "Strictly speaking, we must grant that Reich . . . Marcuse . . . and Brown did not ignore the problem of women's subordination. However, in both Reich and Marcuse the discussion of the problem was always elided into the discussion of the social relations of production; the feminist analysis gave way to the Marxian one. For Brown too, male domination was not an independent issue but instead, a way station in culture's denial of death and the instincts."[38]

Although I do not agree that Marcuse's feminist analysis must be read as giving way to the Marxian one, or that male domination is merely a "way station," I do recognize that a certain tendency to subordinate the issue of gender to that of class survives in Marcuse's argument. Marcuse does equate patriarchy with class domination and fails to provide an extended discussion of the crucial role of gender polarization in the structure of domination. He pays no attention to the inertia of patriarchal structures conceived as separate from the structure of class domination—almost as if men as gender-class containing both ruler and ruled had no significant common interest in the subordination of women. Benjamin's insistence, and that of other feminist theorists, that the structure of gender relations must be treated as an "independent issue" is thus an essential correction of the Marcusean position. But gender relations ought not be treated *only* as an independent issue. In reading Benjamin's *Bonds of Love*, one can easily come to the conclusion that even without class society's requirement for hierarchically organized alienated labor, men's need to establish their masculine identity under the circumstances of mother-monopolized child rearing would require the polarization of subject and object, the domination of nature and of woman as nature—that it is gender polarization which (simply) gives rise to class domination.

The Marxian analysis gives way to the feminist one. But Benjamin's brief critique, toward the end of her book, of the "limitations of the psychoanalytic feminist approach . . . [of] Chodorow and Dinnerstein" suggests that it is not Benjamin's intention simply to turn the tables on the Freudian Marxists: "Chodorow and Dinnerstein conclude . . . that if both men and women raised children, both would become associated with primary oneness. . . . Males would no longer have to . . . repudiate and denigrate . . . nurturance and empathy, and this might begin to dissolve the rationality" of the performance principle (which is, as Marcuse acknowledged, "the male principle"). Benjamin questions this conclusion, believing that gender polarization would persist even with the end of mother-monopolized child rearing. Larger cultural structures are involved "because parents are not only objects of identification: they actively . . . shape the child's identity in accordance with the culture—continuity in girls, discontinuity in boys."[39]

There are a few sentences here about the need for "a radical extension of the feminist critique" to the larger structures of societal rationalization—"the hegemony of formal rules . . . of instrumental knowledge . . . of the accumulation of profit"[40]—which are the materializations of the principle of male domination. Gender polarization is a deep structure of the civilization as a whole; Benjamin seems very close here to acknowledging that subject-object polarization does not simply spread *from* the man-woman relation *to* the larger structures. And in the last endnote, on the last page of the book, she writes, "I have not tried to name the origin of this structure, to locate it in a specific set of social relations."[41] If the attempt were made, it might carry us down to our repressed memories of Freud's theories of infantile sexuality and Marcuse's challenge to patriarchal class domination in the name of the pleasure principle.

Conclusion

Our knowledge of contemporary gatherer-hunter societies points to the possibility that mother-monopolized child rearing, though it has produced in virtually every human culture not only an intense focus on gender identity as the central organizing feature of personal identity but also a substantial degree of tension and hostility between the sexes, gives rise to *subordination* of women—polarization of subjectivity and objectivity—only under certain definite economic and social circumstances. For example, according to Colin Turnbull, the student of the Mbuti pygmies of Zaire (the "Forest People"), there is absolutely no subordination of women among these people. It is in fact the female elders who have "both authority and power," overshadowing that of the males, precisely because it is the woman who is the mother. There is noticeable tension between males and females, but it is resolved by working "hard at emphasizing the complementarity of the sexes without any sense of superordination or subordination."[42] Other anthropologists have made similar observations of other gatherer-hunter cultures, and there is a growing tendency among feminist anthropologists to question our perception of male superiority in still other gatherer-hunter societies as the projection of the male anthropologist.

Mbuti males[43] are so playful, so gentle that Steven Goldberg, author of the infamous *Inevitability of Patriarchy*,[44] has to explain their existence as an exception to his "Iron Law." According to Goldberg, men are biologically foreordained by their endocrine system to be more competitive than women; therefore, all societies that require competition will evoke the superior competitive performance of men, and women will be subordinated "for their own good." Among the Mbuti, however, there is no need for competitive behavior. Man's potential for domination is not evoked. For Goldberg, this exception is trivial, in fact useful, for proving his rule, because modern society "must" be competitive. Competition cannot be abolished without regression to the forest, and no one would want to go back.

From my point of view, the interesting question is this: Could it be that mother-monopolized child rearing, whatever its primitive origins, develops into gender polarization only under certain circumstances having to do with competition, war, the state, and class? Could it be that mother-monopolized child rearing *and* the patriarchal domination that rises on that foundation cannot be abolished without the abolition of toil? Can we use the languages of intersubjectivity and sexuality, and of gender and class, without needing to *derive* one from the other? If so, Benjamin's feminist psychoanalysis could only be greatly enriched and strengthened by a conscious return to the repressed sexual and socialist themes of Marcuse's *Eros and Civilization*.

Notes

1. Jessica Benjamin, *The Bonds of Love: Psychoanalysis, Feminism, and the Problem of Domination* (New York: Pantheon Books, 1988), 7.
2. Ibid., 31.
3. Ibid., 18.
4. Ibid., 20.
5. Ibid., 48.
6. Ibid., 30.
7. Ibid., 47.
8. Ibid., 56.
9. Ibid., 191.
10. Ibid., 177.
11. Gad Horowitz, *Repression: Basic and Surplus Repression in Psychoanalytic Theory—Freud, Reich, and Marcuse* (Toronto and Buffalo: University of Toronto Press, 1977), 203.
12. Herbert Marcuse, *Eros and Civilization: A Philosophical Inquiry into Freud* (Boston: Beacon Press, 1955), 166–69.
13. Herbert Marcuse, "Love Mystified: A Critique of Norman O. Brown," in Herbert Marcuse, *Negations: Essays in Critical Theory*, trans. Jeremy J. Shapiro (Boston: Beacon Press, 1968), 236.
14. Benjamin, *Bonds of Love*, 174.
15. Ibid., 47.
16. Ibid., 126.
17. Ibid., 40.
18. Herbert Marcuse, *An Essay on Liberation* (Boston: Beacon Press, 1969), 10.
19. Stephen Mitchell, *Relational Concepts in Psychoanalysis* (Cambridge, Mass.: Harvard University Press, 1988), 122.
20. Ibid., 87.
21. Ibid., 91.
22. Ibid., 121.
23. Ibid., 119.
24. Benjamin, *Bonds of Love*, 130.
25. Ibid., 63.
26. Ibid., 77–78.

27. Ibid., 165.

28. Ibid., 170–73.

29. Ibid., 109–10.

30. Ibid., 102.

31. Ibid., 87–91.

32. Ibid., 112.

33. Except in one footnote: "The core sense of belonging to one sex or the other is not compromised by cross-sex identifications and behaviors. The wish to be and do what the other sex does is not pathological, not necessarily a denial of one's own identity. The choice of love object, heterosexual or homosexual, is not the determining aspect of gender identity." Ibid., 113.

34. For an analysis of the implications of Marcuse's work for bisexuality, see Horowitz, *Repression*, chapter 4.

35. Ibid., 94.

36. Benjamin, *Bonds of Love*, 47–48.

37. Ibid., 7.

38. Ibid., 247.

39. Ibid., 217.

40. Ibid., 216.

41. Ibid., 294, n. 60.

42. Colin Turnbull, "Mbuti Womanhood," in *Woman the Gatherer*, ed. Frances Dahlberg (New Haven, Conn.: Yale University Press, 1981), 211–12.

43. See Horowitz, *Repression*, 118–19.

44. Steven Goldberg, *The Inevitability of Patriarchy* (New York: William Morrow, 1973).

C. Fred Alford

Marx, Marcuse, and Psychoanalysis: Do They Still Fit after All These Years?

Much has changed in psychoanalysis since the 1954 publication of Herbert Marcuse's *Eros and Civilization*. Object relations theory, which emerged in the 1930s and which has come to dominate psychoanalysis, was apparently unknown to the Frankfurt School, including Marcuse. The choice faced by Marcuse, that between Freud on the one hand and the social-psychological revisionists on the other hand, no longer holds. In addition, new critics have turned to psychoanalysis to support radical social programs, or antiprograms. Psychoanalytic feminists, such as Dorothy Dinnerstein and Nancy Chodorow, are the best known in the United States, but a more radical group has emerged in Europe. Influenced by the psychoanalyst Jacques Lacan, as well as postmodernism generally, scholars such as Julia Kristeva and Luce Irigaray are returning to Freud in an entirely new way. In many respects these women are the true legatees of the Frankfurt School's transformation of psychoanalysis into a medium of radical social criticism. A complete reassessment of Marcuse's appropriation of psychoanalysis would have to include these developments.

My essay is not so ambitious. Instead, I focus on what remains of lasting value in Marcuse's project after its key failure is confronted. That key failure is his insensitivity to human relatedness, to the way in which not eros but relationships fulfull the self—or rather, the way in which eros is always already part of a relationship with another subject. Pleasure, says object relations theorist W. R. D. Fairbairn, is not the object; it is the signpost to a relationship with the object.[1] Is there any way to appreciate this insight, the insight of psychoanalytic object relations theory, while preserving Marcuse's radical, utopian individualism, his "somatization of radical protest, its concentration on the sensibility and feelings of individuals," as he put it in his last address?[2] If these two insights cannot be wedded in some way, then no reinterpretation of Marcuse's project is possible, only a revision that abandons its core. I believe that a genuine reinterpretation is feasible and that it depends on the recognition that the self that relates to others is first of all a body self—a body ego, as Freud calls it. Mutual recognition supports the psyche, so that it can localize itself in its body rather than finding itself in the commodities and fantasies of one-dimensional society. The core of Marcuse's thinking, what remains of lasting value, is his commitment to the reasons of the body. In a postmodern era in which texts seem to have replaced bodies, Marcuse's work is more important than ever.

Eros and Civilization as Response to Instrumental Reason, to the Proletariat, and to Auschwitz

In their critique of the dialectic of Enlightenment, Theodor Adorno and Max Horkheimer, Marcuse's Frankfurt School colleagues, involved every aspect of reason in the domination of nature. Man was once weak and ignorant, nature was powerful and mysterious. Man learned to master nature, but only by transforming reason into an instrument of domination and control. Not even idealistic reason escaped this fate: "Idealism as rage" at a world too sparse to be dominated is how Adorno put it.[3] Unfortunately, Horkheimer and Adorno could conceive of no alternative to reason. Adorno wrote of approaching the world "without velleity (*Willkür*) or violence." Velleity, it will be recalled, is the weakest form of desire, one that does not lead to the slightest action, and the term seems an excellent rendering of Adorno's intent.[4] But not Marcuse's! *Eros and Civilization* may be read as Marcuse's solution to the Frankfurt School's critique of instrumental reason, in which eros, the strongest desire, takes the place of reason—or blends with it.

The "dialectic of civilization," according to Marcuse's interpretation of Freud, stems from the fact that culture demands the repression of eros, so that psychic energy that would otherwise be directed toward gratification can be inhibited and rechanneled into work. The trouble is that in repressing eros, culture represses and weakens the one force that might be able to "bind" aggression. As Marcuse puts it, "Culture demands continuous sublimation; it thereby weakens Eros, the builder of culture. And desexualization, by weakening Eros, unbinds the destructive impulses. Civilization is thus threatened by an instinctual de-fusion, in which the death instinct strives to gain ascendency over the life instincts. Originating in renunciation . . . civilization tends toward self-destruction."[5] *Eros and Civilization* is Marcuse's intervention into this fatal dialectic, which Horkheimer and Adorno called the dialectic of Enlightenment but which Marcuse, playing off the title of Freud's *Civilization and Its Discontents*, calls the dialectic of civilization. Under either rubric the problem is the same: how to contain human aggression against man and nature, even when this aggression masquerades under the title of reason and civilization itself.

Marcuse turned to eros to solve not merely a profound philosophical problem but a more pressing political one as well. Who or what might become the carrier or agent (*Träger*) of the revolution, now that the proletariat had so clearly failed its historical task? The answer is not a social class but a biological dimension within us all. It is a dimension Marcuse calls eros, protected but not immune from social pressure. Rarely has such a desperate, implausible answer inspired such a fine work. Perhaps, too, Marcuse turned to eros as an alternative to the despair reflected in Adorno's famous statement that "to write poetry after Auschwitz is barbaric."[6] *Eros and Civilization* is filled with poetry; it is a type of philosophical poetry.

Drawing on the later psychoanalytic theory of Freud, Marcuse argues that men and women are shaped by two primary drives. One is called eros, or erotic energy, or the life instinct—these terms are roughly synonymous. The other primary drive is thanatos: destructive energy, the wish to destroy life, to annihilate it. Developing this scheme under the shadow of the First World War, Freud held that these two drives are basic, inborn, given, and always in conflict, with death always threatening to gain the upper hand.[7] Marcuse's approach was to recognize that while these drives may be given, the balance between them might depend on the social organization of society and hence be subject to historical modification.

Although Marcuse's argument is complicated, requiring a deep knowledge of Freudian psychoanalytic theory, its basic structure is fairly simple. When considered broadly, both eros, the drive for greater unities, and thanatos, the drive to return to an inorganic state, are derivative. Both are manifestations of a more primal drive to eliminate tension, a drive Marcuse calls the nirvana principle. These instincts are not truly dualistic but instead are composed of a displaceable energy that is able to join forces with either the erotic or destructive impulses. "Never before has death been so consistently taken into the essence of life; but never before also has death come so close to Eros."[8] Since in the advanced industrial world there exist enough resources to satisfy everyone's basic needs, it is in principle possible to relax repression, Marcuse argues. The repression necessary so that people in the First World might continue to have more consumer goods is really surplus repression: necessary to preserve the unequal distribution of scarcity, but unnecessary to support a decent existence. Under decent social conditions, a nonrepressed eros could triumph over destructiveness as a means to approach nirvana. Culture would be driven and expanded not from the energies of repression but from the energies of sublimation.

Under a social order governed by sublimated eros, Marcuse continues, human alienation from labor would be complete. Individuals would no longer have to find satisfaction in their work, for such satisfaction is always incomplete, in some way always false. Elsewhere I have shown that Marcuse's formulation leaves no room for satisfaction in a job well done, even for its own sake.[9] Marcuse is not writing of a world in which individuals would be laborers in the morning and poets in the afternoon. He is writing of a world in which even the writing of poetry would be a detour from genuine gratification. Here I shall let Marcuse speak for himself, and we should take him as literally as he intends: "The more complete the alienation of labor, the greater the potential of freedom: total automation would be the optimum. . . . The realm of necessity, of labor, is one of unfreedom. . . . Play and display, as principles of civilization, imply not the transformation of labor but its complete subordination to the freely evolving potentialities of man and nature."[10]

Eros and Civilization as Rage

"Is our picture in speech any the less beautiful because we can't show how it can be realized in fact?" asks Socrates when describing his ideal Republic (*Republic*, 473e). A traditional answer has been "it depends," and this applies to Marcuse's erotic ideal as well. It depends on whether this picture, even if impossible to achieve, captures the core issues and dilemmas that humans face as they live in this world. It depends, in other words, on whether this picture captures something important about human nature—a beleaguered but important term, especially when employed as Marcuse does as a virtual oxymoron. "There is no such thing as an immutable human nature," he writes in a last address.[11] Yet, if eros is a creature of history, then it loses its great revolutionary virtue, which is its utter demandingness and its desire for real and genuine fulfillment now and forever. It is these qualities that make eros such a potent and permanent revolutionary force, even in exile, so to speak, deep within the alienated body and one-dimensional mind. I do not believe that Marcuse ever solved this dilemma: To make eros historical, so that it might be liberated by changes in technology, labor, and society, is to risk its emancipatory potential, which rests in its immunity to social influences. Nor do I believe that it is important to solve this conflict. On the contrary, the dilemma misleads, because it is based on assumptions about scarcity and satisfaction far too material. In this regard Marcuse's utopia does not adequately incorporate fundamental forces and facts of human existence.

This can best be seen by focusing on Marcuse's difference with Freud on repression. For Marcuse, repression is a consequence of the child's confrontation with the reality principle, as represented by father. Take away the reality principle, expressed in scarcity and labor, and virtually all repression could become surplus. For Freud, on the other hand, repression is a consequence of psychosexual development itself, aimed not so much at preparing the body for labor as at separating the child from his union with mother, a union that would otherwise culminate in incest.[12] Seen from this angle, Norman O. Brown comes closer to the mark in *Life against Death*. For Brown, the "lack of sufficient means and resources" that has always seemed to be the lot of humans on this earth stems not from the way labor, capital, and goods are organized and distributed but from nonmaterial needs so powerful that no conceivable organization of society could meet them. "Scarcity" is not a material lack but an emotional and relational one, a scarcity of undivided mother-love. "It is because the child loves the mother so much that it feels separation from the mother as death," says Brown.[13] All the automation in the world will not overcome this scarcity.

From this perspective, the child seeks a sexual relationship with mother not "only" from sexual desire but from a wish to overcome his own separation and dependence by having a child with his mother and so becoming his own father. The fantasy behind this wish is the desire for absolute self-sufficiency, the *causa sui* project, as Brown calls it, of becoming father to oneself. Incestuous desire, fear of separation and dependence, fear of castration (a separation from a precious part of oneself), fear of death: all run together to express not so much a fear of loss of pleasure as a fear of what it is to be human in this world, to be separate, vulnerable, and alone. Eros, love in all its manifestations, can provide compensation for this experience of humanness, but it can hardly overcome it. Think, for a moment, of what it means to love and lose a loved one. Love does not so much compensate for the loss as cause the pain. Love is the problem, the source of pain, not the solution to it, even though another love, perhaps a later one, may ease the emptiness. But not fully, and not too soon, or we shall know that something was missing in the original love, or in the new one (because it would be easy to make comparisons to the original love).

If we consider Marcuse's culture heroes, those mythical figures who represent Marcuse's erotic ideal, Orpheus and Narcissus, from this perspective, a troubling point arises. Marcuse seeks not merely freedom from labor so that the entire body might remain libidinally cathected—that is, what he calls polymorphous perversity. Rather, Marcuse seeks an erotic relationship to the self so complete that others are unnecessary and become a burden, their presence reminding us of the pain of separation, incompleteness, loss, and death that accompany us throughout life. To escape this burden is indeed an old philosophical ideal, as old as Plato's *Symposium* and *Phaedrus*, in which the eros of the body is supposed to lead young men to a transcendent union with an unchanging beauty that lasts forever. I believe that Marcuse sees, not "idealism as rage," but eros as rage: a rage that humans depend so terribly on unreliable others and our own unreliable bodies.

Marcuse states that the dominant mythic culture heroes are Apollonian figures such as Odysseus and Prometheus. They are clever tricksters who create culture at the price of perpetual pain and at the price of the Dionysian aspiration to transgress boundaries and abandon the self to sleep, paradise, release: death-in-life, life-in-death, nirvana. It is against such culture heroes that Marcuse calls attention to Orpheus and Narcissus. It is the neglect of the orphic and narcissistic element that leads directly to the dialectic of Enlightenment, the transformation of reason into an instrument of rage at a nature that demands so much self-sacrifice as the price of survival. Orpheus and Narcissus, says Marcuse, "have not become the culture-heroes of the Western world: theirs is the image of joy and fulfillment; the voice which does not command but sings; the gesture which offers and receives; the deed which is peace and ends the labor of conquest; the liberation from time which unites man with god, man with nature."[14]

Yet we should not forget the full story of these antiheroes, a story Marcuse only selectively consults. Narcissus rejects the erotic charms of Echo for the autoeroticism of his own image, finding it so attractive that he pines away and dies while admiring it in the still water. Orpheus, Marcuse's other antihero, could charm wild beasts with his lyre. However, after striking a deal with Pluto to recover his wife Eurydice from Hades, he could not control his own desire and anxiety sufficiently to lead her back to this world. Instead, he seeks a reassuring glance of her, and she is snatched away from him forever. Thereafter Orpheus held himself apart from women, dwelling on his lost opportunity. Thracian maidens sought to captivate him, but he resisted their charms, until one day they became so incensed that they drowned out the music of his lyre with their screams and tore him to pieces. Is an erotic hero fixated on himself unto death really an image of fulfillment? Is someone who, through lack of control, fails to reach a genuinely desirable goal and so spends the rest of his life in mourning, rejecting eros utterly, an ideal? Surely the balance can be better struck than this.

In defense of Marcuse it may be argued that he emphasizes that Orpheus and Narcissus illustrate the isolated deeds of individuals, and as such they are bound to be neurotic, aiming at death, not life. "As an isolated individual phenomenon, the reactivation of narcissistic libido is not culture-building but neurotic."[15] Only when the protest against the reality principle is shared may eros become a social force, the builder of culture and communities and a medium of human relationships. It is in this light that Chodorow's criticism in "Beyond Drive Theory" should be read: that Marcuse *intends*, at least, that his erotic utopia be filled with erotic relationships, even if his theory of how this might come about (nonrepressive sublimation) finds no support in Freud. Chodorow argues that the narcissistic mode of relating, typical of Marcuse's erotic utopia, "pre-cludes those very intersubjective relationships that should form the core of any social and political vision." The narcissistic mode described by Marcuse is characterized by a " 'refusal to accept separation from the libidinous object (or subject)' "; thus his " 'union with a whole world of love and pleasure,' denies the object or external world its own separateness and choice."[16] Chodorow concludes that among the "higher values" that Marcuse should include are respect and concern for the needs and autonomy of others.

Radicalism and Revisionism

Although Chodorow's criticism is trenchant, she is nonetheless a "Neo-Freudian revisionist" in the precise sense of the term employed by Marcuse: one who puts harmonious social relationships first.[17] For Marcuse it is the pure revolutionary potential of eros, its utter demandingness, even selfishness, that makes it such a potent force. Is there any way to preserve this revolutionary aspect of eros while at the same time acknowledging that the human being is fundamentally relational, that each person finds deepest satisfaction not in pleasure per se but in being recognized by others for who he or she truly is and in recognizing others accordingly? This, I take it, is the fundamental challenge raised not only by Chodorow but by developments in psychoanalysis and psychoanalytic social theory in the last forty years: to make *Eros and Civilization* an account of human relationships, without diluting its radical, utopian individualism that puts individual happiness first.

There are, I believe, three dimensions of what Marcuse calls eros that are central to his project. Each reflects the importance Marcuse attaches to finding a reliable source of opposition to a totalizing, one-dimensional society.

1. The "somatization of radical protest, its concentration on the sensibility and feelings of individuals," as the ground of revolution. Not revolutionary ideas but revolutionary needs, rooted in the body's desire for satisfaction, are the most profound source of radical social thought and action.

2. The search for a source of resistance to repression and false-consciousness that will not be readily coopted, especially by that smooth,

comforting, attractive society Marcuse writes of in *One-Dimensional Man*.

3. The search for a dimension of human experience that demands the real thing: not satisfaction in labor, or meaningful work, or even creative pursuits, but satisfaction per se. If civilization and memory are just detours from primitive gratification, then forget both civilization and memory and go directly for the gratification.

A successful reinterpretation of *Eros and Civilization* in light of almost forty years of criticism, as well as almost fifty years of developments in psychoanalysis, most of which Marcuse was unaware, will respect and preserve something of this radicalism—a radicalism that is inseparable, I believe, from Marcuse's utopian individualism. If a reinterpretation does not preserve this aspect of *Eros and Civilization*, then it is no real reinterpretation at all. It is a different story altogether, and a less profound one as well.

The Dialectic of Mutual Recognition:
From Hegel to Winnicott

Here I can only sketch the outlines of such a reinterpretation, drawing on the work of psychoanalyst D. W. Winnicott, student of Melanie Klein's and perhaps the most well-known of all the British object relations theorists, as they are called. Elsewhere I have traced the development of object relations theory in some detail, relating its development to the Frankfurt School's appropriation of psychoanalysis.[18] In place of what Freud called drives, object relations theory substitutes a focus on the self's relationship with and use of others in order to become a subject. As Fairbairn puts it, pleasure is not the object. Pleasure is a signpost to a relationship with the object. It is this relationship that counts most, but not simply because people want relationships with others. First and foremost, men and women desire themselves: not as objects of narcissistic satisfaction but as subjects of their own selfhood. This requires the recognition of, and relationships with, others. Jacques Lacan makes a similar argument, even if his conclusions are more despairing. I believe that this insight runs deeper than either Freud's or Marcuse's. Behind the desire for pleasure is a desire to be a genuine or true self, able to be its own subject. This insight is also

139

more profound than Chodorow's; she sees the relationship as fundamental, yet it is not merely the relationship but the way in which the relationship serves the self that is key. This is why my reinterpretation better captures Marcuse's project.

To write of the way in which relationships serve the self sounds as if relationships must always be part of a selfish struggle. This recalls Hegel's dialectic of mutual recognition, in which Ego wishes to affirm himself as absolute and free, utterly independent of Alter's will. Yet to know oneself as absolute and free requires the recognition of Alter, who of course also wishes to be absolute and free, independent of Ego's recognition. Alter withholds his recognition, so as not to be a mere instrument of Ego's will. And so the struggle continues, becoming more and more ironic, as Ego seeks to force Alter to do what Ego should be able to do for himself were he truly free and independent: to recognize himself. Eventually Ego may force Alter to recognize him, so that instead of mutually recognizing each other, Ego becomes Alter's master. However, even this victory must be a hollow one, as it reveals Ego's dependence on Alter's recognition, quite the opposite of Ego's intended goal of demonstrating his absolute freedom.[19]

Just as Marcuse returns to "an imaginary *temps perdu* in the real life of mankind" in order to discover a utopian alternative to Freud's fatal dialectic of civilization, so too shall I return to the young child's earliest relationship, generally with its mother, to characterize a utopian version of Hegel's dialectic. This utopia is a dialectic of perfect recognition, granted so freely and completely that it is never even noticed. Such a utopia is one to which only infants have rights, and even then it is an idealization, never happening quite like this (and perhaps it shouldn't: mothers have needs, too). But this picture in speech need be no less beautiful simply because it is impossible, as long as it is in accord with human nature. And that nature includes Norman O. Brown's insight that the fundamental human scarcity is not material but relational: a scarcity of undivided mother-love, a scarcity of perfect recognition.

Winnicott writes that the child's self is most endangered by precocious adaptation to the environment. The child has a natural right to use the mother ruthlessly for the recognition and gratification that its development demands.[20] Creativity, Winnicott states, stems from an original stage of unconcern or ruthlessness, in which the infant's spontaneous impulse rules the world. This impulse initially stems from fantasy: the fantasy of an infinite supply of food, warmth, and comfort, offered freely even before its absence is noted. The caretaker's job, at first, is to support the illusion by means of an exquisite sensitivity to the infant's needs, so that the infant might be sustained for a little while in its illusion of omnipotence, along the lines of "I am hungry, and milk appears." Gradually, of course, the infant must be disillusioned, painfully so. If, however, the infant has once experienced this illusion, and if it is withdrawn carefully, the infant will have a lifelong source of strength and creativity from which to draw. This is the core of the true self. If, on the other hand, the mother cannot adapt herself to the infant's needs, intrusively demanding that it comply with her needs and demands, the child will develop what Winnicott calls a false self in order to protect the true self, the self that would take it for granted that every need and gesture will be recognized and reciprocated.[21]

Winnicott's formulation is a reversal of Darwin's. For Darwin, survival (of the species) is assured by adaptation to the environment. For Winnicott, human development is a struggle against adaptation: to be spontaneous, genuine, and free, willfully ignorant of the constraints of the environment.[22] Winnicott, though, is not just writing about freedom, even if much of what he says is remarkably similar to some of Marcuse's early works on freedom.[23] Winnicott is writing about what it is to feel fully real and alive, which is not precisely the same as writing about eros. Eros is the life force, and Winnicott is writing about what it means to experience it most fully. Winnicott answers that to be fully alive means "the localization of self in one's body," and he uses a term from Heidegger, "in-dwelling," to characterize how psyche should reside in soma.[24] Not an easy task, it requires that the mind not be constantly preoccupied with adapting itself to a changing, intrusive, and unpredictable environment. Rather, the psyche should take its environment for granted, being held by it so that the body-self that is the first self, the source of spontaneity and vitality, can come to freely inhabit its mind and so experience "the imaginative elaboration of somatic parts, feelings and functions, that is, of physical aliveness."[25] Winnicott considered artistic expression to be one of the most important ways in which adults could experience and express this imaginative elaboration of the body. The alternative, suggests Winnicott, is the repression of soma by a psyche constantly attuned to adaptation, as though the psyche had to "mind" its body as if it were some dangerous natural object.

The connection between this formulation and the Frankfurt School's critique of the dialectic of Enlightenment should not be overlooked. For both, humanity survives only by coming to mimic the harsh, scarce, and unrelenting aspects of nature, imposing on itself an order and discipline as harsh as the one it inflicts on nature: adaptation as mimesis.[26] To this Winnicott adds that when the environment is experienced as unduly severe the psyche attempts to disown the body; because of the pain and neglect it has suffered (again, all experience is originally body-experience), the body is regarded as a persecutor of the self, of the psyche.[27] More fully than the Frankfurt School does, this explains why reason so often approaches the body, particularly those bodies perceived as somehow more natural (those of women, so-called primitive peoples, and the like), as one last piece of unconquered nature. For Winnicott, mind-body dualism is not so much a philosophical problem as a psychological one, a failure of development, a reaction to the pain and insecurity of experience. Unfortunately, one way this "philosophical" problem is experienced is for the psyche of one group to impose the pains and desires of its members' bodies on other groups. Postmoderns have written of this extensively but have not always explained the connection between philosophy and psychology.[28] Between philosophy and psychology Marcuse interposes the body, making both disciplines more real. In an intellectual world in which the aesthetics of language has driven out the aesthetics of the body, Marcuse's interjection is more important today than ever before.

Winnicott's ideal is appropriate only for infants. Adults who continually expect or demand such perfect responsiveness would no doubt be monsters. Nevertheless, Winnicott's ideal can help us rethink the specifications of social relationships that support the true self. Infants and children must grow up, which means recognizing that they live in a world with other selves who also make a legitimate claim to recognition. Chodorow seems correct in observing that Marcuse does not fully appreciate this fact. Or rather, she is correct that his theory does not allow him to grant recognition of others the importance it deserves. This, however, does not mean that the ideal of the true self is irrelevant, or that

Hegel's dialectic of mutual recognition is the only way to formulate relationships among adult selves.

On the contrary, society is best judged by how well its members cooperate to foster and protect each other's true self. Here is a standard of social development, justice, and legitimacy as fundamental as any other proposed by Marcuse (such as his pacification of existence). Are the culture, economy, and politics of a society organized to promote the true selves of its members, or to repress and distort them? What more important question can be asked about a society than this? In practice, of course, this will be a difficult judgment. Certainly this formulation does not avoid many of the most difficult questions of distributive justice raised by Aristotle and debated for over two millennia. As Norman O. Brown implies, even recognition of one's self is a scarce resource, perhaps the ultimate one. It too will have to be institutionally distributed, at least when questions of access to the means of self-development are at stake, for example. And this means politics, not just the administration of selves! Nevertheless, there are generalizations and principles readily available, and as far as Marcuse is concerned, most are found in *One-Dimensional Man*, the book that introduced the Frankfurt School to a new generation and a new culture. (I bought my first copy in an airport bookstore on my way back to college after my freshman year.) One-dimensional man *is* the false self, the self that finds its soul in its possessions and its reason in its insistence that things cannot be different from the way they are now. One-dimensional society is the society that preserves and extends itself at the expense of the true self. This thesis thrilled and shocked me when I first read it, even if I hardly understood it. Now I understand it a little better, and it still has the same effect.

Preserving Marcuse's Radicalism

Reinterpreting *Eros and Civilization* in terms of a utopian dialectic of perfect recognition preserves the radicalism of Marcuse's project while overcoming its key defect, its inability to find a place for human relatedness. Doing so in terms of Winnicott's theory possesses the great advantage of continuing to make the body central, so that the true self is its body, imaginatively elaborated as though it were a work of art. To ask of society that it support, not exploit, the true selves of its members is no small demand. It is as radical a standard as anything Marcuse ever proposed. Finally, a focus on the self and its vicissitudes, to use a favorite Freudian word, draws attention to Marcuse's psychoanalytic studies of society undertaken after *Eros*, particularly "The Obsolescence of the Freudian Concept of Man."[29] Nothing to rejoice about, the obsolescence of this concept means that now not even the presumably most antisocial (and hence potentially radical) elements of the psyche are immune to social exploitation and control. Although a focus on the true and false self obviously does not solve this problem, it allows its more precise formulation, and it holds out a hope: that no matter how deeply hidden and suppressed, the true self will continue to wait for recognition. This is, of course, precisely what Marcuse hoped for from eros in the first place.

That the self is not just a fiction, not merely one more metanarrative, not just one more symptom of the endlessly desiring subject, as Lacan would put it:[30] all this is assumed by any program that takes Marcuse seriously. That the self is a value, so that a true self is more valuable than a false one, is an implication of this assumption, one not widely shared by postmodern thought. In the end it is Marcuse's great contribution to have turned to the body: not to texts about bodies, though *Eros* is certainly a text about bodies, but to the suffering and desiring body. Mine is not the only way to draw on Marcuse's marriage of psychoanalysis and radical social criticism. There is no *echt* Marcusian approach. However, any approach that takes his teachings seriously will stay close to the body—which means, I believe, staying close not merely to its sufferings and desires but to *individual bodies*. History, philosophy, and political theory, as well as psychoanalysis, are properly stories of the almost infinite suffering and desire of individual men and women. Texts are the medium of this passion play, not its object and certainly not its subject. It is a simple and obvious point, perhaps, but one frequently forgotten in the academy today. Marcuse was not an academic writer in this sense, and *that* is his great virtue.

Notes

1. W. R. D. Fairbairn, *An Object Relations Theory of the Personality* (New York: Basic Books, 1952), 33.

2. Herbert Marcuse, "Ecology and the Critique of Modern Society," *Capitalism, Nature, Socialism* 3, 3 (September 1992): 29–38.

3. Theodor Adorno, *Negative Dialectics*, trans. E. B. Ashton (New York: Seabury Press, 1973), 22–23.

4. Theodor Adorno, *Minima Moralia*, trans. E. F. N. Jephcott (London: NLB, 1974), 247.

5. Herbert Marcuse, *Eros and Civilization: A Philosophical Inquiry into Freud* (Boston: Beacon Press, 1966), 83.

6. Theodor Adorno, *Prisms*, trans. Samuel Weber and Shierry Weber (Cambridge, Mass.: MIT Press, 1983), 34. Later Adorno would soften this view, specifying that he was referring to lyric poetry and recognizing that "literature must resist this verdict." "Commitment," *New Left Review* 87-88 (September–December 1987): 84.

7. See Sigmund Freud, *A General Introduction to Psychoanalysis* (New York: Garden City Publishing, 1943), 130–31, on the influence of the First World War. It was not just external events but Freud's study of the repetition compulsion in *Beyond the Pleasure Principle* that led him to postulate the *Todestrieb* (death drive). Probably these theoretical considerations were more important. Freud asked why individuals would seek to restore an earlier state, the earliest state of all being, of course, nonexistence. Something in the organism itself must seek nonbeing. *The Standard Edition of the Complete Psychological Works of Sigmund Freud*, 24 vols. (London: Hogarth Press, 1953–1974), 18:7–66.

8. Marcuse, *Eros and Civilization*, 28–29.

9. C. Fred Alford, *Science and the Revenge of Nature: Marcuse and Habermas* (Gainesville: University Presses of Florida, 1985), 40–45.

10. Marcuse, *Eros and Civilization*, 156–57, 195.

11. Marcuse, "Ecology and the Critique of Modern Society."

12. Sigmund Freud, *An Outline of Psycho-Analysis*, trans. James Strachey, rev. ed. (New York: W. W. Norton, 1969).

13. Christopher Lasch makes this point well in *The Minimal Self* (New York: W. W. Norton, 1984), 235. Marcuse's harsh criticism of Brown in "Love Mystified: A Critique of Norman O. Brown" (*Negations: Essays in Critical Theory*, trans. Jeremy J. Shapiro [Boston: Beacon Press, 1968], 227–42) addresses only Brown's later and more mystical *Love's Body*, not *Life against Death: The Psychoanalytic Meaning of History* (Middletown, Conn.: Wesleyan University Press, 1959).

14. Marcuse, *Eros and Civilization*, 162–63.

15. Ibid., 209.

16. Nancy Chodorow, "Beyond Drive Theory," *Theory and Society* 14 (1985): 293.

17. Marcuse, *Eros and Civilization*, "Epilogue: Critique of Neo-Freudian Revisionism," 238–74.

18. C. Fred Alford, *Melanie Klein and Critical Social Theory* (New Haven, Conn., and London: Yale University Press, 1989), 2–4, and throughout.

19. G. W. F. Hegel, *Phänomenologie des Geistes* (Hamburg: Felix Meiner Verlag, 1952), 143.

20. Adam Phillips, *Winnicott* (Cambridge, Mass.: Harvard University Press, 1988), 4. I follow Phillips quite closely at several points. This is a marvelous book, capturing Winnicott's poetry and paradox without succumbing to it.

21. D. W. Winnicott, *The Maturational Processes and the Facilitating Environment* (London: Hogarth Press and Institute of Psycho-Analysis, 1965), 148.

22. Phillips, *Winnicott*, 3–5.

23. See particularly Marcuse's "Über die philosophischen Grundlagen des wirtschaftswissenschaftlichen Arbeitsbegriffs," in *Kultur und Gesellschaft*, 2 vols. (Frankfurt am Main: Sukrkamp, 1965), 2:7–48. I review Marcuse's early works on freedom in *Science and the Revenge of Nature*, chapter 2.

24. Winnicott, *The Maturational Processes*, 65; Phillips, *Winnicott*, 78.

25. D. W. Winnicott, *Collected Papers: Through Paediatrics to Psycho-Analysis* (New York: Basic Books, 1958), 244.

26. This is the thesis of Max Horkheimer and Theodor Adorno's *Dialectic of Enlightenment*, trans. John Cumming (New York: Herder and Herder, 1972).

27. Winnicott, *Collected Papers*, 246–54.

28. For example, William E. Connolly, *Identity/Difference: Democratic Negotiations of Political Paradox* (Ithaca, N.Y., and London: Cornell University Press, 1991).

29. "Obsolescence" was first delivered in 1963. In *Five Lectures: Psychoanalysis, Politics, and Utopia*, trans. Jeremy J. Shapiro and Shierry M. Weber (Boston: Beacon Press, 1970), 44–61.

30. Jacques Lacan, "Some Reflections on the Ego," *International Journal of Psycho-Analysis* 34 (1953): 11–17.

Part III

Artful Thinking

Shierry Weber Nicholsen

The Persistence of Passionate Subjectivity: Eros and Other in Marcuse, by Way of Adorno

It sometimes happened that despite its chocolate and its toy model of a mine, the salon inside my Aunt Lehmann's flat did not have as much to say to me as the vestibule in which the old servant woman took my coat from me as though it had been a burden, and pressed my cap down on my head as though she were trying to bless me.
—*Walter Benjamin,* A Berlin Childhood ca. 1900

When I asked myself, as I was preparing to write this essay, what relevance Marcuse does indeed have for us in the 1990s, I remembered both how immediately Marcuse spoke to us in the 1960s and 1970s and how a few years ago, realizing that I had "forgotten" Marcuse, I began asking colleagues and friends, "What happened to Marcuse?"—meaning, of course, "Have we really forgotten Marcuse, and if so, why?" In reflecting on Marcuse's at least partial or temporary oblivion, I was struck with the fact that the work of his colleague and contemporary Theodor Adorno has maintained a high profile in contemporary critical thought, and this despite the fact that Marcuse lived for a decade after Adorno's death. Witness to this apparent contrast between the fate of Marcuse's work and the fate of Adorno's is Fredric Jameson's recent book on Adorno, to which my title alludes: *Late Marxism: Adorno, or, the Persistence of the Dialectic.* Labeling Marcuse the thinker of the 1960s, Jameson proposes that Adorno may provide an appropriate model of dialectical thought for our own time: "There is some chance that [Adorno] may turn out to have been the analyst of our own period, which he did not live to see, and in which late capitalism has all but succeeded in eliminating the final loopholes of nature and the Unconscious, of subversion and the aesthetic,

149

of individual and collective praxis alike, and, with a final fillip, in eliminating any memory trace of what thereby no longer existed in the hence-
forth postmodern landscape."[1] Although my reflections have not led me
to disagree with Jameson about Adorno, they have also convinced me
that we cannot relegate Marcuse to the alleged oblivion of the 1960s.

Here I will recapitulate the train of thought that arose in me in response to the question of Marcuse's contemporary relevance. My train of
thought surprised me, I must admit, not so much because of the views of
Adorno and Marcuse that emerged but because it took me into two
spheres—that of aesthetic experience and textual form on the one hand
and that of nature, science, and technology on the other—whose connection has certainly been noted but not explored in depth by the Frankfurt
School. My reflections suggest both that this conjunction can be profit-
ably explored on the basis of the "critical theory of experience" implicit
in the Frankfurt School's work and that the divergence between the two
spheres can provide the motor for further development in that critical
theory.

What my essay represents, then, is a meditation on the truth of Adorno's and Marcuse's work as it emerges in the afterlife of that work and as
it becomes visible through an examination of the relationship of the two
men's work. The meditation covers a great deal of ground, certainly, and
in the brief scope of the present essay I can do no more than sketch out
the various points in its trajectory, leaving, of necessity, some gaps, some
sharp curves and rough edges, and some points in embryonic form.

The Trajectory of Marcuse's Eclipse

Let me begin by noting some of the common ground Marcuse and
Adorno share. It includes the basic premises of Frankfurt School critical
social theory and ranges from the critique of instrumental reason in the
name of another reason more compatible with the sensuous and the nonidentical, to the explication of the aesthetic dimension as a locus of utopian potential, as a *promesse de bonheur*, or promise of happiness, in
Stendhal's phrase. For both men subjective experience is the locus of an
experiential dialectics of oppression and liberation. It is the experiential

arena of one-dimensionalization and administratization—Marcuse's concept of one-dimensional society and Adorno's concept of the totally administered society are congruent—but also the arena of reflection, critical awareness, and thought in its objectivity. It is the locus of aesthetic experience and the locus of the experience and definition of needs and possibilities for political praxis. Central to both Marcuse's and Adorno's explication of subjective experience is the relationship of eros to other—hence the phrase "passionate subjectivity" in my title. For both men, in short, the critique of a totalizing and leveling social reality and of the deformations of consciousness that accompany and support it has as its reverse side an attempt to uncover the dimension of erotic, sensuous, subjective experience and to link that dimension with an alternative and more utopian future for humankind.

And yet, during at least the 1980s, Adorno in some sense eclipsed Marcuse. This can be understood as a quasi-deliberate move on Marcuse's part to hide the innermost core of his thought behind Adorno's aesthetics in order to protect it during a particularly repressive phase of intellectual and cultural history and also as a fate curiously reflected in and appropriate to the presentational forms of the two men's work. Marcuse's own thought in fact furnishes a useful description of the trajectory that leads to his apparent oblivion and to the importance of Adorno as the carrier of the Frankfurt School's conception of a relationship between eros and other. As we know, *Eros and Civilization* and *One-Dimensional Man*, arguably Marcuse's most important works, which date from the 1950s and 1960s, as a pair expound the tradition within psychoanalytic theory of the possibility of a reconciled sensuous subjectivity—the spread of erotic relationships in a positively sublimated, as opposed to a repressively desublimated, form. Imagination and fantasy, the same aspects of subjective experience that can serve as a bridge between sensuousness and reason, provide a vehicle for the new demands and needs expressed by a rebellious subjectivity. The conjunction of imagination, eros, and a rebellious subjectivity seemed to describe well important aspects of the experience of those who participated in the social movements of the 1960s. At the same time, *One-Dimensional Man* in particular described the forces within the affluent society that worked to eliminate from awareness precisely that dimension of subjectivity. These forces, whose strength became increasingly evident after the decade of the 1960s, were also at least initially recognizable in the experience of those same participants.

Given how well Marcuse's two major books articulate the play of forces at work in the 1960s and then the 1970s, it is not surprising that in the 1970s, the last decade of Marcuse's life, his work should in its own way articulate the next turning in the historical dynamic. And this is what I believe we see in *The Aesthetic Dimension*, Marcuse's last book, published in 1978. In this brief volume, Marcuse offers his counterposition to orthodox Marxist theories of art. He takes the position, consonant with *Eros and Civilization*, that the kind of sublimation that occurs through submission to artistic form produces a consciousness whose affinity is with eros and that transcends specific historical situations, thereby approaching the universal. Although Adorno himself would not appeal to universals in this way—a point to which I will return later—in this assertion of the validity of art *as* art Marcuse concurs with Adorno. In fact, he explicitly acknowledges his general debt to Adorno's aesthetic theory at the beginning of his book.

The Aesthetic Dimension had, if I am not mistaken, very little impact in comparison with Marcuse's earlier works, however dear the topic was to Marcuse personally. It did not seem to speak directly to the rebellious subjectivity as his previous work had. Further, while its presentational form is in many respects similar to that of Marcuse's earlier books, in a work devoted to art as such it draws attention to itself with its striking plainness. It is only a slight exaggeration to say that *The Aesthetic Dimension* is a set of assertions without detail or argumentation, neither social-scientific, nor directly political, nor literary.

The contrast between the presentational form of *The Aesthetic Dimension* and that of Adorno's work on aesthetics, to which Marcuse links his, is compelling. This contrast signals, I believe, the very specific culturally and historically determined purpose that Marcuse was following in *The Aesthetic Dimension*. He was attempting, I would argue, to take the imagination and its utopian potential, as explicated in *Eros and Civilization*, and to lodge it within the aesthetic dimension in the narrower sense of the aesthetic experience of works of art and culture. So lodged, it would be safe to some degree both from the ideological battles of a troubled Left and from one-dimensionalization. And he placed it explicitly—and, by virtue of the contrast in presentational form, emphatically—under the aegis of Adorno's aesthetic work, which, for reasons I shall examine shortly, could be expected not to lose its impact.

Marcuse himself indicates that the ascendance of a negatively totalizing one-dimensional society in the 1970s has made political action far more problematic than it hitherto seemed and has consequently made it more necessary to turn to the aesthetic as the repository of emancipatory potential:

> What appears in art as remote from the praxis of change demands recognition as a necessary element in a future praxis of liberation—as the "science of the beautiful," the "science of redemption and fulfillment." Art cannot change the world, but it can contribute to changing the consciousness and drives of the men and women who could change the world. The movement of the sixties tended toward a sweeping transformation of subjectivity and nature, of sensibility, imagination, and reason. It opened a new vista of things, an ingression of the superstructure into the base. Today, the movement is encapsulated, isolated, and defensive, and an embarrassed leftist bureaucracy is quick to condemn the movement as impotent, intellectual elitism.[2]

"Encapsulated, isolated, and defensive": from the conjunction of these statements about art and the movement, we can infer that like Brecht, whom he admired more than Adorno did, Marcuse resorted to a kind of "peasant cunning" to deal with one-dimensionalization. He hid his thought under an almost platitudinous shell where it would remain inconspicuous, and he counted, one might say, on Adorno to bring the explosive force of the link they had forged between the imagination, the erotic, and emancipation through to another time.

Adorno's work does in fact preserve the experiential force of this link, thus demonstrating the shrewdness of Marcuse's move. The images of encapsulation and protective shell should call to mind an image that Adorno himself repeatedly invoked with regard to critical theory: that of *Flaschenpost*, the message in the bottle, cast upon the waters, perhaps to reach an audience and perhaps not, perhaps to be acted on and perhaps not. It is as though virtually all of Adorno's work, with its reliance on the interpretation of *geistige Gebilde*, cultural-intellectual works, incorporated the stance that Marcuse expressed in his last book. Hence, of course, it is not surprising that Adorno is repeatedly charged with the "impotent, intellectual elitism" that Marcuse mentions.

But in Adorno's case the encapsulation, the form, is not only appropriate to the demands of the historical period but also part of the content of the thought: The bottle is part of the message, so to speak. The very form of Adorno's work embodies the possibility of something definitively other, a more reconciled existence, which is linked with the possibility of authentic negative experience in a situation in which consciousness is threatened with the dismantling of its very capacity for critical reason. This is not only what allows Adorno's thought to survive but also what gives it its fascination and, as Jameson points out, its unique role in a postmodern period that is fascinated with form but unable to critically conceive of something other. Adorno's message is kept alive in the experience of reading him, and in this sense the *Flaschenpost* has reached land.

The Eros of Language in Adorno's Writings

Adorno's work highlights the role of presentational form in a critical theory of experience. The fundamental notion of Adorno's aesthetic theory is that aesthetic form, in embodying the essence of a negative reality, also negates that reality in the name of another possibility, that of a reconciled existence. The complex structures of negation that make up aesthetic form do not of themselves constitute a utopian reality, nor do they represent a political practice; they only point negatively to something other. In this regard, the affirmative qualities of art have an ideological as well as a utopian moment, and conversely the hermeticism and meaninglessness of modern art have a negative but utopian import. The break with meaning, Adorno tells us, "which the work does not bridge but rather, lovingly and hopefully, makes the agent of its form, remains, the figure of a substance that transcends it. It expresses meaning through its ascetic stance toward meaning."[3] This is the means by which the mere edge of a critical consciousness can be maintained in the present situation.

Adorno's own writing participates in this dialectic. It has a distinctly hermetic quality in that it refuses to participate fully in standard academic discourse, creating instead a repertoire of quasi-private imagistic terms. It refrains from orderly argumentation and the standard paragraphing that reflects it, proceeding instead through conjunctions of paradoxical formulations related by association.⁴ It combines essayistic form with an impersonal, abstract aphoristic form which permits no semblance of an easy give-and-take between writer and reader.

The hermetically evoked reconciliation that characterizes utopia for Adorno is also a quasi-Kantian reconciliation of reason and sensuousness, in which the "nonidentical"—which for Adorno means the individual, concrete and embodied—can find a place. Reconciliation in this sense occupies a prominent place in Adorno's theory and practice of aesthetic form, primarily in terms of language. For Adorno, in the ongoing struggle between a deductive, logical-conceptual communicative language and a pure expressive, sensuous language, the debased communicative form of language tends more and more to get the upper hand. In Adorno's own writing, rebellion against the hegemony of communicative language is embodied in a movement away from argumentation and example and toward what he calls "logicity," in which the writing maintains both the semblance of logical coherence and the sense of a quasi-sensuous aesthetic connectedness. This logicity is another face of Adorno's hermeticism.

If the utopian moment is a moment of reconciliation, both among humans and between reason and the sensuous, then in a world that hinders reconciliation, erotic reconciliation is itself the object of erotic longing. In Adorno's work, it is the other within language, that which is present only as possibility, that stands in for this erotic reconciliation and becomes the object of erotic longing. Adorno evokes the other within language in the image of *Rauschen*, the German word for such murmuring, expressive, but indistinct sounds of nature as the rustling of trees, the rushing of a brook, or the surging of the surf. A line from the German poet Rudolf Borchardt that Adorno cites repeatedly may be taken as his touchstone: *Ich habe nichts als Rauschen,* (I have nothing but murmuring). *Rauschen*, which is akin to *Rausch* (ecstasy), evokes the essence of language as an erotic object in itself; this is the utopian and nonidentical element concealed beneath the surface of a language that appears to be pressed inexorably into the service of an administered world. In a similar way, a foreign language is the other of one's own language, and Adorno defends his use of *Fremdwörter*, foreign or loan words, in terms of their erotic appeal. His rebellious use of foreign words as a schoolboy during the First World War, when there was an effort to "Germanize" all words, was, he tells us, "hardly due to political considerations. Rather, since language is erotically charged in its words, at least for the kind of person who is capable of expression, love drives us to foreign words. . . . The early craving for foreign words is like the craving for foreign and if possible exotic girls; what lures us is a kind of exogamy of language, which would like to escape from the sphere of what is always the same."[5]

The experience of negation and utopian possibility, of potential erotic reconciliation, that is sedimented in the work of art, and in analogous ways in Adorno's work as well, enables the reader (or viewer, or listener) to have the same kind of subjective experience. Such experience, which is what authentic aesthetic experience and, in its own way, authentic philosophical experience would be, requires a mimetic activity on the part of the reader. The reader must imitate in his own experience the process and structure that are sedimented in the work's form, in much the same way that the work itself imitates not the surface but the essence of reality and possibility. The way in which Adorno describes this mimetic activity evokes a relationship, one of cooperation rather than domination: Aesthetic understanding, he says, needs to be thought of as "a kind of following along afterward [*Nachfahren*], as the coexecution [*Mitvollzug*] of the tensions sedimented in the work of art, the processes that have congealed and become objectified in it. One does not understand a work of art when one translates it into concepts . . . but rather when one is immersed in its immanent movement."[6] This is the kind of interaction to which the aesthetic work, and Adorno's own work, invites the reader. It is both ascetic and sensuous, for it is through an asceticism that recognizes the sensuous dimension and the longing for it, and an asceticism toward meaning for the sake of a meaningfulness that may someday be realized, that Adorno embodies, negatively, the possibility of erotic relations with the other. He embodies it in both the content and the formal aspects of his writings, which include his abstention from philosophical argumentation and his use of foreign words. It is in this form that the *Flaschenpost* engages the subjective experience of the contemporary reader.

The Eros of Solidarity and
Participation in Marcuse's Writings

Adorno's viability derives, I believe, from the aspects of his presentational form I have just explicated. But this raises the question of what role Mar-

156

cuse's presentational form plays in his early success, his eclipse, and his potential reemergence from under Adorno's skirts, so to speak. Marcuse's writing does not itself encapsulate the aesthetic experience and ensure its survival, but an examination of his presentational form can help us to see why he spoke to us in the 1960s and can suggest the role he may play in the present. I have already noted Marcuse's appeal to universals in his defense of the aesthetic. The universal has a crucial place in Marcuse's project, and I will use a passage from his argument about the philosophical value of universals, which appears in *One-Dimensional Man*, to explore the way his presentational form embodies his conception of the relationship of eros to other. We shall see that an appeal to the universal is part of the formal structure of his writing.

In his argument Marcuse attacks analytic philosophy's dismissal of universals in its attempt to dissolve them into specific acts and processes. The universal, he argues, represents the totality that, as background, restricts the nature of individual acts. It is "the concrete objective ground of their functioning in the given social and historical context, . . . the established state of affairs which determines the life of individuals." The mind, accordingly, is different from specific mental processes or dispositions:

"Negatively present" [in an individual] are the specific "environmental" forces which precondition his mind for the spontaneous repulsion of certain data, conditions, relations. They are present as repelled material. Their absence is a reality—a positive factor that explains his actual mental processes, the meaning of his words and behavior. Meaning for whom? Not only for the professional philosopher, whose task it is to rectify the wrong that pervades the universe of ordinary discourse, but also for those who suffer this wrong although they may not be aware of it—for Joe Doe and Richard Roe.[7]

Striking in this passage is the conjunction of a "negative-positive" dialectical pattern of thought with a simple and straightforward vocabulary that avoids technical definitions, as Adorno's does, yet is, unlike Adorno's, amply redundant in such a way as to appeal to ordinary understanding. Also striking are the question "meaning for whom?" and the direct appeal to the suffering of the ordinary individual, for whom Joe Doe and

Richard Roe stand in. There is no careful crafting of sentences and no use of metaphor or figurative speech. Instead, we find an interesting conjunction of a rhetoric of direct appeal, of solidarity invoked between speaker and audience, with an appeal to the absent totality as a tool of critical thought. The presentational form, in other words, is not itself an embodiment of aesthetic experience, as Adorno's is, but rather a conjunction of the philosophical with what we might call the political. Whereas Adorno appeals to the otherness in language, which the reader is to experience by reconstructing aesthetic experience, Marcuse uses an eros of empathy to establish a bridge of solidarity across the reader's otherness.

We might expect to see a more aesthetic element in Marcuse's discussion of the universals of beauty. In the case of beauty, he argues, the universal encompasses not the forces of repression so much as the disjunction between what is and what might be: "The irreducible difference between the universal and its particulars seems to be rooted in the primary experience of the unconquerable difference between potentiality and actuality—between two dimensions of the one experienced world."[8] What we see, however, is that Marcuse focuses not on *geistige Gebilde*, works of culture and intellect, but rather on aesthetic experience in the broadest sense, the range of aesthetic experiences that ordinary people may have (just as in *Eros and Civilization* his focus was on fantasy and imagination as such rather than on works of art):

> Talking of a beautiful girl, a beautiful landscape, a beautiful picture, I certainly have very different things in mind. What is common to all of them—"beauty"—is neither a mysterious entity, nor a mysterious word. On the contrary, nothing is perhaps more directly and clearly experienced than the appearance of "beauty" in various beautiful objects. The boy friend and the philosopher, the artist and the mortician may "define" it in very different ways, but they all define the same specific state or condition—some quality or qualities which make the beautiful contrast with other objects. In this vagueness and directness, beauty is experienced in the beautiful—that is, it is seen, heard, smelled, touched, felt, comprehended.[9]

Marcuse's presentation, which has its own kind of "vagueness and directness," appeals to ordinary experience as already containing a sense of something other, and it also shows the universal of beauty spanning the range of subjective experience, from the mental to the sensory—"seen, heard, smelled, touched, felt, comprehended." In terms of classical aesthetics, Marcuse is bridging this *Kunstschöne* and the *Naturschöne*, the beauty of art and the beauty of nature. He is also bridging the "lower" sphere of direct sensuous experience and the "higher" sphere of reason, concepts, and metaphysics. Direct, qualitative experience is the locus of this reconciliation of opposites: "The unpurged experience seems to be more familiar with the abstract and universal than is the analytic philosophy: it seems to be embedded in a metaphysical world."[10] While in one sense the plainness of Marcuse's form seems to reflect his insistence on bridging a spectrum that reaches from direct sensuous experience to the most abstract sphere, it is also important to note that the sensuous element as such is not present in his writing; it must be supplied by the reader's experience. Again, just as Marcuse is interested in linking the extreme ends of the spectrum rather than focusing on works of art, arguably at the center of the spectrum, so his eros reaches outward to the reader rather than being contained as a murmuring within his writing.

The universals in Marcuse, which are both qualitative and abstract, bridge not only sensuousness and reason but also the possible and the empirical, in a way that is quite different from Adorno's project. For Marcuse, the universals, as tools of critical social thought and indicators of human potential, are discussable in terms of objective historical potentialities. This is why, unlike Adorno, he talks not about utopia but rather about empirically demonstrable possibilities for a qualitatively different life in society (for example, in "The End of Utopia" in *Five Lectures: Psychoanalysis, Politics, and Utopia*).[11] If the necessary material and intellectual forces for a qualitative transformation are at hand, then the free society is not unfeasible or impossible; it is simply that strong counterforces have hitherto prevented its realization. The "criteria for the rationality of a transcendent project" that Marcuse lays out at the end of *One-Dimensional Man* show very clearly the nature of his bridging of the empirical and the universal. On the one hand, a transcendent project (that is, a project for qualitative social change) "must be in accordance with the real possibilities open at the attained level of the material and intellectual culture"; on the other hand, the project's rationality will be indicated by the fact that "its realization offers a greater chance for the pacification of existence, within the framework of institutions which offer a greater chance for the free development of human needs and faculties."[12] For Marcuse, then, historical empirical assessment considers both the "resources" available and human needs and faculties, i.e., the "subjective factor" of direct experience. In addition, both needs/faculties and resources span the range between the physical and sensuous and the mental and social. Again, however, the empirical itself is not present in Marcuse's writing but is rather invoked in connection with the reader's historical situation on the one hand and the universal as absent possibility on the other.

To recapitulate: If we consider *One-Dimensional Man* and the essays on related topics collected in *Five Lectures* to represent the most advanced aspects of Marcuse's project, it becomes apparent that his use of universals is indicative of an important strategic difference between his and Adorno's attempts to keep the experience of unrealized possibility alive and in awareness. Marcuse's attempt is more broad-based, appealing more directly to the solidarity of individuals linked through eros while at the same time evoking the possibility—a negative or absent one for which he provides no specific images—of an extension to some intuitively felt need that people sense in their current subjective experience. For Marcuse, the relationship of eros to other, the relationship of exogamy that Adorno embodied in aesthetic form, is formulated as the "pacification of existence." What this means is the extension of peaceful, life-supporting relationships in all directions. The extension of eros to other also means that the absent other, the possibility of freedom, is linked with the qualitative dimensions of current empirical existence. Accordingly, just as Adorno's project of creating aesthetic form in language is meant to embody and demonstrate a direct erotic linking with the other, so Marcuse's linking of an absent, abstract, metaphysical other with the qualitative and empirical dimensions of his readers' ordinary experiencing is meant to project an erotic link with the absent other, a link that is mediated by the imagination as the locus in which subjectivity, sensuousness, and possibility coexist.

The Conjunction of Subjective Experience,
Nature, and Technology as the Context
for Marcuse's Reemergence

If Marcuse's form directs itself to the reader, to the reader's engagement with her own emergent experience, and also to empirical possibilities, then it makes sense that Marcuse would have spoken to us in the 1960s, when such new dimensions of experience were indeed emerging and when new empirical possibilities were being explored. But what this consonance with the memory of the 1960s hides from us is the fact that by its very form, by virtue of its appeal to the reader "out there" and to what is empirically possible in a specific historical period, Marcuse's form demands and requires readers in whom these possibilities can emerge. Thus it both resonates with such readers and provides an incitement for any reader to become such a reader. In a way strikingly different from the hermetic Adorno's, the project of Marcuse's work requires readers in the present to participate in undertaking it. His project, which might be termed a "critical theory of sensuous experience," takes the form, as it were, of a proposal. Accordingly, although it emphasizes empirical possibility, it does not contain the empirical work itself but rather appeals to whatever empirical possibilities are currently being explored or can emerge into exploration.[13] On the other hand, this kind of open communicative appeal may leave the dimension of language itself unreflected in a way that is problematic; this is a point to which I will return.

One of the reasons Marcuse's work is now ripe for reemergence is that this conjunction of the erotic, the empirical, and the universal has been and is under discussion side by side with the postmodernist fascination with aesthetic form and *jouissance* to which Adorno seems to speak. Empirical questions concerning environmental issues, along with what might be thought of as qualitative universal questions of the relationship of human to nonhuman "nature"—the erotic or sensuous question of our participation, via sensibility, desires, needs, the body, in the larger natural environment—have become central to one version of the present crisis. Accordingly, we can expect that Marcuse's project of a critical theory of sensuous experience will appeal to and engage with those who are open to experience in this area or involved in empirical work in this area. And in fact the suggestions Marcuse makes in *One-Dimensional Man* and elsewhere about science and the domination of nature have prompted a great deal of response over the years.[14] Those suggestions illustrate the kind of partnership between experience and empirical work that Marcuse's project implies and evokes.

Marcuse explicitly links the imagination with science and technology (which he does not, as Andrew Feenberg has pointed out, differentiate):[15]

"In the light of the capabilities of advanced industrial civilization, is not all play of the imagination playing with technical possibilities, which can be tested as to their chances of realization? The romantic idea of a 'science of the imagination' seems to assume an ever more empirical aspect."[16] Essential to Marcuse's argument is the claim that a "pacified existence" is an empirical possibility, a possibility that is linked with the capacities of science and technology: "Science and technology has rendered possible the translation of values into technical tasks."[17] There are sufficient resources currently available to provide a pacified existence for all, albeit at a lesser standard of living than that currently enjoyed or aspired to by some.

At the same time, Marcuse argues that science as we know it "has projected and promoted a universe in which the domination of nature has remained linked to the domination of man."[18] Thus he proposes a shift in the scientific project: "Its hypotheses, without losing their rational character, would develop in an essentially different experiential context (that of a pacified world); consequently, science would arrive at essentially different concepts of nature and establish essentially different facts."[19] He adds, however, that he does not intend by this notion of a different scientific project any such "obscurantist ideas" as some sort of "qualitative physics."

Marcuse's statements raise the question of whether a different, erotic attitude toward nature—"the project of nature as opposing partner instead of object," in Habermas's words[20]—would provide the basis for a different kind of science or rationality altogether, or whether in fact there is only one kind of rationality on which science must necessarily be based, even though we might find alternative ways of fulfilling human needs and develop alternative technologies within the context of the one and only scientific rationality. Although some readers argue that Marcuse's suggestions are ambiguous or contradictory, I would propose another interpretation: that Marcuse's lack of resolution reflects the fact that he is directing our attention to the *conjunction* of the imaginative, the sensuous, the empirical, and the universal in his statements about nature, science, and technology. His emphatic rejection of "obscurantist ideas" indicates that his project calls not for a specific radical alternative to current science so much as for an imaginative meditation on and further development of the relationships suggested by this conjunction. It calls, in other words, for further reflection, and imagining of the interaction between an altered experiential relationship to nature and alternative forms of scientific and technological activity.

The conjunction with which I am concerned can be seen in the interweaving of two slightly different trains of thought in Marcuse's suggestions. Both involve notions of human needs (nature) and of technical possibilities. The first train of thought, which has its starting point in felt needs, can be summarized as follows: 1) it is possible for genuine (universalizable) human needs to emerge in subjective experience; 2) how to satisfy those needs is in some sense an empirical, technical question; and 3) empirically, it seems to be the case that current resources are adequate to satisfy genuine needs, though not false needs.

The second train of thought originates in science: 1) science as we know it has evolved in the social context of the domination of both human beings and nature; 2) science as we know it is not leading to the satisfaction of genuine human needs; 3) science can be redirected in the service of a pacified life; and 4) this would involve different goals, which would lead to the construction of different concepts and the discovery of different facts.

Each of these trains of thought is itself fraught with ambiguity and in need of empirical investigation, and each of them involves slightly different linkages between the erotic, the universal, the empirical, and the technical. Their sequence is more a suggestive juxtaposition than an attempted proof. This is consonant with the form of Marcuse's work, which invites and requires the reader's experiential reflections and empirical activities.

If we formulate Marcuse's suggestions in terms of possible relationships rather than in terms of claims, we arrive at the following: A different attitude toward nature in the broadest sense could result from as well as facilitate different subjective experiences, which could in turn suggest different investigative methods and raise different questions for theorizing and for empirical examination. Such work could in turn suggest different technical possibilities, which would again in turn require evaluation, through empirical examination and rational discourse, in the context of reflection on emergent experience.

Since, as I have said, all these suggestions depend on the collaboration of the readership, let me now provide a small sample of some of the reflections and empirical work that in my view contribute to the further development of the project Marcuse is proposing. The examples are taken from the domain I have been discussing: that of our relationship to nature (which, again, in the present context includes human needs) and the role of science and technology in that relationship.

1. There is a body of work that attempts, from a socially critical perspective, to empiricize the range of human needs and render them quantifiable as a preliminary step to pursuing their fulfillment. A recent example is Len Doyal and Ian Gough's *Theory of Human Needs*,[21] which attempts to delineate the spectrum of human needs—from food and shelter, to psychological security in childhood, to political systems that permit critical thought. Doyal and Gough then present the various schemata currently used to measure these needs. Clearly their work is directed precisely toward the calculation of what Marcuse calls "the available range of freedom from want."[22] An example of a very focused study along similar lines is the work of Roger Colton for the National Consumer Law Center on the appropriate criteria for measuring fuel needs in low-income groups in the United States.[23]

2. There is work in environmental philosophy that attempts to redefine our relationships with animals and the nonhuman environment in general by drawing on the dimension of emergent or generally unacknowledged experience. Marcuse's notion of an erotic relationship with nature has been explicitly invoked in this connection by Bill Devall, an American spokesperson for the deep ecology movement. In a discussion of the "ecological self," Devall asserts that "recalling eros from banishment and integrating it through our practice requires moving from our minimal self further into wild territory. . . . In Marcuse's terms, what is required is a new radical sensibility that draws on the qualitative, elementary, preconscious world of experience."[24]

Extending erotic relationships to nonhuman nature involves, as Devall indicates, transformations in the sphere of sensuousness and in the sphere of psyche or self. J. Baird Callicott, an environmental philosopher, gives an eloquent personal example of the kind of solidarity toward which it is possible to move, and the kind of altered physical and psychic experience this solidarity entails:

> If the world is one's body, and not only does one's consciousness live in its specific content the world around, but the very structure of one's

psyche and rational faculties are formed through adaptive interaction with the ecological organization of nature, then one's self, both physically and psychologically, merges in a gradient from its central core outwardly into the environment. One cannot thus draw hard-and-fast boundaries between oneself, either physically or spiritually, and the environment.

For me this realization took concrete form as I stood, two decades and an ecological education later, on the banks of the Mississippi River where I roamed as a boy. As I gazed at the brown silt-choked waters absorbing a black plume of industrial and municipal sewage from Memphis, and as my eye tracked bits of some unknown beige froth floating continually down from Cincinnati, Louisville, or St. Louis, I experienced a palpable pain. It was not distinctly locatable in any of my extremities, nor was it like a headache or nausea. Still, it was very real. I had no plans to swim in the river, no need to drink from it, no intention of buying real estate on its shores. My narrowly personal interests were not affected, and yet somehow I was personally injured. It occurred to me then, in a flash of self-discovery, that the river was part of me. And I recalled a line from Leopold's *Sand County Almanac*—"One of the penalties of an ecological education is that one lives alone in a world of wounds."[25]

Here an altered attitude, itself shaped in interaction with knowledge and experience, gives rise to a new dimension of bodily need, a new capacity for felt suffering that serves as an indicator of a dimension in which existence is not pacific.

3. In the philosophy of environmental ethics and animal rights, we see how arguments about such an erotic relationship with nonhuman nature can lead directly to a critique of false scientific assumptions about relationships between humans, other species, and the nonhuman environment. The philosopher Mary Midgeley's *Animals and Why They Matter*, which involves an extensive critique of behaviorism in psychology, is a case in point. Midgeley argues, for instance, that science incorrectly assumes that a rigid "species barrier" exists between humans and other species, in which consciousness is denied to species other than our own; on the contrary, there is abundant evidence that both humans and animals rely on "reading" one another's signals with great accuracy and that such

mutual reading is the basis for relationships between humans and domestic animals and pets. Midgeley goes on to distinguish between social duties, which we have toward those animals with whom we have formed social or kinlike bonds, and ecological duties, which we have toward all manner of other beings, arising from the fact that we are one species among many. While the former duties might be experienced in terms of a "response to consciousness," the latter, which embraces other species as well as rivers, mountains, and so on, might require a still-wider imaginative extension of our point of view.[26] Such arguments can contribute to the fleshing out of our conception of a pacified existence, which may then furnish goals to be served by empirical investigation.

4. A particularly striking example of such empirical investigation is found in the agroecological work carried on at the Land Institute in Salina, Kansas, under the direction of Wes Jackson. The underlying assumption of this work is that there can be an erotic relationship between humans and nature and that this would entail a human agriculture modeled on natural ecosystems, as indicated by the title of a book expounding these ideas, *Farming in Nature's Image*. (Remember that for Adorno aesthetic experience requires that the reader or spectator "follow along," reconstructing the work in her own experience.) The authors make it quite clear that the Land Institute's work is concerned with a redirection of science that would explore different concepts and yield different facts:

> If we approached agriculture with more of a nurturing attitude, we would create a fundamentally different research program, right down to the questions researchers ask. For instance, pests would no longer be seen as the enemy that must be eliminated, but as an inevitable part of the agroecosystem, albeit a part that must be controlled. High numbers of pests would become the fever, the warning symptom that all is not well within the system. Researchers would seek the causes of ill health rather than seeking simply to eliminate the symptoms. They would no longer ask, "How can we kill this pest?" but rather, "Why is this species population so high? What happened to its natural enemies? What is it about our crop system that is so attractive to this species? What can we do to bolster the health of the system, improve its resistance to this pest, and reduce the pest's numbers?"[27]

The focus of the Land Institute's efforts is an agriculture appropriate for prairie areas, based on the key aspects of the natural prairie ecosystem, which features polycultures of perennial grasses mixed with legumes and composites. The specific technical work of the institute, then, is directed toward finding appropriate mixtures of these species for a polyculture agriculture so that an overabundance of seed will be produced, which can then be harvested. The differences between this work and current biotechnological research seem to constitute a redirection rather than a dramatic rejection of "normal science." The Land Institute's work involves, for instance, more interdisciplinary cooperation over longer time periods (since the behavior of the species mixtures over a period of years must be investigated), the participation of a broader range of constituent groups (such as farmers), and different patterns of funding suitable to this more broadly participatory and longer-term research.

Such are the diverse but interrelated kinds of work about which Marcuse's project asks us to think in conjunction. Their vitality and abundance bodes well for Marcuse's reemergence. He suggests—and my examples are intended to underline that suggestion—the possibility of a traversable path from emergent experience in these areas to revised technical efforts to fulfill redefined human needs. This will be a difficult path to map, given that it must traverse the complex terrain sketched out in the debates around Marcuse's suggestions about science and technology. It is difficult in another way as well, in that the whole dimension of sensuous experience that is crucial here—the dimension I have been referring to as "eros and other"—poses problems of how that experience may be expressed in words and in what modes it may be communicated.[28] It is here that Adorno, with his refined dialectic of aesthetic experience and textual form, can again contribute to Marcuse's project. The emergence of new needs and new forms of experience involves a moment of reflection and articulation as well as a moment of experimentation, and that reflection and articulation may well require a language that will share some features with Adorno's notion of the erotically foreign element in language. Adorno's notion of logicity may prove valuable in suggesting what an attempt to communicate about the experience of landscape would sound like, or in articulating the kind of intersubjectivity among species that would form the basis for considerations of environmental ethics, or in describing the kind of pain that J. Baird Callicott experienced in viewing the polluted Mississippi. Conversely, the emergence of new needs and new experience takes place against the background of a reexperiencing of pain, deprivation, suffering, and numbness that have been occluded from consciousness—a reemergent negative awareness whose most accurate formulation may require the kind of textual dialectics we find in Adorno.

The dialectic of sensuous and aesthetic experience found in the implicit partnership between Marcuse and Adorno suggests that a critical theory of experience should be a central part of the Frankfurt School's contribution to redefining and fulfilling human needs in a more pacified world. How fruitful Marcuse's project eventually becomes, and the extent to which it can help lay the foundation for that kind of critical theory of experience, will depend in turn on our own efforts to pursue his call for imaginative and experiential reflections.

Notes

1. Fredric Jameson, *Late Marxism: Adorno, or, the Persistence of the Dialectic* (London and New York: Verso, 1990), 5.
2. Herbert Marcuse, *The Aesthetic Dimension: Toward a Critique of Marxist Aesthetics* (Boston: Beacon Press, 1978), 32–33.
3. Theodor W. Adorno, *Notes to Literature*, vol. 2, trans. Shierry Weber Nicholsen (New York: Columbia University Press, 1992), 108.
4. Cf. Adorno's own presentation and justification of his textual form in "The Essay as Form," in *Notes to Literature*, vol. 1, trans. Shierry Weber Nicholsen (New York: Columbia University Press, 1991), 3–23.
5. Ibid., 1:187.
6. Ibid., 2:297.
7. Herbert Marcuse, *One-Dimensional Man: Studies in the Ideology of Advanced Industrial Society* (Boston: Beacon Press, 1964), 209.
8. Ibid., 209–10.
9. Ibid., 210.
10. Ibid., 211.
11. "The End of Utopia," in Herbert Marcuse, *Five Lectures: Psychoanalysis, Politics, and Utopia*, trans. Jeremy J. Shapiro and Shierry M. Weber (Boston: Beacon Press, 1970), 62–82.
12. Marcuse, *One-Dimensional Man*, 220.
13. As Jürgen Habermas puts it in another context, "The investigation of social-scientific hypotheses is not Marcuse's goal. Marcuse's arguments have to be construed instead as part of a grand practical discourse in which the point is not the verification of empirical assertions but the identification and justification of universalizable interests." "Herbert Marcuse: On Art and Revolution," in Jürgen

Habermas, *Philosophical-Political Profiles*, trans. Frederick Lawrence (Cambridge, Mass.: MIT Press, 1988), 171–72.

14. Cf. for instance, Habermas's "Technology and Science as 'Ideology,'" in his *Toward a Rational Society*, trans. Jeremy J. Shapiro (Boston: Beacon Press, 1979), 81–122, and Andrew Feenberg, *Critical Theory of Technology* (New York: Oxford University Press, 1991).

15. Cf. Feenberg, *Critical Theory of Technology*, 165f. Feenberg argues that one can explore the question of alternative technologies without deciding the question of a possible successor science.

16. Marcuse, *One-Dimensional Man*, 248–49.

17. Ibid.

18. Ibid., 166. Of the possibility of a science not based on the domination of nature, Habermas has this to say: "The concept of a categorically different science and technology is as empty as the idea of a universal reconciliation is without basis." "Theodor Adorno: The Primal History of Subjectivity—Self-Affirmation Gone Wild," in *Philosophical-Political Profiles*, 110.

19. Ibid., 166–76; see also the discussion in David Ingram, *Critical Theory and Philosophy* (New York: Paragon Books, 1990), 87ff.

20. Habermas, *Toward a Rational Society*, 88.

21. Len Doyal and Ian Gough, *A Theory of Human Needs* (New York: Guilford Press, 1991).

22. Marcuse, *One-Dimensional Man*, 232.

23. Roger Colton, *Credit and Collection Activities under Different Utility Low-Income Programs* (Boston: National Consumer Law Center, 1992), provides a multistate evaluation of low-income energy needs, using different definitions of the term "need."

24. Bill Devall, *Simple in Means, Rich in Ends* (Layton, Utah: Peregrine Smith Publishing, 1988), 53–54.

25. J. Baird Callicott, "The Metaphysical Implications of Ecology," in *Defense of the Land Ethic* (Albany: State University of New York Press, 1989), 114.

26. Mary Midgeley, *Animals and Why They Matter* (Athens: University of Georgia Press, 1983), esp. 141ff.

27. Judith Soule and John Piper, *Farming in Nature's Image* (Washington, D.C.: Island Press, 1992). For a short summary of the Land Institute's underlying ideas and research, see Wes Jackson, "Nature as the Measure for a Sustainable Agriculture," in *Ecology Economics Ethics: The Broken Circle*, ed. F. Herbert Bormann and Stephen R. Kellert (New Haven, Conn.: Yale University Press, 1991), 43–58.

28. Contemporary reexaminations of the history of science in terms of narrative and metaphor are relevant here. See, for instance, in two very different veins, Donna J. Haraway, "The Contest for Primate Nature: Daughters of Man-the-Hunter in the Field, 1960–80," in her *Simians, Cyborgs, and Women: The Reinvention of Nature* (New York: Routledge, 1991), and James Hillman, "On Psychological Femininity," in his *Myth of Analysis* (New York: Harper, Collins, 1978).

Carol Becker

Surveying *The Aesthetic Dimension* at the Death of Postmodernism

> If pressed on the subject of political correctness and art, Marcuse often recounted an anecdote that pleased him a great deal. It was about the painter Victor Neep, who, when "challenged" to explain the "alleged element of protest" in Cezanne's "A Still Life with Apples," responded, "It is a protest against sloppy thinking."
>
> —*Barry Kātz,* Herbert Marcuse and the Art of Liberation

The Last Decade

The eighties were a contradictory time for the art world. The market went wild, rewarding with fame and fortune those artists deemed fashionable, while others who had not as yet "made it" waited nervously, caught in a dream of imminent possibility. Students entered art schools optimistic and idealistic about their futures. New galleries sprang up everywhere, and more people seemed interested in the art displayed than ever before. Openings were flooded with non–art world types like investment bankers who all seemed to be "collecting." Writing about art proliferated. Museum attendance was on the rise. From the outside it seemed like a boom. However, from the inside, there was a definite sense that something had gone askew. Although many people did seem preoccupied with looking at art, few really understood what they were looking at. That which did succeed in galleries and museums often referenced itself only to art. If one were not part of that world, the allusions to the work of other artists past and present were difficult to uncode, as were the extreme innovations in form that renounced traditional conventions and left viewers asking, "But is it art?" It was easy to think that much on display, although marketable, had lost a sense of social purpose. There seemed to be a great aesthetic and political demoralization manifested in the confusion of many artists over what to make work about.

Other trends were also observable. Among those not pulled by the art world's capricious lure were those more socially conscious artists who also emerged in great strength in the eighties with a clear critique of an art world that mirrored the larger social system and appeared to them as insular, elite, intellectually corrupt, and exclusionary. Women artists in particular recognized the full extent of the power of patriarchy to reinforce and reward male artists. Their work no longer remained silent about these conditions. Artists of color began to make their art overtly expose how entrenched and insidious the racism of the art world actually was. Gay and lesbian art appeared with confidence and strength. At the same time, artistic articulations of the horrors of AIDS were to be found in all media.

The enthusiastic adoption of theory—writing about gender, race, class, media studies, psychoanalysis—also changed the character of the art world in the eighties. It constructed a parallel universe of ideas from which the art world took sustenance and to which it added image, metaphor, and its own discourse. The new emphasis on theory within the "postmodern" period has proved to be a mixed blessing. It undoubtedly infused the art world with complex ideas and helped formulate the concept of political correctness. However, theory also created a split between past generations trained to work intuitively on aspects of form and a new generation clearly driven by content and metadiscussions about the nature of content. As the art world attempted to make sense of these complexities, such political figures as Jesse Helms and Alfonse D'Amato complicated matters by taking the law into their own hands, questioning the "morality" of more controversial work and the legitimacy of government funding to art that some found "offensive" and downright "anti-American." Fueled by these issues, the art world entered the nineties immersed in debate about what artists should be doing, how they should be doing it, and why they might do it at all.

If the present period of the early nineties can be categorized as post-postmodern, it is because artists have recognized the limits of postmodernism and have come to a point where they are no longer content to remain on the edge making radical statements to the art world alone. Rather, many artists now want to intersect with the center and to address the concerns of a larger audience. As a result we have come to an exciting, if difficult, moment: The art world has assimilated the lessons of postmodernism—its irreverent mocking of form, challenge to the notion of a coherent subject, political sophistication, cynicism, and isolation—yet out of this assimilation an analysis has evolved that incorporates the realities of the economic and political crisis, the capriciousness of the gallery, the market system, as well as the alienation artists feel. The sense of why people make work, how they make it, and to whom it is addressed are all affected. At this time there is no doubt that many artists want to be relevant to the world in which they live and comprehensible to those with whom they share this world.

Because the art scene has changed in these often seemingly contradictory ways, it is now time to do a serious exploration of the phenomena of the artist in society and the impact of art within a social context. This exploration should be useful to those writers, intellectuals, and artists who struggle to combat regressiveness in the art world while defending it against the reactionary puritanism of "outsiders" who would abuse it as a scapegoat for all that is wrong in contemporary society. The art world needs to further its understanding of how conflicting tendencies come together. Unfortunately, there are few places to turn for such a vision. It is therefore a fortuitous moment to revisit the work of the Frankfurt School—those intellectuals whose historical and philosophical mission was to make sense of a senseless world. In particular it is useful to rethink the importance of Herbert Marcuse's last book, *The Aesthetic Dimension*, and to consider how his ideas might be reinterpreted in this difficult post-postmodern era, in this time of political urgency and despair. Perhaps we can take from his analysis a much-needed sense of possibility, or as Marcuse himself might say, "hope."[1]

A Return to *The Aesthetic Dimension*

The Aesthetic Dimension begins with a disarming apology: "In a situation where the miserable reality can be changed only through radical political praxis, the concern with aesthetics demands justification. It would be senseless to deny the element of despair inherent in this concern: the retreat into a world of fiction where existing conditions are changed and overcome only in the realm of the imagination."[2]

In this statement, published in 1978, Marcuse admits that he was beginning to lose faith in the possibility that the "miserable" political environment could be changed. At such a point of crisis, as his own optimism waned, he returned to aesthetics—his early, great love. He focused primarily on literature, about which he could speak with an unhesitating authority that was lacking in his knowledge of the visual arts. And when he went back to what in the beginning had fed his own utopian ideals, he did so with a deliberate agenda. He was attempting to use this reexamination to refute Marxist notions about the function of art in society, which he saw as limited, didactic, and naive. He railed against the idea that art, which focuses on the "declining class" (i.e., the bourgeoisie), is decadent and that consequently all art should focus on the "ascending class" (i.e., the proletariat). He was quite clear that art need not represent the social relations of production directly. In fact, the indirect ways in which art does represent these social relations may well prove to be the more significant and profound:

> I shall submit the following thesis: the radical qualities of art, that is to say, its indictment of the established reality and its invocation of the beautiful image . . . of liberation are grounded precisely in the dimensions where art transcends its social determination and emancipates itself from the given universe of discourse and behavior while preserving its overwhelming presence. Thereby art creates the realm in which the subversion of experience proper to art becomes possible: the world formed by art is recognized as a reality which is suppressed and distorted in the given reality.[3]

In its refusal to be absorbed within the reality principle or to adhere to the rules of the reality principle, in its insistence on addressing the issues of subjectivity and the presentation of contradiction, art refuses the notion that there can be any simple transformation of society or that "all of that which art invokes and indicts could be settled through the class struggle."[4] But if art does indict, what comprises its indictment?

According to Marcuse, all humans have been forced to repress basic instincts in order to survive within civilization as it has been constructed. Such is the premise of *Eros and Civilization*, in which Marcuse asks, "How can civilization freely generate freedom, when unfreedom has become part and parcel of the mental apparatus?"[5] In Marcuse's sense art is a location—a designated imaginative space within which the experience of freedom is allowed to exist. Art "challenges the monopoly of the established reality" by creating "fictitious worlds" in which one can see mirrored that range of human emotion and experience that does not find an outlet in the present reality. In this sense the fabricated world of art becomes "more real than reality itself."[6] It presents the possibility of a fulfillment that in truth only a transformed society could offer. It is the reminder of what a truly integrated experience of oneself in society might be. Art can embody a tension that keeps hope alive about a "memory of the happiness that once was, and that seeks its return."[7] In such a configuration there must be a sense that there is something beyond the reality principle, even if the existence of such a different condition can only exist within the imagination. In its ability to conjure those dimensions of the individual's emotional life not dominated by the social system, art, according to Marcuse, is able to sustain an image of humanness—an image of human beings as "species beings" capable of living in that community of freedom that is the potential of the species. The recognition of this potential is the "subjective basis of a classless society."[8] The image of the liberated human psyche can be communicated by art not only through a literal representation of the utopian dream, as has been the case in socialist realist work, but in the emotions such work is able to elicit.

This range of emotional response can be transmitted by the struggles depicted in content and their embodiment in form. The manifestation of these ideas within a form that has integrity is the achievement of art. Through form, art can portray humanness on a grand scale, beyond the class struggle. At the point where form becomes content, the artist lives best, and individuals can experience a spectrum of imaginative possibilities crucial to envisioning and manifesting a revolutionary process.

Marcuse believed that a great deal of the radical potential of art lies in its ability to play with and yet exist outside of the reality principle. Because art actually serves no demonstrable function within the society, its purpose must be articulated from outside the immediate experience it generates. The act of observing art may have a transformative effect on a person, but within a society of alienation its actual use value is often discounted. In fact, Marcuse might say that within a capitalist system the deepest purposes of art go against the basic premises on which capitalism is constructed. Its only really justifiable place would be as an object that can be bought, speculated on, and sold for a profit within the art market. Its worth as a tool to regenerate the lost, hidden, creative, spiritual, intuitive aspects of human life will never be given their proper value under capitalism.

At its best, art serves a different master than capitalism, one whose values are not as readily discerned. Although its place in the order of things is not always clearly articulated, no one would publicly advocate a society that did not, at least in theory, encourage creative expression as manifested in art. The idea of a society without art seems impoverished. The necessary tension between the longing embedded in people's desire for a fuller life, or a more complete self, and the world in which they live would be obliterated. That which is almost unspeakable, that which cannot be contained, is allowed to live through the form of art. This is why art at times is perceived as subversive: not simply because it presents a world that appears immoral, or licentious, as is often thought, but because it reminds people of buried desires that their deepest selves actually dream and cannot manifest within the existing system.

Marcuse locates this vision of possibility within the well-articulated space of the aesthetic dimension. It is a place that stands in negation to the reality principle. It does not embody what is, but what wants to be. "One of the foremost tasks of art," writes Walter Benjamin, "has always been the creation of a demand which could be fully satisfied only later."[9] "Later," within Marcuse's system, could only be realized within a revolutionary society.

Art need not necessarily exist only within the domain of the pleasure principle. If successful, it could also be found wherever human potentiality is able to manifest itself. Art allows for this actualization through the vehicle of form—a physical organization that captures a range of intangible experience. Artists, Marcuse says, are those for whom form becomes content. This becomes the source of their strength and alienation. Those outside the art-making process may not consciously understand why they respond to the work as they do. They may be unaware that the work's embodiment of beauty, coherence, properties of elegance, or deliberate refusal to allow for the experience of elegance does affect their ability to understand the content of the work intellectually and emotionally. Well-executed art stands as both part of and not part of the society out of which it has emerged. It has not bought into the demands of the "miserable reality." It has not accepted the limiting prejudices of race, class, gender. While commenting on such issues, it is also capable of moving beyond them. Thus, when art is effective, in Marcuse's terms, it appeals to progressive people. It may well contain within it a critique of the prevailing ideology. Or, as in Neep's understanding of Cezanne's *Still Life with Apples*, the clarity and integrity of form itself may prove subversive, especially when all else in society seems in disarray.

There is no doubt that this is a utopian vision of the place of art in society, because it allows for the possibility that art itself could embody utopia and in so doing annihilate the reality principle. Marcuse is not naive about how this transcendence will occur. He does not expect or want the experience of art to be easy. On the contrary, he rejects the notion that art should try to reach a large audience directly. He does not think that art is life or that it should attempt to appear to be life. According to Marcuse, its strength is its otherness, the fact that it cannot readily be assimilated. If art comes too close to reality, if it strives too hard to be comprehensible or accessible, then it runs the risk of becoming mundane. If this occurs, its function as negation is lost. To be effective, art must exert its capacity for estrangement. It must dislocate the viewer, reader, audience by its refusal and inability to become part of the reality principle or to in any way anticipate the needs of the performance principle. It should not help people to assimilate into the existing society but at each turn challenge the assumptions of that society, whether it is through the intellectual and visual rigor it demands and/or the heightened recognition of pleasure and pain it provides.

Political Correctness and Uncompromising Estrangement

The ideas of *The Aesthetic Dimension*, ideas that might have seemed dated only a few years ago, now present themselves as useful once again. As the debates about political correctness rage in the art world, current thinking about the question of how artists can make a significant statement and how best to fight against the prevailing ideology often seems naive and oblivious of the fact that the same debates have already occurred and been recorded by the literary world. If the pressure of the eighties was to make pastiche, engage in appropriation, and primarily reference the art world itself, the pressure of the nineties is to make politically correct work. But what constitutes politically correct work? The art world often confers this definition on art whose content is overtly and clearly about political concerns. Marcuse takes issue with the simplicity of these assumptions: "The political potential of art lies only in its own aesthetic dimensions. Its relation to praxis is inexorably indirect, mediated and frustrating. The more immediately political the work of art, the more it reduces the power of estrangement and the radical, transcendent goals of change. In this sense, there may be more subversive potential in the poetry of Baudelaire and Rimbaud than in the didactic plays of Brecht."[10]

These would be fighting words were they written today, because the art world, for the most part, does not tolerate such juxtapositions. It has often simplified the nature of the political to reward certain content. But this has also meant that it has denied the possibility that work too easily designated as "bourgeois" might actually serve a significant, political purpose. The American Left in particular has always had a restricted understanding of form. The same audience that can tolerate extremes in content, that actually desires a revolutionary message, cannot grasp the degree to which innovations in form can also be radical when those formal innovations change the scope of what people are able to see. If the content is not overtly, directly, simply about social concerns, and the work is not easily accessible in a formal sense, then it is not thought to be political.

Within this paradigm, art, to be acceptable, must be "anti-art"—art that refuses to be art, refuses to take pleasure in its own formal properties, or denies conventional forms and therefore defies traditional expectations. But within Marcuse's particular understanding, art that becomes anti-art closely aligns with the reality of day-to-day life and not with the conventions of art making. This art only recreates fragmentation in its simulation of reality and, in so doing, runs the risk of losing its subversive potential. We have seen such anti-art in the sixties, seventies, and eighties. It was often work in which the statement was more significant than its execution, or complexity was sacrificed to a sense of what would be readily understood. It was work often lacking in metaphor. In the nineties it is often linked to the idea of political correctness. Of this complex issue Marcuse writes: "While the abandonment of the aesthetic form may well provide the most immediate, most direct mirror of a society in which subjects and objects are shattered, atomized, robbed of their words and images, the rejection of the aesthetic sublimation turns such work into bits and pieces of the very society whose anti-art they want to be. Anti-art is self-defeating from the outset."[11]

Marcuse clearly rejects the notion that art can effectively comment on the degeneration of society by merely recreating that degeneration, or that it can attack the one-dimensionality of society by reproducing that one-dimensionality. Such art, in its refusal to develop a transcendent form and in its mirroring of the "miserable reality," reflects that which already exists and is in a sense too familiar. It does not allow for the factor of estrangement. We have witnessed this in video, performance, and installation art, as well as in painting. The key to its failure, Marcuse might say, is not its content but rather its refusal to embody that content in an aesthetically challenging form which would further the question and push the viewer or the reader to a more complex, more emotional, or more revelatory understanding of the problem posed by the work.

This particular aspect of Marcuse's analysis is the most controversial for those who see his refusal to accept what he calls anti-art as an attempt to suffocate art and artists within conventional, formal, "bourgeois" boundaries. But it would seem that Marcuse is not so much interested in restricting form as he is in fostering work that refuses to simulate the present reality and hence encourages people to imagine something else. His analysis is also founded on the idea that however radically it may at first seem to smash traditional forms, the shock value will ultimately be lost if the form later appears to be too similar to the experience of daily life. Even today these issues are still not sufficiently discussed within the art world. The need to make formally effective work is more than an abstract idea within Marcuse's system. For him it is *the idea*, essential to the meaning of art itself: "In this sense, renunciation of the aesthetic form is abdication of responsibility. It deprives art of the very form in which it can create that other reality within the established one—the cosmos of hope."[12]

Within Marcuse's concept of the artist, there are two fundamental principles: First, the artist has a responsibility to society; and second, art must embody hope. But Marcuse does not legislate *how* these principles should be achieved. Moreover, his sense that art should be hopeful does not reflect a simple optimism but rather expresses his notion that a much-needed psychic space is created when contradictions are confronted within the aesthetic dimension. For Marcuse, hope lies within the imagination, within the peculiarly human ability to envision that which does not exist and give that imaginary dimension shape. He believes that this shape, this original organization, whether it is in painting, literature, or music, is precisely what is necessary to transcend the limitations of the reality principle. It is the task of all serious writers, artists, and intellectuals to attempt this feat. It is not simply that Marcuse wants art to exist on an elevated plane. There is tolerance within Marcuse's vision to embrace contemporary issues of daily life, as long as those issues are presented in a form that embodies their ability to transform themselves—that reveals their complexity and their emotional and political resonance. Even "death and destruction" should invoke the need for hope, "a need rooted in the new consciousness, embodied in the work of art."[13] In Marcuse's system, the "new consciousness" seems to be that realm of the imagination which has not yet been colonized by the reality principle, that aspect of the psyche which has managed to retain a desire for wholeness and has remained untouched by the oppressiveness of the reality principle or the deadening defeatism of the prevailing ideology.

The Accusation of Romanticization

It is easy to see why Marcuse has been called a romantic and why his work has received so little recent direct acknowledgement from the contemporary art world. Marcuse believed that there was a part of the human psyche that remained somehow invulnerable to the repressiveness of society. If art could tap into this part, then the psyche could be given shape and articulation, its wholeness explored no matter how fragmented the reality that surrounded it. But Marcuse's concept assumes a unified subject and a coherent sense of self that can escape alienation. It also assumes the existence of a universal subject from which one could extrapolate the idea that, at the core, humans can locate an arena of common experience. In the same vein, Marcuse implies that art can transcend racial, gender, and cultural differences through certain aesthetic forms. These forms are undoubtedly Eurocentric, grounded exclusively within the Western tradition. This was the world out of which Marcuse evolved; it was the only world he really knew.

For these reasons *The Aesthetic Dimension* can be attacked and even dismissed. Clearly, after all the collective theoretical work that has resulted from postmodernism, certain aspects of Marcuse's thesis do stand in need of qualification. But even given such reservations, the issues raised in this, his last book are actually very timely and surprisingly synchronized with issues absorbing the contemporary art world.

At the center of Marcuse's theory, for example, is the issue of "the Beautiful," which he says appears time and again in progressive movements and is understood "as an aspect of the reconstruction of nature and society."[14] Even when social upheaval is on the agenda, beauty often has been defined in a limited, benign way as "plastic purity and loveliness" and as "an extension of exchange values to the aesthetic-erotic dimension."[15] Marcuse's philosophical understanding of beauty situates it in a more profound relationship to the issues of revolutionary change.

The beautiful, for Marcuse, is sensuous and is preserved in "aesthetic sublimation." The autonomy of art and its political potential rest in this sensuousness. Marcuse rails against a crude form of Marxist aesthetics which has rejected the idea of the beautiful as the central category of "bourgeois aesthetics" and has failed to grasp its subversive element. This leaves those artists anxious to make a strong statement about society without the possibility of creating work both political and beautiful, in Marcuse's sense. This is often why artists resist committing themselves to political movements. They fear the degree to which such alignments will deny them the right to engage in the sensuousness of the art-making process, as experienced in the love of materials and structure and the pleasure of translating abstract concepts into form. For most artists, these were the reasons they were drawn to art making in the first place.

Artists fear they will be forced to replace their love of this process for guilt derived from the enjoyment and pleasure they take in line, color, texture. In fact, the work considered most "subversive" is often filled with unpleasure, which is only a negation of the beautiful. This art is certainly not a vision of what is possible, not a vision capable of seducing anyone into believing either the more progressive philosophical understandings it represents or the future world it portends. In this sense Marcuse's understanding of the sensuousness of art could be subversive, especially if it is understood that mass culture, as it exists in the United States, cannot comfortably tolerate that which is truly beautiful in his terms—that which exudes a deep resonance of originality and strong formal properties that allow complex meaning to evolve. Work fitting this definition of the beautiful would force people to consider what no longer exists except in dreams: memory of a time (whether real or imagined) when life was fulfilling and people's relationship to it seemed less estranged. It is not necessary to prove or disprove the historical existence of such a time. Rather, it is important to note that throughout many social movements, the seemingly retroactive emotion of *longing* has proved to be a force propelling people forward. This feeling can be elicited through an appeal to the senses and to the emotional and psychological life of an individual. There is little in mass culture that attempts to touch people at all these levels. When longing does exist, it appears as melodrama and/or nostalgia. Such manifestations often homogenize difference by settling for a banal version of human experience. The result is a form of sublimation we tend to think of as "entertainment," not the complex interaction of form and content we call art.

Art is too layered and, at times, too difficult to lend itself easily to mass appeal. That which profoundly moves the senses, the intellect, and the unconscious is essential to the well-being of the collective imagination. Yet, in American society, it only really receives mainstream attention when it has come under attack "in the name of morality and religion."[16] It is to its credit that some art can generate such an extreme response. Moralists, whether they know it or not, are fearful that such work will arouse people, not in a simple, sexual way, but in a sensual, provocative manner. They fear it might touch people's deepest desires and challenge the mundaneity, conformity, and repressiveness—the dissatisfaction— they actually feel in their daily lives, work, environment, and relationships. Consequently, there have always been some who have tried to silence it.

Artists know the power of creating art that is directly sensual and erotic. They often do it precisely because it fights against the tyranny of delayed gratification, of unfulfilled needs—a repression at the core of capitalist society. But within the art world, work often becomes explicitly and provocatively sexual because artists assume their audience is composed of moralists who are offended by sexuality and who therefore need to be shaken up. Artists rarely imagine an audience actually hungry for real sensuality and receptive to all its possibilities—an audience with whom it would be a challenge to communicate. Were they to make work with such an audience in mind, art might be able to fulfill the types of demands Marcuse has presented. Indeed, instead of being sympathetic to the anxiety produced in viewers when their work violates conventional expectations, artists at times opt for the easiest form of provocation—the sexual or pornographic—and then become hostile and confrontational when their work elicits extreme reactions because it is in fact upsetting to its audience. The result is alienation between the audience and the artist. Perhaps this is the manifestation of a larger issue, namely, that the artist has forgotten that the oppressive forces he or she is battling are not necessarily embodied in the individual viewer. They are, rather, embedded in the social system, which not only refuses to make a place for the artist within society but also refuses to recognize the real concerns of human well-being. Were artists to actually imagine their viewers as real people in need of positive stimulation, perhaps their intent would be more deliberately to engage and provoke rather than to shock.

"Art for the People"

The appropriation, pastiche, and at times parodic cynicism that characterized the postmodern period have left a vacuum. Curiously, it now seems that the pendulum has swung fiercely in the opposite direction: There is almost the sense that artists "should" serve as social workers, moving in unfamiliar communities and making work that talks to and has meaning for people other than themselves. Certainly, this turn of events could be useful, but more often than not these ideas have become demands placed on artists by other artists for whom making politically correct work is a moral issue.

Surveying *The Aesthetic Dimension*, it is clear that Marcuse has given a great deal of thought to this kind of mandate. On the other hand, Marcuse is dubious about anything that might come across as "art for the people." He fears a too-deliberate type of populism would diminish and dilute the impact of art, which must help develop "a new morality and a new sensibility."[17] However, "the more the exploited classes, 'the people,' succumb to the powers that be, the more will art be estranged from 'the people.' "[18] The more alienated people are from their own deepest selves, the more fragmented they are from the society in which they live and work, the more they need an experience of art that is powerful—yet the more they might turn away from it, because the deep concerns such art elicits could seem too remote and obscure to touch their daily lives. Therefore, it often happens that the audience most in need of such work might reject its content or find its form unattainable. Nonetheless, excessive attempts to suit the work to the audience can defeat the necessary tension that actually allows work to be subversive.

Marcuse's position on this issue shows a clear understanding of the contradictions in which artists find themselves. His willingness to confront these ambiguities is a trait often lacking in the critical thinking of the art world today. The contemporary approach tends to encourage artists to make work with a strong political orientation and then rewards that work in art-world terms of success even though it has no impact on a larger arena. Meanwhile, work that is not overtly political but perhaps deeply subversive is too easily dismissed and criticized for not extending beyond traditional confines. Ironically, the success of art might be measured, not in how favorably it is received, but rather in how it is attacked or ignored, how "other" it appears when measured against the predominant cultural values or, for that matter, the predominant subcultural values of the art world.

In a similar vein, Marcuse believes that even though the masses may have increasingly bought into the prevailing cultural values which make complex thought intolerable and fearsome, the artist should not be forced to create art, or the writer to write, in a way that is easily assimilated by an audience embedded in the dominant one-dimensionality. If "art cannot change the world," it can help to change "the consciousness and drives of the men and women who would change the world."[19] It may appeal to those who see through the veil of Maya, who move beyond the myths of their own civilization. Artists can make a choice "to work for the radicalization of consciousness." In Marcuse's terms this might mean "to make explicit and conscious the material and ideological discrepancy between the writer and 'the people' rather than to obscure and camouflage it. Revolutionary art may well become 'The Enemy of the People.' "[20] It may antagonize and confuse. Its ability to rupture continu-

183

ity may well be its strength, but it may be misunderstood, ahead of its time, beyond its audience, even when its message is intended to liberate those who passively ignore or actively oppose it. Its function is not to be easily absorbed but rather to challenge and disrupt. We have certainly seen this concept play itself out fiercely within the last thirty years. Art that might have helped free its audience from repressive conventions was met with great hostility by precisely those people who could have been moved to greater understanding had they opened themselves to the possibilities it offered. But the work was finally too unnerving to find acceptance in non–art world audiences.

In truth, even artists and intellectuals have trouble absorbing the deeply controversial work of others or allowing multiple points of view to coexist. Artists who make such work can deal with negative responses if they accept the fact that they will face a certain degree of rage when they challenge aspects of society that people have internalized as correct, moral, and legitimate. They need to understand that there is a political function to the uproar their work has caused. Too often success is measured by work "fitting in," even fitting into the nontraditional world of art. In fact, neither the dominant culture nor even the supposedly more sophisticated subculture of the art world may be able to absorb the most profound work produced, especially when the work refuses to tolerate the politically correct line.

To make work too easily acceptable to an audience for whom the work must inevitably be challenging is to homogenize the work and ultimately to render it impotent. William Blake believed that his own poetry had to be difficult to read, that it was in the act of struggling to understand the text that transformations of consciousness actually occurred. To simplify the effect, to translate the form, would have meant diluting the power of the work to reach deeply into the psyche and challenge the values of society at a fundamental level.

Within the notion of political correctness, there is often a desire to simplify not just the form but the content of the work as well, to reduce it to a message that can be easily "gotten." This frequently results in a heavy-handedness and an almost insulting condescension in the work that is quite off-putting to the audience. "Getting" the message might not be the problem; they may not like the message they are getting. It is also humiliating to the artist, whose function—unlike that of the television scriptwriter, newscaster, journalist, cabaret dancer, or popular singer—may not be to seduce by entertaining. Perhaps one clear, significant role of the artist of the future is, as Susan Sontag says of her own intent, "to keep alive the idea of seriousness, to understand that in the late 20th Century, seriousness itself could be in question."[21]

Marcuse understood this aspect of art. Knowing the indigenous anti-intellectualism that progressive Americans have always had to confront, Marcuse was not sympathetic to any movement that forced art to serve the god of political correctness through oversimplification. He could easily see the limitation of this tendency and also the repressiveness of forcing artists into any one position. I think he might also have grasped the irony of the art world's attempts to prescribe for itself what is legitimate, what work can and cannot be made, and how it should be made. Nor is it coincidental that this movement of self-regulation has followed so closely on the heels of a postmodernism in which artists isolated themselves from a more general audience. It seems a dramatic swing to err in the other direction, to overcompensate and in the process destroy, in the name of relevance and accessibility, what is uniquely important about art—its commitment to play and freedom of expression. This crisis of purpose is also a crisis of vision. Artists and writers, insecure about what art should be and how to justify its existence, attempt to impose a meaning on it from the outside in the hope that a set of political criteria will make art somehow more scientific, objective, and therefore more legitimate.

In the beginning of *The Aesthetic Dimension*, Marcuse notes that only radical political praxis can change the political situation and that his concern with aesthetics "demands justification." If his final work retains nothing else useful for us today, it demonstrates the importance of aesthetics as an area of exploration and the importance of art as a crucial force for liberation within a repressive society. The debate Marcuse entered into almost twenty years ago is in fact still relevant and under discussion today. As the world artists live in becomes more complex, as the demands made on us all increase, his work on aesthetics can provide an endless source of inspiration, not necessarily for the answers it provides but rather for the range of questions it fearlessly asks. Postmodernism may well have changed the discourse and terms of the debate, may have introduced issues of identity, postcolonialism, and the notion of the disunified subject. But no matter. In this post-postmodern moment, as the art world moves into the next decade in search of a meaningful identity, Marcuse's last book is still one of the finest justifications for the significance of art in society.

Notes

1. Herbert Marcuse, *The Aesthetic Dimension: Toward a Critique of Marxist Aesthetics* (Boston: Beacon Press, 1978), 52.

2. Ibid., 1.

3. Ibid., 6.

4. Ibid., 14.

5. Herbert Marcuse, *Eros and Civilization: A Philosophical Inquiry into Freud* (New York: Vintage Books, 1961), 206.

6. Ibid., 66.

7. Marcuse, *The Aesthetic Dimension*, 68.

8. Ibid., 17.

9. Walter Benjamin, *Illuminations*, ed. Hannah Arendt, trans. Harry Zohn (New York: Schocken Books, 1968), 237.

10. Marcuse, *The Aesthetic Dimension*, xii–xiii.

11. Ibid., 49.

12. Ibid., 52.

13. Ibid., 7.

14. Ibid., 62.

15. Ibid.

16. Ibid., 66.

17. Ibid., 28.

18. Ibid., 32.

19. Ibid.

20. Ibid., 35.

21. Susan Sontag, "Susan Sontag Finds Romance," *New York Times Magazine*, 2 August 1992, 23–43.

Part IV

Ecofascists and Cyberpunks

Timothy W. Luke

Marcuse and Ecology

Why return to Marcuse, especially now in the 1990s? What can his writing possibly offer to those desperately seeking new alternatives to the prevailing social order? Since the collapse of the New Left in the 1970s, Marcuse has been largely forgotten as the theory community stampeded from craze to craze during its successive infatuations with Habermas, Foucault, Lyotard, Baudrillard, Derrida, and Heidegger. Marcuse perhaps had something to do with this fall from favor after he brooded over the demise of the various New Left movements in *Counterrevolution and Revolt* and then apparently turned away from direct political strategies toward the aesthetic alternatives promised by "a new sensibility" in *The Aesthetic Dimension*.[1]

For new audiences caught up in the postmodernism debates of the 1980s, Marcuse's most mature theoretical formulas often seemed to lack cultural resonance or political closure. As a result, his project was largely shelved, if not forgotten, by the time of his death in 1979. Although up against the allure of French poststructuralists and deconstructionists, Habermas basically held on to his market share without slipping too much. In a world, however, that has heard everything Habermas has had to say about philosophical discourses of modernity and theories of communicative interaction throughout the 1980s, it seems increasingly strange that advanced industrial society remains totally bogged down in serious new crises associated with the end of nature and tribal wars of fascistic ethnic cleansing. The French poststructuralists and deconstructionists are not much help in this department either, but something else beyond Habermas's colorless and ineffectual "critical theory" definitely seems needed. With regard to the ecological crises embedded in the ending of nature, Marcuse can still be quite helpful.

Marcuse and the Ecological Issue

As this collection of essays reveals, however, Marcuse always has been problematic. His conceptualizations of social contradictions, historical forces, and political conflicts in broad categories drawn from Freudian metapsychology often lack any sense of subtle nuance or real complexity. Similarly, his commitment to a Marxian vision of class domination and his Hegelian notion of human needs also run against the grain of more recent postmodernist readings of these philosophical codes, which are rife with those allegedly suspicious metanarratives. Nonetheless, Marcuse's acute sense for providing an always challenging critique of advanced industrial society is sharp, thorough, and relentless. And it is this dimension of his project, particularly inasmuch as he frames the environmental crises of advanced capitalist society, that remains as vital today as it was three decades ago. Things on the environmental front have not changed much; and, if there has been change, it has been mainly for the worse.

Marcuse's influence on the New Left during the 1960s and 1970s was significant, and to the extent that elements of the New Left were concerned with issues of ecology and the environment, Marcuse has had some impact on today's ecological criticism. Hazel Henderson's *Politics of the Solar Age: Alternatives to Economics* marks this dimension of Marcuse's work, and Langdon Winner in *The Whale and the Reactor* notes how Marcuse, as an ecological thinker, "had begun building a bridge between Frankfurt School critical theory and the possibility of an alternative technology"[2] in the 1960s and 1970s. This side of Marcuse is also noted in Koula Mellos's *Perspectives on Ecology*, which casts Marcuse as an important "theoretical inspiration" for the ecology movement through the New Left.[3] Even so, Marcuse rarely ends up being cited or discussed as a decisive intellectual influence by radical ecologists. In contemporary terms, his project is read by most ecological activists as being either too anthropocentric or too socialistic to be taken seriously by most participants in the environmental politics of the 1990s.[4] This neglect of Marcuse is unfortunate, because he initially raised in a very cogent and highly coherent fashion most of the central concerns preoccupying ecological activists today.

At the same time, it is clear that the themes of ecology and the environment, as they are understood, for example, by today's deep ecologists or bioregionalists, are not prominent features in Marcuse's theoretical project. Like Marx, Marcuse continually throws out many off-hand asides about nature in his writings. He basically affirms the general importance of respecting the environment's essential integrity and order, but he is also committed to rationalizing and humanizing nature. What this means concretely, however, is less obvious. The topic of ecological destruction per se is taken up by Marcuse only during and after 1970. Even then, his published considerations are relatively few and unsustained. *Counterrevolution and Revolt*, which was presented initially as lectures at Princeton and the New School for Social Research during 1970, includes as its second chapter some thought on ecology, entitled "Nature and Revolution."[5] Yet this text was not published until 1972. During the same year, he made some short remarks at a Paris conference on ecology that were published in *Liberation* as "Ecology and Revolution" a few months later.[6] Finally, a lecture that Marcuse presented in California to a group of students in 1979 was published recently by *Capitalism, Nature, Socialism* as "Ecology and the Critique of Modern Society."[7]

Beyond such scant attention in Marcuse's published *oeuvre*, ecological issues are mainly worked into the background of his writings. This curious ecological aporia in Marcuse's work can even be documented indirectly by returning to the two major, book-length analyses of Marcuse published in the United States during the 1980s by Schoolman and Kellner. Neither *The Imaginary Witness* (1980) nor *Herbert Marcuse and The Crisis of Marxism* (1984) specifically identifies the ecology question with Marcuse in their tables of contents.[8] Likewise, neither study makes a concerted effort to think about or even document Marcuse's approach toward ecology, the environment, or nature with individual index entries. Of course, Marcuse's environmental concerns are raised occasionally by both Schoolman and Kellner, but neither one of them develops a truly focal concentration on Marcuse's complex approaches to environmental topics.

On the one hand, this silence is understandable. Despite his reputation for being the all-knowing guru of the New Left, Marcuse did not consider the ecology a distinct issue as such until other figures and forces associated with New Left movements popularized ecological questions during the months leading up to the first Earth Day in 1970. Even then, the environmental question remained wrapped up in Marcuse's essentially Marxian reading of nature and his Freudian take on human subjectivity. On the other hand, however, much of Marcuse's theoretical project does focus on ecology and the environment. Much of his most important work ends up assessing the negative impact of excessively destructive social institutions on what he identifies as "human nature," or the primary impulses and experiences underlying anyone's rationality and emotions, and "external nature," or the existential environments of nature that frame everyone's survival. These preoccupations are central to his analysis of domination in *Eros and Civilization, One-Dimensional Man*, and *An Essay on Liberation*.[9] In *Counterrevolution and Revolt*, for example, Marcuse asserts that "in the established society, nature itself, ever more effectively controlled, has in turn become another dimension for the control of man: the extended arm of society and its power."[10] Consequently, the revolutionary task of the present era is quite clear: "The radical transformation of nature becomes an integral part of the radical transformation of society."[11]

Like many of today's radical ecologists, Marcuse argues in *One-Dimensional Man* that "contemporary industrial society tends to be totalitarian."[12] Totalitarian forms of rule include not only the political forms of terroristic, one-party dictatorships but also an ecological and psychosocial form tied to "a non-terroristic economic-technical coordination which operates through the manipulation of needs by vested interests."[13] Marcuse admits that the character, satisfaction, and intensity of human needs have always been historically preconditioned and that the question of what are true and false needs ultimately can only be answered by the individuals expressing these needs. In today's advanced industrial societies under late capitalism, Marcuse contends that the socio-historical definition of needs, the politico-economic demands that promote the repressive or liberatory development of individual needs, and the technical-administrative satisfaction of socially defined/personally accepted needs must all be "subject to overriding critical standards."[14] Marcuse's criticisms of advanced industrial society essentially explore one of the more perplexing issues raised by this new totalitarianism in the guise of technological reason, namely, "how can civilization freely generate freedom, when unfreedom has become part and parcel of the mental apparatus."[15]

Subjectivity and Productivity

The critical standards for Marcuse's judgments are to be found in the promise of liberation from the deadening toil of unending labor. For Marcuse, everything in society must be gauged by the degree to which actual freedom from material want is turning into a real possibility. Under these conditions, Marcuse never ceased believing in the utopian hopes of Marx's leap from the realm of necessity into the realm of freedom:

> The very structure of human existence would be altered; the individual would be liberated from the work world's imposing on him alien needs and alien possibilities. The individual would be free to exert autonomy over a life that would be his own. If the productive apparatus could be organized and directed toward the satisfaction of the vital needs, its control might well be centralized; such control would not prevent individual autonomy, but render it possible. This is the goal within the capabilities of advanced industrial civilization, the "end" of technological rationality.[16]

All of these emancipatory promises are actually possible for Marcuse, but they are not being realized. The vested interests controlling the state, the productive apparatus, and the institutions of society manipulate psychosocial expectations in strategies of repressive normalization that impose false needs on individuals and collectivities. "Such needs," Marcuse notes, "have a societal content and function which are determined by external powers over which the individual has no control; the development and satisfaction of these needs is heteronomous."[17] True needs, as opposed to such false needs, are those vital human needs for food, lodging, clothing, and meaning at some attainable level of culture.

In keeping with the critiques advanced by many radical ecologists, Marcuse attacks false needs, or "those which are superimposed upon the individual by particular social interests in his repression: the needs which perpetuate toil, aggressiveness, misery, and injustice."[18] Marcuse notes that "their satisfaction might be most gratifying to the individual, but this happiness is not a condition which has to be maintained and protected if it serves to arrest the development of the ability (his own and others') to recognize the disease of the whole and grasp the chances of curing the disease. The result then is euphoria in unhappiness. Most of the prevailing needs to relax, to have fun, to behave and consume in accordance with the advertisements, to love and hate what others love and hate, belong to this category of false needs."[19]

With these arguments about individual subjectivity and social productivity, Marcuse presents a comprehensive vision of how and why an advanced industrial society functions on deeply anti-ecological terms. By exploiting nature, it produces a short-range, material surplus that allows its vested controlling interests to coopt, buy off, or immobilize "those needs which demand liberation—liberation also from that which is tolerable and rewarding and comfortable—while it sustains and absolves the destructive power and repressive function of the affluent society."[20] Everyday material existence in contemporary society can be quite tolerable, rewarding, and comfortable, because it permits deep, long-run ecological disaster to sustain its shallow, short-run institutional reproduction. False needs become the cause of and excuse for continuing such environmental destruction, as everyday life is presented as the vindication of "the freedom to choose." What is chosen, however, is the perpetuation of a false repressive totality in which liberty is transformed to happily accept the mechanisms of domination. At that point, Marcuse observes, "the social controls exact the overwhelming need for the production and consumption of waste; the need for stupefying work where it is no longer a real necessity; the need for modes of relaxation which soothe and prolong the stupefication; the need for maintaining such deceptive liberties as free competition at administered prices, a free press which censors itself, free choice between brands and gadgets."[21] This waste represents not only the signs of serious social irrationality but also a complete environmental disaster.

Marcuse's understanding of the ecological crisis is closely tied to his reading of subjectivity, which parallels the basic scripts of Freudian metapsychology. For Marcuse, human beings are shaped by two primary drives (also referred to as basic instincts or essential drives). One is Eros, or erotic energy and the life instincts; the other is Thanatos, or destructive energy and the death instincts. Unfortunately, the major reality principles of advanced industrial society—that is, the sum total of those norms and values that regulate moral behavior—are based upon the destructive energies of Thanatos. Following Freud, the death instincts of Thanatos express a human drive to live in a state of painlessness, the life existence in the womb before birth. Its force, as Marcuse argues, "is the destruction of other living things, of other living beings, and of nature."[22] These drives are at the heart of the repressive false needs of one-dimensional society; hence, they also anchor the performance principles of toil and sacrifice at the core of technological rationality. To oppose its workings, Marcuse looks to Eros, or to the life instincts, for the basis of resisting this entire social order. This drive, according to Marcuse, seeks to attain not the painlessness before the beginning of life but the full, flowering majority of life: "It would serve to protect and enhance life itself. The drive for painlessness, for the pacification of existence, would then seek fulfillment in protective care for living things. It would find fulfillment in the recapture and restoration of our life environment, and in the restoration of nature, both external and within human beings."[23]

The constellation of false needs presented to the inhabitants of advanced industrial society creates a conformist character structure and at the same time blocks the emergence of a radical character structure that might transform this order by reopening human subjectivity to nature. The radical character structure threatens this entire social order, because in looking to restore natural forces, it represents "a preponderance in the individual of life instincts over the death instinct, a preponderance of erotic energy over destructive drives."[24] Given this organic basis for radical subjectivity, Marcuse connects the liberatory agendas of the ecology movement to the expression of Eros as an organized political force: "This is the way in which I view today's environmental movement, today's ecology movement. . . . A successful environmentalism will, within individuals, subordinate destructive energy to erotic energy."[25] The various ecology movements embody the politicization of erotic energy, even though at present they may lack the institutional power to overthrow the ruling reality principle. With these observations, Marcuse sums up the current plight of most environmental movements during the 1980s and 1990s. Even though their rank-and-file membership may express a desire for radical change, the diverse and divided movements basically remain stuck in an ineffectual strategic mode of organizing nonconformist protest campaigns rather than striking out to totally reconstitute society from the ground up.

Timothy W. Luke

Technology and Ecology

Marcuse's reading of science and technology in one-dimensional society echoes the Frankfurt School's general critique of the Enlightenment.[26] Ultimately, Marcuse sees science, as it operates in contemporary advanced industrial society, in terms that underscore its intrinsic instrumentalism. The procedures of abstraction, calculation, formalization, and operationalization lead him to affirm "the *internal* instrumentalist character of this scientific rationality by virtue of which it is *a priori* technology, and the *a priori* of a specific technology—namely, technology as a form of social control and domination."[27]

This inherent instrumentalism is a problem, because the value-free objectivism of science leaves it open to adopt and serve ends external to it. Emerging along with modern European entrepreneurial capitalism and nationalistic statism, the technological instrumentalism of science soon applied its operations to destructive social ends. As Marcuse suggests:

The principles of modern science were *a priori* structured in such a way that they could serve as conceptual instruments for a universe of self-propelling, productive control; theoretical operationalism came to correspond to practical operationalism. The scientific method which led to the ever-more-effective domination of nature thus came to provide the pure concepts as well as the instrumentalities for the ever-more-effective domination of man by man *through* the domination of nature. Theoretical reason, remaining pure and neutral, entered into the service of practical reason. The merger proved beneficial to both. Today, domination perpetuates and extends itself not only through technology but *as* technology, and the latter provides the great legitimation of the expanding political power, which absorbs all spheres of culture.[28]

Caught up within these operational constraints and instrumental goals, science works so that "the liberating force of technology—the instrumentalization of things—turns into a fetter of liberation; the instrumentalization of man."[29]

Humanity's increasing control over the environments of nature through technological means necessarily results in a greatly increased ability to dominate human nature. The two spheres are intimately con-

196

nected inasmuch as the complex technical controls implicit in advanced technology demand that everyone exercise greater discipline over their own labor and patterns of consumption. By preconditioning the behavioral patterns of individuals, Marcuse sees technological reason introjecting its technical demands into each person's somatic-psychic constitution, which "becomes the psychological basis of a *threefold domination*: first, domination over one's self, over one's nature, over the sensual drives that want only pleasure and gratification; second, domination of the labor achieved by such disciplined and controlled individuals; and third, domination of outward nature, science, and technology."[30]

The key political point about science and technology, which Marcuse continually stressed, is that they have become an anti-environmental system of domination. He sees this recognition as critical: "Science, *by virtue of its own method* and concepts, has projected and promoted a universe in which the domination of nature has remained linked to domination of man—a link which tends to be fatal to this universe as a whole. Nature, scientifically comprehended and mastered, reappears in the technical apparatus of production and destruction which sustains and improves the life of individuals while subordinating them to the masters of the apparatus."[31] Consequently, the rationalizing technical hierarchy based on humans dominating nature merges with the disciplinary social hierarchy of humans dominating other humans.

However, Marcuse also sees the possibilities for changing the direction of progress for the scientific project. The reconciliation of Logos (science and technology as a global system) and Eros in a new metaphysics of liberation might assist science in developing essentially different concepts of nature, facts, and experimental context. Were it not for the reification of technology, which reduces humans and nature to merely fungible objects of organization, neither the worlds of nature nor the systems of society would be the stuff of total administration. Marcuse believes this break is possible, if a new idea of reason, attuned to a new sensibility capable of guiding its theoretical and practical workings, could be developed. This moment, which would reverse the relationship between existing science and the metaphysics of domination, would come with the completion of technological rationalization, or "the mechanization of all socially necessary but individually repressive labor."[32] This moment of technological liberation would also make possible the pacification of existence—a new

Timothy W. Luke

social condition marked by qualitatively different relations between humans and between humans and nature—if such newly freed individuals effectively work to realize it.

The "New Sensibility" and Pacifying Nature

Marcuse's ecological engagements are totally intertwined with his advocacy of both "a new science" and "a new sensibility" as paths for society to take out of its current environmental crises. Since the old science of instrumental operationalism is an essential factor behind the domination of nature and humans, new scientific practices, linked not to a metaphysics of domination but rather to a metaphysics of liberation, might well alter everything. Here, a new sensibility—aesthetic, life affirming, and liberatory in character—would play a vital role. Most important, a new sensibility, based on the aesthetic dimension with its regard for beauty as a check against aggression and destruction, would mark the ascendance of life instincts/Eros over death instincts/Thanatos in the pacification of existence.

Marcuse sees the powers of the imagination unifying the faculties of sensibility and reason and so becoming productive and practical. A new sensibility of emancipatory freedom would work as "a guiding force in the reconstruction of reality—reconstruction with the help of a *gaya scienza*, a science and technology released from their service to destruction and exploitation, and thus free for the liberating exigencies of the imagination."[33] The new science, when combined with the sensuous aesthetic awareness of the new sensibility, would reintegrate labor and leisure, science and art, work and play so thoroughly that humanity and nature would also become one: "Such a world could (in a literal sense) embody, incorporate, the human faculties and desires to such an extent that they appear as part of the objective determinism of nature."[34] By unchaining reason from domination and exalting Eros over Thanatos, humans with the new sensibility would mobilize the aesthetic to develop freedom hand-in-hand with emancipation, as art merges with technology and science serves liberation.

The aesthetic universe is the *Lebenswelt* on which the needs and faculties of freedom depend for their liberation. They cannot develop in an environment shaped by and for aggressive impulses, nor can they be envisaged as the mere effect of a new set of social institutions. They can emerge only in the collective *practice of creating an environment*: level by level, step by step—in the material and intellectual production, an environment in which the nonaggressive, erotic, receptive faculties of man, in harmony with the consciousness of freedom, strive for the pacification of man and nature. In the reconstruction of society for the attainment of this goal, reality altogether would assume a *Form* expressive of the new goal. The essentially aesthetic quality of this Form would make it a work of *art*, but inasmuch as the Form is to emerge in the social process of production, art would have changed its traditional locus and function in society: it would have become a productive force in the material as well as cultural transformation.[35]

Art, then, would cancel the positive facticity of technological domination with its negative visions of technological emancipation. In the development of society and the subject, Marcuse argues that human pacification of existence can be repressive or liberating. Nature is not seen as some benevolent, all-knowing fount of positive goodness; it is instead constructed by Marcuse as a combination of ferocious, inventive, blind, fertile, and destructive processes. A liberating pacification of nature would reduce the misery, violence, and cruelty of nature in the face of its scarcity, suffering, and want.

"Nature and Revolution" in *Counterrevolution and Revolt* brings Marcuse directly to the issues of ecology and the environment through his commitment to creating "a new sensibility."[36] Trapped by psychosocial performance principles no longer needed to produce the material needs of civilization, individuals are seen by Marcuse as having new hope for attaining liberation by consciously and intentionally developing new sensibilities about the unlimited potentialities of all modern technology and the liberatory promise of collective action. On this count, Marcuse asks Freud only for some preliminary directions about metapsychology. He does not accept Freud unquestioningly as an omniscient guide into these murky realms of analysis. In advanced industrial society, Marcuse argues, "the performance principle enforces an integrated repressive organization of sexuality and of the destruction instinct."[37] However, if the unintended consequences of technological rationalization have rendered the institutions of the performance principle obsolete, then "it would also tend to make obsolete the organization of the instincts—that is to say, to release the instincts from the constraints and aversions required by the performance principle."[38]

On the one hand, this claim could imply the eventual elimination of such destructive surplus repression in new emancipatory forms of life; on the other hand, it might explain why ruling social forces generate false needs to be satisfied by adhering to the performance principle long after it has served its purpose in meeting true, vital needs. To transcend and destroy the performance principle of advanced capitalism, Marcuse believes, "individuals themselves must change in their very instincts and sensibilities if they are to build, in association, a *qualitatively* different society."[39] These changes require not only the emancipation of consciousness but also the emancipation of the senses to envelop the totality of human existence.

At the heart of this new sensibility, Marcuse affirms Marx's vision of transforming society. However, the revolution *he* sees is to be made in accordance with "laws of beauty" by underscoring the importance of aesthetic needs and impulses. In reversing capitalism's repressive containment of the aesthetic dimension and redirecting aesthetic awareness as a subversive force, Marcuse sees the active, aggressive destructiveness of capitalism being upended and overthrown by the passive, receptive productiveness of a new socialist community. This outcome would, in part, reflect the unleashing of more positive, but repressed and distorted, "female" qualities to recombine with the negative, but also oppressive and contorted, "male" qualities. Ultimately, what Marcuse wants to see come into realization is "the ascent of *Eros* over aggression, in men *and* women; and this means, in a male-dominated civilization, the 'femalization' of the male. It would express the decisive change in the instinctual structure; the weakening of primary aggressiveness which, by a combination of biological and social factors, has governed patriarchical culture."[40]

Nonetheless, Marcuse hopes that these fundamental alterations in consciousness and the senses would also, in part, reanimate the aesthetic adherence to the laws of beauty at the center of his new sensibility. These shifts would work toward emancipating nature from the exploitative domination of destructive technologies. With it would come, according to

Marcuse, "the ability to see things in their own right, to experience the joy enclosed in them, the erotic energy of nature—an energy which is there to be liberated; nature, too, awaits the revolution."[41] Human emancipation would also entail a historical transformation of nature; nature would become integrated into the human world and would in turn become expressive of human historical qualities. With the fusion of Eros with *techne*, Marcuse believes a new aesthetic realization should take place. This revolutionization by aesthetic means would bring with it a new ecological order. On the one hand, "cultivation of the soil is qualitatively different from destruction of the soil, extraction of natural resources from wasteful deforestation; and, on the other hand, poverty, disease, and cancerous growth are natural as well as human ills—their reduction and removal is liberation of life."[42] The pacification of existence, therefore, becomes the truly postmodern condition in which modern, aggressive, technological society no longer struggles to dominate and exploit nature. Instead, it should become fully humanized, civilized, pacified in the conquest of necessity; thus, "Nature ceases to be mere Nature to the degree to which the structure of blind forces is comprehended, and mastered in the light of freedom."[43]

Marcuse's ecological sensitivities allow him to see how the technological means to conquer scarcity have also become the tools for forestalling liberation. The obscene levels of overproduction and the excessive consumption enjoyed in many advanced industrial areas cannot furnish an acceptable model for the pacification of existence, because they are accompanied "by moronization, the perpetuation of toil, and the promotion of frustration."[44] The environment is plundered to provide the materials needed for the one-dimensional society; and, as Marcuse claims, "it is the sheer *quantity* of goods, services, work, and recreation in the overdeveloped countries which effectuates this containment. Consequently, qualitative change seems to presuppose a *quantitative* change in the advanced standard of living, namely, *reduction of overdevelopment*."[45] Only the existing material base of overdeveloped advanced industrial society can provide the rational foundations for beginning the pacification of existence; but, at the same time, it is this material base that perpetuates the dehumanizing ravages of one-dimensional society.

This program for pacifying nature is neither ridiculous nor impossible. Marcuse's vision of the process is fragmentary and incomplete, but he discusses it in plainly historical and political terms. In contrast to one-dimensional society, marked by "the increasing irrationality of the whole; waste and restriction of productivity; the need for aggressive expansion; the constant threat of war; intensified exploitation; dehumanization," Marcuse chooses to pursue an alternative, rooted in "the planned utilization of resources for the satisfaction of vital needs with a minimum of toil, the transformation of leisure into free time, the pacification of the struggle for existence."[46]

Unlike most of today's ecofeminists or deep ecologists, who travel around the world on jumbo jets burning tons of jet fuel in order to decry the pollution of the atmosphere, the evils of modern technology, and corruptions of consumerism, Marcuse is much more honest about his vision of pacifying nature. Since nature is a human construct in both theory and practice, a truly nonanthropocentric society or posttechnological economy is pure fantasy. Hence, the pacification of nature presupposes the mastery of nature, which is and remains the impassive objectivity opposed to the formation of liberating institutions. A new science would need the guiding illusions of a new sensibility from art. At this juncture, "the rationality of art, its ability to 'project' existence, to define yet unrealized possibilities could then be envisaged as *validated by and functioning in the scientific-technological transformation of the world*. Rather than being the handmaiden of the established apparatus, beautifying its business and its misery, art would become a technique for destroying this business and this misery."[47]

Marcuse and Ecological Criticism Now

Today's ecology and environmental movements are very complex, quite diverse, and openly pluralistic. Ideas that influence one faction, such as animal rights philosophy, ecological economics, deep ecology thinking, or global energy accounting, often are completely disdained or wholly ignored by other groups in what most outsiders would regard as the same basic cause. Marcuse's influence on any faction of the ecology and environmental movements is difficult to document, even though his ideas closely parallel many intellectual positions taken by various elements in these movements.

In the 1960s, neither Barry Commoner nor Murray Bookchin, for example, give any indication of being influenced directly by Marcuse in their work, although Bookchin's *Ecology of Freedom* mocks Marcuse's visions for realizing the pacification of nature.[48] Somewhat more conventional readings of ecological crises developed by Rachel Carson, Herman Daly, and David Browder also do not acknowledge Marcuse.[49] Likewise, in the 1970s and 1980s, new ecological thinkers—including Arne Naess, Bill Devall, George Sessions, E. F. Schumacher, David Foreman, Ivan Illich, Thomas Berry, Carolyn Merchant, Henryk Skolimowski, Wendell Berry, Bill McKibben, and Kirkpatrick Sale—give few signs of being affected by Marcuse.[50] Of the three major histories of the ecology and environmental movement either published or revised in the 1980s—Nash's *Wilderness and the American Mind*, Hays's *Beauty, Health, and Permanence: Environmental Politics in the United States, 1955–1985*, and Bramwell's *Ecology in the 20th Century*—only Bramwell even mentions Marcuse, and then it is mainly in passing when discussing the New Left of the 1960s.[51] Regardless, Donald Edward Davis includes Marcuse's *One-Dimensional Man* in his 1989 overview of ecological thought, *Ecophilosophy: A Field Guide to the Literature*, calling it an important influence on ecological philosophers and environmentalist thinkers.[52]

Clearly, Marcuse's new political theories about technology, subjectivity, and nature are not without some serious problems. Marcuse's quest to discover new organic sources of social negativity and political resistance in late capitalism ultimately led him through classical Marxism to Heidegger and Freud. This search culminates, in turn, with his phenomenological critique of technological rationality and the psychoanalytic theory of history. Marcuse's adaptation of these heterogenous perspectives as his own style of immanent critique resulted in some problematic misrepresentations of present-day political realities and of their emancipatory possibilities. Marcuse perhaps proved insufficiently critical of technological rationality when he attributed its domination largely to its misuse by exploitative groups. Similarly, he ends his critique of modern technological society by grounding his emancipatory politics and his theory of negative collective subjectivity in the organic instinctual energies of each human individual. In his search to supplant the historical negativity of the identical subject-object of *labor*, or the emancipated proletariat, Marcuse turns to an equally unsatisfying solution, namely, a new naturalistic, presocial, and prehistorical collective subjectivity—the identical subject-object of *pleasure*, or the individual's and the human species' erotic instincts.[53]

Nonetheless, Marcuse cannot be easily dismissed or forgotten. He anticipates virtually every critique made by contemporary radical ecology groups. First, as in the discourses of deep ecology, he identifies the destruction of nature with instrumental reason, or "a concept of reason which contains the domineering features of the performance principle,"[54] in order to ground all of his ecological arguments. Second, as in the narratives of ecofeminism, he connects the workings of the performance principle with the destructive drives of the death instinct and male needs for domination. Third, as in social ecology, he sees that the domination of nature flows out of the domination of human beings as ruling forces and vested interests in society, subjecting internal human nature and external environmental nature to the same instrumentalities of domination. Fourth, like many soft-path technologists, he suggests that modern technology possesses the power and productivity to overcome material scarcity, if only its techniques and instrumentalities were organized in more rational, emancipatory forms of application. Fifth, like advocates of voluntary simplicity, he ties waste, ruin, and despoliation of the environment to false needs imposed on individuals, not to meet true vital requirements but to perpetuate the powers and privileges of vested interests that benefit from such domination and destruction. And, finally, like the new nature poets and philosophers, Marcuse expects a new sensibility—one that is life affirming, aesthetic, female, erotic, and liberatory—to provide the conceptual categories and moral values needed to reintegrate humanity with nature in an environmentally rational society where technology is art, work can be play, and ecology provides freedom.

Despite all his many shortcomings, Marcuse continues to be a theoretical force to be reckoned with. Much of today's debate within deep ecology, ecofeminism, social ecology, and bioregionalism is addressing the issues of political conflict, cultural contradiction, and individual struggle that Marcuse first raised in *Eros and Civilization*, *One-Dimensional Man*, *An Essay on Liberation*, and *Counterrevolution and Revolt*. The question of a new science, a new technology, and a new aesthetics as the basis for realizing an ecological transformation of society has still never been addressed as sharply as Marcuse did, even if his critical and analytical discourses about all these forces are flawed. For this reason alone, his work needs to be considered again. And, as these discussions continue, Marcuse's vision of a pacified existence for an ecological society might begin to prevail socially and politically over the dour green visions presented by today's more penitential ecoauthoritarians, ranging from Lester Brown's disciplinary Worldwatchers to Garrett Hardin's ecofascist rational-choice environmentalism.[55]

Notes

1. See Herbert Marcuse, *Counterrevolution and Revolt* (Boston: Beacon Press, 1972), and *The Aesthetic Dimension: Toward a Critique of Marxist Aesthetics* (Boston: Beacon Press, 1978).

2. Langdon Winner, *The Whale and the Reactor: A Search for Limits in an Age of High Technology* (Chicago: University of Chicago Press, 1982), 69. See also Hazel Henderson, *The Politics of the Solar Age* (Garden City, N.J.: Anchor Press, 1981).

3. Koula Mellos, *Perspectives on Ecology* (New York: St. Martin's Press, 1988), 4.

4. For examples of these readings, see Murray Bookchin, *The Ecology of Freedom* (Palo Alto, Calif.: Cheshire Books, 1982), and Christopher Manes, *Green Rage: Radical Environmentalism and the Unmaking of Civilization* (Boston: Little, Brown, 1990).

5. See Marcuse, *Counterrevolution and Revolt*, 59–78.

6. Herbert Marcuse, "Ecology and Revolution: A Symposium," *Liberation* 17, 6 (1972): 10–12.

7. Herbert Marcuse, "Ecology and the Critique of Modern Society," *Capitalism, Nature, Socialism* 3, 3 (September 1992): 29–38.

8. Morton Schoolman, *The Imaginary Witness* (New York: Free Press, 1980); and Douglas Kellner, *Herbert Marcuse and the Crisis of Marxism* (Berkeley: University of California Press, 1984).

9. See Herbert Marcuse, *Eros and Civilization: A Philosophical Inquiry into Freud* (Boston: Beacon Press, 1955); *One-Dimensional Man: Studies in the Ideology of Advanced Industrial Society* (Boston: Beacon Press, 1964); and *An Essay on Liberation* (Boston: Beacon Press, 1969).

10. Marcuse, *Counterrevolution and Revolt*, 60.

11. Ibid., 59.

12. Marcuse, *One-Dimensional Man*, 3.

13. Ibid.

14. Ibid., 4.

15. Marcuse, *Eros and Civilization*, 225.

16. Marcuse, *One-Dimensional Man*, 2.

17. Ibid., 5.

18. Ibid., 4–5.

19. Ibid., 5.
20. Ibid., 7.
21. Ibid.
22. Marcuse, "Ecology and the Critique of Modern Society," 36.
23. Ibid.
24. Ibid., 32.
25. Ibid., 36.
26. See Max Horkheimer and Theodor W. Adorno, *Dialectic of Enlightenment*, trans. John Cumming (New York: Herder and Herder, 1972).
27. Marcuse, *One-Dimensional Man*, 157–58.
28. Ibid., 158.
29. Ibid., 159.
30. Herbert Marcuse, *Five Lectures: Psychoanalysis, Politics, and Utopia*, trans. Jeremy J. Shapiro and Shierry M. Weber (Boston: Beacon Press, 1970), 12.
31. Marcuse, *One-Dimensional Man*, 166.
32. Ibid., 230.
33. Marcuse, *An Essay on Liberation*, 31.
34. Ibid. Also see Marcuse, *The Aesthetic Dimension*, 54–69.
35. Marcuse, *An Essay on Liberation*, 31–32.
36. See Marcuse, *Counterrevolution and Revolt*, 59–78.
37. Marcuse, *Eros and Civilization*, 131.
38. Ibid.
39. Marcuse, *Counterrevolution and Revolt*, 74.
40. Ibid., 75.
41. Ibid., 74.
42. Marcuse, *One-Dimensional Man*, 240.
43. Ibid., 236.
44. Ibid., 242.
45. Ibid.
46. Ibid., 252–53.
47. Ibid., 239.
48. See Barry Commoner, *Science and Survival* (New York: Viking, 1963); *The Closing Circle: Nature, Man, and Technology* (New York: Knopf, 1971); *The Poverty of Power* (New York: Knopf, 1976); and Murray Bookchin, *Post-Scarcity Anarchism* (Berkeley, Calif.: Ramparts Press, 1971).
49. See Rachel Carson, *Silent Spring* (Boston: Houghton Mifflin, 1964); Herman Daly, *Toward a Steady-State Economy* (San Francisco: W. H. Freeman, 1973); and David Browder, *Not Man Apart* (San Francisco: Sierra Club Books, 1965).
50. See Arne Naess, *Community, Ecology, and Lifestyle* (Cambridge: Cambridge University Press, 1989); Bill Devall and George Sessions, *Deep Ecology* (Salt Lake City, Utah: Peregrine Smith Books, 1985); Bill Devall, *Simple in Means, Rich in Ends: Practicing Deep Ecology* (Salt Lake City, Utah: Peregrine Smith Books, 1988); George Sessions, "Shallow and Deep Ecology: A Review," *Ecological Consciousness: Essays from the Earthday X Colloquium* (Washington, D.C.: University Press of America, 1981); E. F. Schumacher, *Small Is Beautiful* (New York: Harper and Row, 1973); Dave Foreman, *Confessions of an Eco-Warrior* (New York: Harmony Books, 1991); Ivan Illich, *Energy and Equity* (New

York: Harper and Row, 1974); Thomas Berry, *The Dream of the Earth* (San Francisco: Sierra Club Books, 1989); Carolyn Merchant, *The Death of Nature: Women, Ecology and the Scientific Revolution* (New York: Harper and Row, 1980); Henryk Skolimowski, *Living Philosophy: Eco-Philosophy as a Tree of Life* (London: Penguin, 1992); Wendell Berry, *The Unsettling of America: Culture and Agriculture* (New York: Avon Books, 1977); Wendell Berry, *Standing by Words* (San Francisco: North Point Press, 1983); Wendell Berry, *What Are People For?* (San Francisco: North Point Press, 1990); Bill McKibben, *The End of Nature* (New York: Random House, 1989); Kirkpatrick Sale, *Human Scale* (New York: Coward, McCann and Geoghegan, 1980); and Kirkpatrick Sale, *Dwellers in the Land: The Bioregional Vision* (Philadelphia, Pa.: New Society Press, 1991).

51. See Roderick Nash, *Wilderness and the American Mind*, 3d ed. (New Haven, Conn.: Yale University Press, 1982); Samuel Hays, *Beauty, Health, and Permanence: Environmental Politics in the United States* (Cambridge: Cambridge University Press, 1987); and Anna Bramwell, *Ecology in the 20th Century* (New Haven, Conn.: Yale University Press, 1989).

52. See Donald Edward Davis, *Ecophilosophy: A Field Guide to the Literature* (San Pedro, Calif.: R. and H. Miles, 1989).

53. See Timothy W. Luke, "A Phenomenological/Freudian Marxism? Marcuse's Critique of Advanced Industrial Society," *Social Theory and Modernity: Critique, Dissent, and Revolution* (Newbury Park, Calif.: Sage Publications, 1990), 128–58.

54. Marcuse, *Eros and Civilization*, 130.

55. See, for example, Lester R. Brown, *Building a Sustainable Society* (New York: Norton, 1981); Lester R. Brown, Christopher Flavin, and Sandra Postel, *Saving the Planet: How to Shape an Environmentally Sustainable Economy* (New York: Norton, 1991); Garrett Hardin, *The Limits of Altruism* (Bloomington: Indiana University Press, 1977); and Garrett Hardin, *Filters against Folly: How to Survive despite Economists, Ecologists, and the Merely Eloquent* (New York: Viking Press, 1985).

Andrew Feenberg

The Critique of Technology: From Dystopia to Interaction

> The task to be accomplished is not the conservation of the past, but the redemption of the hopes of the past.[1]
>
> —*Theodor Adorno and Max Horkheimer*

Prologue: Obstinacy as a Theoretical Virtue

As a good Hegelian, Marx considered any merely moral critique of capitalism to be arbitrary. He measured the system instead by reference to an immanent criterion, the unsatisfied needs of the population. Although the argument was persuasive for its time, it becomes no longer relevant after capitalism proves itself capable of delivering the goods. Then the (fulfilled) needs of the individuals legitimate the established order. Radicalism means opposition, not just to the failures and deficiencies of that system, but to its very successes.

From what standpoint can society be judged once it has succeeded in feeding its members? It takes astonishing nerve to persist in radical social criticism at this point. But, as Marcuse once wrote, "obstinacy [is] a genuine quality of philosophical thought."[2] To be obstinate means to reject the easy reconciliation with society, to keep *a sense of reality* based on longer time spans, deeper tensions, higher expectations and goals.

Marcuse's solution to the problem had two parts. First, he believed that the historically evolved ideals of peace, freedom, and happiness still provide criteria for measuring the existing society. These ideals are not to be dismissed as merely subjective, because they have roots in the very nature of the human psyche. They drive the historical process forward through the formation of new needs reflecting as-yet-unrealized human potential. New needs are not arbitrary or willful in Hegel's sense because—and this is the second part of Marcuse's solution—the unrealized technical potential of advanced industrialism provides a basis on which to concretize them as historical projects. Advanced society, Marcuse argued, is capable of "pacifying" existence but artificially maintains competition and violence as the basis for domination and inequality. That society is, in a certain sense, *technically* outmoded by its own achievements. As he put it in his last speech on ecology, "The specter which haunts advanced industrial society today is the obsolescence of full-time alienation." Moreover, radical political struggle today consists in "existential revolts against an obsolete reality principle."[3]

The revolutionary historical judgment has always been made in the future anterior tense, as when Saint-Just imagined what "cold posterity" *will have said* concerning the absurdity of monarchy.[4] Marcuse's concept of "obsolescence" gave that judgment a technological twist. Thus he was not merely complaining about a system he didn't like. He was imagining how it will appear to a backward glance rooted in the wider context of values evolved over past centuries and destined to achieve realization in the very technology of a future society. The obsolescence of the present system will be obvious in this hypothetical future, justifying the obstinacy of those who persisted in critique through these difficult times.

With the collapse of Soviet communism, the last apologia of historicist opposition to capitalism has died. We can no longer rest our case for change, if we ever did, on historical necessity or the achievements of "socialism." We are one step closer to a world in which only Marcuse's type of principled opposition is available. His thought has never been more relevant, but its limitations have also become more obvious. In particular, it has become increasingly clear that Marcuse had no adequate account of how historical ideals are to be effectively realized in technical potential.

In this chapter, I will explore Marcuse's contribution to the question of technology, which he, more than anyone in the last thirty years, placed on the agenda of political discussion. In an earlier article, I presented a detailed account of his theory of technology.[5] Here I will attempt to situate that theory in the larger framework of the emergence of a mass critical culture of technology, to which he contributed so significantly. I will also sketch a new approach, linking the tradition of radical critique with a new "interactivist" perspective emerging in recent years as an alternative to both the Old and the New Left.[6]

Andrew Feenberg

Rationality and Dystopia

Marcuse's radical critique of technology had a tremendous impact on the New Left. Much of it has been so thoroughly confirmed by subsequent experience that he would no doubt feel right at home in contemporary discussions of technology, far more so than in the atmosphere of the 1960s when his ideas were often rejected as reactionary and irrationalist. Marcuse would agree, for example, with the now-commonplace view that despite its grandiose achievements, scientific-technical rationality has endowed us with an extraordinarily destructive way of life. And he would surely applaud us for losing our naive faith in the disinterestedness, competence, and relevance of expertise.

These developments have opened a space for public debate about technical issues that were long thought to be above—or beneath—politics. But the recent news from the East seemed to close down the debate before it began: If in fact there is no alternative to capitalism as we know it, then, for better or worse, technology is destiny and social critique is as outdated as alchemy. History, in the words of one recent commentator, is over. Once again, Marcuse would not be surprised to find us confronting a one-dimensional rationality that forecloses the alternatives.

Other recent developments might awaken disturbing memories of the 1930s for someone with Marcuse's background. As the Left collapses and hope for a more rational administration of technological societies fades, a variety of fundamentalisms and nationalisms flourish, all too often with war and civil war on the horizon. These reactionary attacks on modernity are usually characterized by total technical conformism: Duplicating the pattern of early Japanese and Russian industrialization, anti-Western regimes busily import Western technology and install it unchanged while denouncing the civilization that produced it. The chances of anything truly original emerging from such a combination of resentment and imitation are slim.

In sum, although old assumptions about progress are losing ground, no equally convincing new ones have appeared to replace them. This situation is not merely a function of historical events, confusing though these are, but reflects deeper problems in the very foundation of modernity, that is, in the project of building a rational society. This project, in all its various forms—political, economic, technological—is in crisis today.

210

Formerly, the distinction between modernity and tradition was supported by a naive faith in rationality. Modernity was said to be rational in the strong sense that its cognitive foundations—science and technology—were superior to those of any earlier society. According to positivism, rationality was beyond any social or historical conditioning and was therefore a true universal. To question or criticize it was not only to challenge the legitimacy of the modern age but to undermine the only reliable standpoint from which to make judgments about nature and history.

But in recent years, that legitimacy has appeared more and more doubtful, and rationality is increasingly explained as a product of culture and society. New social interpretations of science and technology flourish today amid the shattered technocratic illusions of an earlier generation. Tradition, insofar as it supports cultural variety against the "false universality" of the West, is now granted a dubious reprieve. Differences of race and gender recover an importance they had lost in the melting pot of rational universality.

To understand Marcuse, we must disregard this startling breakdown of Enlightenment assumptions and transport ourselves back in thought to an earlier time when rationality went practically unchallenged. His position comes into focus against the backdrop of those assumptions and the sparse and necessarily eccentric attacks on them by marginal writers and social critics like himself.

Until recently all but a few cranky social critics took it for granted that humanity was in control of its technologies. I will call this consensus view the instrumental theory of technology, or instrumentalism.[7] Instrumentalism holds that technology is neutral: As a transparent medium, it adds nothing substantive to the activities it serves but merely accelerates those activities, or realizes them on a larger scale or under new conditions. Because technology is neutral, the decision to employ it can be made on purely rational grounds, such as measurable, verifiable improvements in efficiency.

This view has political implications. Rationality has always been considered a basis for truly free association; when common goals emerge from debate and argument, people cooperate without coercion. Modern life has taught us how difficult it is to share goals, but efficiency too is a kind of universal value and, as such, subject to rational agreement. And as concern with efficiency spreads to more and more domains, its constraints supply a common framework for social life. Perhaps, the argument goes, consensus can be reached over means despite the unresolvable contention over goals characteristic of the modern world. That would at least make for a well-ordered society in which the areas of disagreement were reduced to manageable proportions. Instrumentalists therefore hold out the hope of general reconciliation—social integration—in an advanced society.

The proposal sounds innocuous in this form, but taken to the limit, it describes a technocracy in which expertise replaces citizenship as the basis of the political order. The idea has been around for over a century in one form or another, but only in the 1960s did it become the legitimation of actually existing historical states. Ideology was supposed to be exhausted; the emerging "Great Society" was to be justified by its success in delivering the goods. At that point, the critique of technocracy, already adumbrated in Dostoyevski (see *Notes from Underground*), was transformed from a conceit of a few literary intellectuals into a mass cultural phenomenon.

Long before this period, science fiction had articulated the fear of technocracy with particular effectiveness in stories that depicted the horrors of life in a perfectly rationalized society. At stake in "dystopias" (negative utopias) like *Brave New World* or *1984* is the destiny of the human spirit in a world based on scientific enlightenment. The issue is not simply the destructive misuse of scientific discoveries but the fate of individuality in a scientized world. The successful integration of modern mass society provokes a nostalgic backward glance toward lost freedoms. The isolated individualistic hero of these tales stands for the human values inevitably ground under foot by the march of reason.

From this dystopian standpoint, technical progress is not just a value-neutral increase in efficiency but a whole new way of life. This is also the view of philosophers who propose what I will call substantive theories of technology. They reject the notion that technology is neutral and argue that it is actually a distinct cultural framework embodying its own particular values. This new form of critique is present in the background of Marcuse's work. As Heidegger put it, "The outstanding feature of modern technology lies in the fact that it is not at all any longer merely 'means' and no longer merely stands in 'service' for others, but instead . . . unfolds a specific character of domination."[8]

The grounds for substantive critique vary. Some social critics claim that technology as such is limited and biased by its Prometheanism or abstraction; others argue that technology is neutral in its own sphere but distorts essentially noninstrumental domains such as the family or the public sphere. Heidegger, Jacques Ellul, and Ivan Illich are the most prominent representatives of the first view, and they are joined by feminists who criticize modern technology as an inherently "masculinist" enterprise.[9] Jürgen Habermas has become the best known defender of the second view. All these critics agree that technology fundamentally transforms activities hitherto regulated by tradition and human values, so much so that its specific accomplishments matter little by comparison. The content of the choices made under the rule of efficiency is less important than the fact that efficiency criteria play a role in making those choices. That in itself creates a new kind of society, not simply a streamlined version of the old.

The flavor of these various theories can best be gathered from Heidegger, who was in fact Marcuse's teacher. Consider, for example, his formulation of the distinction between traditional tools and modern technologies. As noted before, means are supposed to operate not on the substance of desire but on the pace, scale, and conditions of its fulfillment. But beyond a certain point, changes in pace, scale, and conditions transform means into contexts independent of the particular ends they serve. Heidegger called this the "giganticism" of modern technology.[10]

A city traversed by freeways is not the same place as the old pre-automotive urban center. This obvious fact indicates the limits of the neutrality of technology. Of course, the automobile is indifferent to its driver's destination, but it requires infrastructural preconditions in order to be operated at all. Supplying those preconditions actually reshapes the world in which destinations are chosen, transforming fields and neighborhoods into roadbeds. This example is characteristic: What in modern societies we call progress in efficiency is precisely the employment of means with such massive impacts.[11] Our world is in the grip of them, "enframed," in Heidegger's terms.

Now it is true that premodern artifacts are also occasionally gigantic—for example, late medieval architecture. But they usually leave nature as they found it, and their social reach depends less on their technical than on their symbolic power. Today the sheer size and pervasiveness of our machines makes it impossible to confine their effects to particular applications. Devices that were supposed to transparently realize preexisting ends have become so massive that they assault the natural landscape and impose their own requirements on the human beings they were made to serve. Tradition can flourish in the shadow of a Gothic cathedral, but not under a freeway overpass.

Thus, modern means already change the world "immanently," independent of the purpose for which they are employed. Our tools have become the environment in which we live; increasingly, we are incorporated into the apparatus that we have created, and we are subordinated to its rhythms and demands. Heidegger called this the "peril" of the age.

Radical Critique of Technological Society

Dystopian literature and the substantive critique of technology opened the space within which we speculate today about the meaning and nature of modernity. From them we learn that we are *inside* the machine, that technology is not merely a tool extending our capabilities. This realization is a necessary condition for understanding contemporary culture.

Traditional Marxism, if not Marx himself, appears hopelessly beside the point in this context. However, radical social criticism does not disappear as technology advances but instead becomes ever more uncompromising and eventually inspires resistance to the dystopian universe it denounces. The Frankfurt School, and especially Marcuse, enjoyed real popularity in the one-dimensional society that, it charged, had made critique all but impossible. Both the American and German New Left were influenced by its dystopian perspectives. Somewhat later, after the May events of 1968, French social theory also turned antidystopian in the work of Deleuze and Foucault. Today's "new social movements" grew out of these currents of the 1960s and 1970s.

Although strongly influenced by substantive critique, Marcuse and Foucault did not despair of the future in technological societies. Rather than identifying an essence of technology that condemned human beings eternally to servitude, they sought historical causes for the undesirable effects of technical progress. They concluded that technology-based domination is contingent and might be overthrown in a process involving not only political change but also fundamental shifts in the form of rationality.

This approach marked a sharp break with traditional Marxism. Marxists had denounced capitalism as inefficient; the new radicals rejected the authoritarian consequences of the very pursuit of efficiency in modern societies. These societies, they claimed, have made a bargain with the devil: their increasing order and prosperity are invariably accompanied by new forms of control from above. That control does not depend on traditional social distinctions in status, wealth, age, or gender but employs social technologies of training, therapy, medicine, advertising, management, administration, etc. The new authority system is rooted in the gap between the operators of these technologies and their human objects.

The nexus between efficiency and authority suggested to Marcuse a new interpretation of Marxism as an antidystopian critique of *rationality*.[12] This in turn led him back to the work of Weber, the great theorist of rationalization, whose conception of modernity was influenced by Marx but who probably did more than anyone to dash hope in a socialist solution to its problems. Weber defined modernity in terms of the spread of markets, formal law, democracy, bureaucracy, and technology. He called these "rationalized" institutions because they share certain qualities normally associated with reason: They appear more abstract, more exact, more value- and context-free, better grounded in scientific knowledge, and more efficient than traditional institutions.[13]

Weber founded an influential sociological tradition in which the notion of rationality has continued to play a central role. In the work of Talcott Parsons, for example, history culminates in the substitution of "universalistic" values for older "particularistic" ones as science and democracy replace traditional forms of belief and politics.[14] In the postcolonial era, theories of modernization extended the range of such arguments, cheerfully predicting the passage to modernity on a global scale.[15] It is this view, suitably modified to take into account neoliberal economics, that has become the common sense of the West and the passionate hope of the East.

The concept of "formal rationality," which was the distinguishing trait of modernity in the work of Weber and his successors, suggests a pejorative evaluation of the "irrationality" of tradition. Although rationality/ modernity has not eradicated inequality and injustice, liberals and most

Marxists split with dystopian radicals over the cause: Is it the incomplete rationalization of modern societies a consequence of such rationalization that has occurred? Marcuse defended the latter view and in the process called attention to aspects of Marx's thought that had been largely forgotten.

Traditional societies do not hide the substantive consequences of the exercise of authority, the inequalities it inevitably creates, the favoritism that is its prerogative. But modern formal rationality serves similar social purposes under an appearance of neutrality. No longer does the monarch decide fates by tipping his fan toward this or that subject. Instead, purely objective criteria, such as examinations, hearings, or measurements, discriminate between individuals. Markets know no persons but only commodities and money. Scientific and technological discovery depends on objective proof, not subjective preferences. Yet science and technology form the basis of a new type of social hierarchy in which new inequalities in the distribution of social power replace the traditional order.

It was Marx who first discovered how to construct an effective critique of this new hierarchy. He argued that markets are not merely neutral mediators between those who have and those who need; their generalization submits society to a new power, the power of capital. What is true of markets is equally true of the labor process. Capitalism reshapes production technology to reinforce its control of workers. Marx argued that external supervision of work only emerges when ownership and management are separated from the work itself. Soon discipline is tightened through deskilling labor, i.e., replacing skilled workers performing traditional crafts with unskilled workers each of whom performs a tiny fraction of the whole job. In the industrial era, control functions are transferred to machines, the design of which is determined by the preexisting division of labor and authority into which they are inserted. Mechanization finally perfects the hitherto clumsy, personalized techniques of industrial discipline by objectifying the split between conception and execution.[16]

Marcuse concluded from Marx's analysis that the capitalist *technical* system is not universal but reflects particular class interests.[17] Needless to say, it was not a conclusion many Marxists reached before the 1960s. Marcuse was one of the first to take this dimension of Marx seriously. He argued that science, technology, and indeed all the formally rational, supposedly neutral structures of modern society are politically biased. He emphasized the practical dimension of what are usually taken to be essentially theoretical activities, such as scientific and technical research. If one sees modern rationality as a social activity, then it is plausible to ask *what else* this activity entails besides the pursuit of pure knowledge. The answer to this question tells us something important about how power is accumulated and applied in modern societies through the acquisition and control of knowledge and technology.

Why does formal rationality have such consequences once it escapes the narrow confines of natural science and technique and begins to shape a whole society? Marcuse argued that in splitting up its objects analytically into manipulable parts a rationality of this type predestines these objects to domination. Hence the organization of advanced societies around such a rationality is politically loaded. This can be seen in the very structure of Weber's theory of rationalization. Weber never questioned the extension of formal rationality from technology to administration. It did not occur to him that there might be a more appropriate form of rationality for handling human relations than technical control. In this regard, he uncritically adopted the capitalist point of view. As Marcuse concluded, "The highly *material*, historical fact of the private-capitalist enterprise thus becomes . . . a *formal* structural element . . . of *rational* economic activity itself."[18] Weber smuggled a whole system of domination into his definition of rationality. Today, what Marcuse called a one-dimensional society extends the same sort of mystification to an ever-larger number of rationalized spheres, including leisure, education, sexual life, and so on.

Here we have the intuition that informs Habermas's theory of the "colonization of the lifeworld."[19] Modern societies are threatened by the measureless expansion of technically rational means, a process that is not itself rational because it obliterates the all-important distinction between the communicative and the technical dimensions of human experience. Unlike Marcuse, Habermas was no critic of science and technology per se, rejecting only their institutionalization as the foundation of a *total* social order. He argued that this totalization of technique is irrational even though our society's sciences are true and its technologies neutral.[20]

Despite his success in reviving critical Marxism and undermining rationalistic justifications of social hierarchy, Marcuse lacked an adequate account of how change might be brought about. Although sometimes accused of technophobia, he never called for the dismantling of modern industrial society. On the contrary, he argued that

> if the completion of the technological project involves a break with the prevailing technological rationality, the break in turn depends on the continued existence of the technical base itself. For it is this base which has rendered possible the satisfaction of needs and the reduction of toil—it remains the very base of all forms of human freedom. The qualititative change rather lies in the reconstruction of this base—that is, in its development with a view of different ends. . . . The new ends, as technical ends, would then operate in the project and in the construction of the machinery, and not only in its utilization.[21]

But how can this be achieved? Marcuse advocated uncompromising opposition to racist violence and imperialist war, but nothing comparable makes sense in the technical sphere. He occasionally mentioned such notions as the "long march through the institutions" and working within the "interstices" of the system, but he never developed them in any detail or applied them to technology. Marcuse's most explicit remarks on the transformation of technology consist in interesting but very abstract claims for aestheticizing the technical sphere.[22]

Thus his critique of capitalist technological rationality contained a kind of promissory note on which he failed to deliver. We ought to be able to extract an alternative theory of rationality from it that would show how human values could be incorporated in the very structure of technicity. Unfortunately, his gestures in this direction were so sketchy that they cannot easily be linked to any concrete practice. And as practical attempts to grapple with technology in fact proliferate, this flaw seems more and more fatal. Nevertheless, there are certain recent theoretical shifts that may help to carry the critical movement Marcuse did so much to initiate beyond the limitations of his position.

Interactive Strategies of Change

The dystopian model inspired what Marcuse called a "Great Refusal" of advanced industrial society, but today the idea of such uncompromising opposition rings false. Notwithstanding the growing distrust of technocracy, dependence on technology continues to increase. There is no disguising the alienation but no getting away from the system, no psychic or political retreat from which to assemble and mobilize the disalienating energies of a subject of history. What is more, the breakdown of faith in rationality, already apparent in Marcuse, has proceeded much further in the work of Foucault and the recent constructivist sociology of science and technology. Thus we are drawn to a different type of strategy that plays on the tensions in modernity. The aim is not to destroy the system by which we are enframed but to alter its direction of development from within through a new kind of technical politics. Such strategies have appeared both globally and locally. They characterize certain non-Western encounters with modernity (e.g., the Japanese) and are also beginning to appear in the West itself, most obviously around environmental problems but also in domains such as computers and medicine in which the technocratic conception of modern life is increasingly contested by what I call an *interactive* politics of technology.[23]

Foucault's critique of the social limits of rationality is one of the key theoretical innovations that lies in the background of current technical struggles. Foucault claimed that the imposition of a rational order gives rise to "subjugated knowledges": particular, local standpoints from which the dominated perceive aspects of reality obscured by the universalizing standpoint of the hegemonic sciences.[24] These subjugated knowledges offer a basis for progressive change. Thus like Marcuse, Foucault distinguished at least implicitly between a particular form of hierarchical rationalization, which was characteristic of modernity until now, and a variety of subversive rationalizations adapted to a more humane and democratic society.[25] However, Marcuse's critique aimed at total transformation; Foucault called only for new forms of local action without any overall plan.

Although apolitical so far in its brief history, constructivism in the sociology of science and technology offers support for Foucault's position by linking all types of scientific-technical achievements to a social background. Roughly sketched, the constructivist argument holds that the route from a bright idea to a successful application is long and winding, strewn with inherently viable alternatives abandoned for reasons having more to do with local circumstances than with the intrinsic technical superiority of the final choice. This position marks a sharp break with instrumentalism, which generally assumes that technical development provides uniquely efficient solutions to clearly defined problems rooted in basic human needs. In this view, social factors intervene in the technical sphere only marginally, deciding, for example, the pace of development or the priority assigned to different types of problems. Constructivism argues, on the contrary, that development involves negotiation and struggle between a variety of social interests with different conceptions of both problems and solutions. The choice of each gear or lever, the form of each circuit or program, are determined not just by an inherent technical logic but by some configuration of social agents and their culturally specific needs. At issue is not simply the pace of technical progress or who benefits from it but the very content and meaning of progress itself.

Constructivism is a "network" theory of technical development that exposes the reciprocal relations and interconnections between social alliances and technical systems.[26] It counts among significant technological actors not merely inventors and engineers but also managers, workers, government agencies, consumers, users, everyone involved with technology. Effective alliances are bound together by the very structure of the artifacts they create, which provide in turn a kind of platform for further activities.

Technology is neither the neutral tool of instrumental theory nor the autonomous power of substantive theory but is just as social as other institutions. If this is so, it should be possible to give a precise account of the social dimension of technology and hence its role in modern hierarchies, which are supported by networks of technical artifacts and associated practices rather than by myths and rituals, or by ideologies and the exercise of coercive power, as in premodern societies. This would be the ultimate refutation of one-dimensionality: the illusion that there is a unique form of technical rationality that sanctions domination under the rule of efficiency.

But most constructivist research is so narrowly focused on the specific local groups involved in particular cases of technological development that it lacks any sense of the larger social context in which these cases may play a politically significant role.[27] And as Donna Haraway remarks, studies in the history of science and technology are distorted by the view, now widely accepted, that the break with positivism was due to a purely internal scholarly evolution beginning with Kuhn. She notes that this ignores the contributions of the various antitechnocratic struggles of the 1960s and, I would add, of radical thinkers such as Marcuse.[28] Ironically, the currently dominant social theory of science and technology seems to have no grasp of the social conditions of its own credibility.

Yet precisely because the rise of constructivism is so closely, if unconsciously, linked to increased resistance to the dominant technological institutions of our society, it can help to sharpen oppositional thinking about technology. Both Foucault and constructivism focus on what makes the "System" a system, on the manifold ways in which it integrates human beings into the technological conditions of their social reproduction. This analysis suggests strategic possibilities Marcuse overlooked.

In the 1960s, the conception of resistance was shaped by peak struggles and large-scale simultaneous political mobilizations, such as May 1968, the waves of urban rioting in the United States, and the national student strike against the invasion of Cambodia. In this context, the struggle against technocratic oppression was conceived in terms drawn from the history of political revolutions. Technology was the enemy in the way the state had been in an earlier era; to revolt was to reclaim humanity against the machine.

Today's political movements are dispersed across traditional boundaries between the political, the social, and the personal. Arguably, today more people than ever before are actually influenced by the Left regarding issues of race, gender, and the environment. But simultaneous mobilizations have become few and far between in the advanced capitalist world. At the same time, we have learned to recognize politics in small interventions that modify the life environment without directly confronting the state. This approach is sometimes called "micropolitics," a situational politics based on local knowledge and action. It presupposes no overall strategy, no global challenge to the society, only a multitude of converging activities that have long-term subversive impact.

Although it is surely not a sufficient response to all the manifold problems of our society, micropolitics has promise in the technical sphere because it is particularly difficult to conceive totalizing strategies there. It describes new forms of concrete political protest that aim to transform technologies one by one through pressure from the grass-roots activities of users, clients, victims. This is rather different from Marcuse's view. He concluded that technologically advanced societies were so successfully integrated that opposition could only come from their margins, for example, from minorities, students, or the Third World. By contrast, technical micropolitics is based on the assumption that marginality is one aspect of everyone's condition in a technological society. Opposition must be "immanent," implied somehow in the very contradictions of the system. The way out must be a way through.

Micropolitics works because the technical environment of our daily lives is not the inhuman oppressor we imagined it to be in the 1960s, but a "soft machine," a loosely organized and highly vulnerable structure *that includes us*. Although we are integral parts of a social machinery and cannot separate ourselves from it to challenge it through the classic gestures of revolutionary politics, we are not helpless: We are discovering how to perform as *inter-actors* in society's technical systems.

I have studied several cases that reveal just how vulnerable technical systems are to transformation from within.[29] However, the movements I discuss are so different from traditional political ones that they are easily overlooked. They are not based on ideologies or clienteles but on technical networks. Technocratic hierarchies are founded on such networks by restricting and channeling communication. The stakes in these struggles are thus also unexpected: not wealth or administrative power, but control of the technical procedures and designs structuring communicative practice.

Let me briefly offer three examples to concretize my argument.

1. The environmental movement has had a major impact on the understanding of technology, transforming privately held, supposedly neutral "technical" information into grist for public controversy. "Right to know" legislation, leaks from concerned technical personnel, the skillful use of publicity, such as for Environmental Protection Agency hearings, have all opened access, and corporations and government agencies are gradually losing the veil of secrecy under which they escaped responsibility for their actions in the past. Increasingly, questions of technological design in such domains as nuclear power and toxic waste disposal are subject to public discussion. As individuals redefine themselves as potential victims of pollution, they close the political circle by claiming their right to control industrial processes in which they are unwittingly involved.

2. The evolution of the computer offers a striking instance of new types

of public participation in technical development. In the past decade, two large-scale computer networks involving millions of users have been created. They are Internet, an international research network, and Teletel, the French domestic videotext network. Both networks were intended by their creators to facilitate the flow of such information as research data and airline schedules. Both networks were hacked by their users and transformed into media of personal communication. These users have literally changed the meaning of the computer as a technology and affected the type of society it is gradually creating. The strategy was not a "Great Refusal" but a subtle hybridization that gave an unexpected twist to the technical system.

3. The medical field offers abundant examples of patients modifying medical practice and technique from within the medical system itself. The revolution in childbirth education that occurred in the early 1970s resulted in significant changes in the role of women in childbirth, although these changes have been eroded by a new technological offensive in recent years. From passive patients, isolated, anesthetized, and controlled, women became for a time active participants in childbirth. More recently, AIDS patients have demanded improved access to experimental treatments and in the process have challenged the organization and rationale of clinical research. In both these instances, patients have altered their roles in the medical system, demanding information and control in ways subversive of the established technocratic hierarchy of medicine.

It may seem that movements of the sort described here result merely in dystopian co-optation, since they do not extract us from the machine and restore our autonomy. No doubt certain values and spheres of life need to be saved from pointless technologization, but general hostility to technology is not only futile but disarms any less totalizing critique. The new interactive politics of technology, on the contrary, reveals the human implications of different technological designs and strategies of development. It defines us as moral and political subjects in the midst of the devices and systems that form our daily environment and shape our future. From that standpoint, the demand for communication represented by these movements is so fundamental that it can serve as a touchstone for a concept of politics adequate to the technological age.

Although Marcuse was right to argue that technical networks of the sort constructed everywhere by advanced societies expose their members to new forms of control, these networks are themselves exposed to transformation by the human groups they enroll. We are interactive subjects in the midst of our technologies, where we represent their still unrealized potential. Immanent resistances arising in the technical sphere are significant bearers of new values, imposing a new form on technical institutions. These transformations can accumulate and build on one another, altering the direction of development and resolving the dystopian crisis.

Notes

1. Theodor Adorno and Max Horkheimer, *Dialectic of Enlightenment*, trans. John Cumming (New York: Herder and Herder, 1972), xv.

2. Herbert Marcuse, *Negations: Essays in Critical Theory*, trans. Jeremy J. Shapiro (Boston: Beacon Press, 1968), 143.

3. Herbert Marcuse, "Ecology and the Critique of Modern Society," *Capitalism, Nature, Socialism* 3, 11 (1992): 35, 37.

4. Louis-Antoine de Saint-Just, *Oeuvres Choisies* (Paris: Gallimard, 1968), 77.

5. Andrew Feenberg, "The Bias of Technology," in *Marcuse: Critical Theory and the Promise of Utopia*, ed. Robert Pippin, Andrew Feenberg, and Charles P. Webel (South Hadley, Mass.: Bergin and Garvey, 1988).

6. For a fuller account of the author's theory of technology, see Andrew Feenberg, *Critical Theory of Technology* (New York: Oxford University Press, 1991).

7. The distinction between instrumental and substantive theories of technology developed here is drawn from Albert Borgman, *Technology and the Character of Contemporary Life* (Chicago: University of Chicago Press, 1984), 9.

8. Quoted in Michael Zimmerman, *Heidegger's Confrontation with Modernity: Technology, Politics, Art* (Bloomington and Indianapolis: Indiana University Press, 1990), 214. Cf. Jacques Ellul, *The Technological Society*, trans. J. Wilkinson (New York: Vintage, 1964).

9. Carolyn Merchant, *The Death of Nature: Women, Ecology, and the Scientific Revolution* (New York: Harper and Row, 1980).

10. Martin Heidegger, *The Question concerning Technology*, trans. William Lovitt (New York: Harper and Row, 1977), 135.

11. Marshall Berman, *All That Is Solid Melts into Air: The Experience of Modernity* (New York: Simon and Schuster, 1982), 166–68.

12. Foucault also developed a critique of the social limits of dystopian rationality in the 1970s. He analyzed the technical basis of social domination in several different institutions and concluded that industrial alienation is a variation on a more general cultural theme: the emergence of a "disciplinary" society. In that society, science and technology are not simply instrumental but play their part in the institutionalization of new forms of social hierarchy. See Michel Foucault, *Discipline and Punish*, trans. Alan Sheridan (New York: Vintage, 1979), 221. For a comparison of Foucault and Marcuse, see Feenberg, *Critical Theory of Technology*, chap. 4.

13. Weber's concept of rationalization is ambiguous. On the one hand, he frequently writes as though modern societies were *in fact* more rational than their predecessors. This is the Enlightenment view according to which modern methods are better than traditional ones and modern individuals are free from the ancient prejudices of their ancestors, better informed and educated, and so on. But on the other hand, Weber seems to say that "rationality" attaches more to the sociologists' "ideal-type" of modern society than to its messy realities. See Weber, *The Methodology of the Social Sciences*, trans. Edward A. Shils and Henry A. Finch (New York: The Free Press, 1949), 39. And he worries that bureaucratic rationality becomes increasingly ritualized with time. Weber concluded that we are headed not toward enlightenment but toward "mechanized petrification" interrupted periodically by charismatic convulsions. Weber, *The Protestant Ethic and the Spirit of Capitalism*, trans. Talcott Parsons (New York: Scribners, 1958), 182.

14. Talcott Parsons, *The Social System* (New York: Free Press, 1964), 61–63.

15. For a critique of the ethnocentric assumptions underlying such theories, see Samir Amin, *Eurocentrism*, trans. Russell Moore (New York: Monthly Review Press, 1989).

16. For a review of various interpretations of Marx's theory of the labor process, see Paul Thompson, *The Nature of Work* (London: Macmillan, 1983).

17. Marcuse, *Negations*, 201–26.

18. Ibid., 212.

19. See Jürgen Habermas, *The Theory of Communicative Action: Lifeworld and System: A Critique of Functionalist Reason*, trans. Thomas McCarthy (Boston: Beacon Press, 1987), and Jürgen Habermas, *Toward a Rational Society*, trans. Jeremy J. Shapiro (Boston: Beacon Press, 1970).

20. Habermas's position on the neutrality of technology has by now worn pretty thin. But when he first proposed it, so strong was the prejudice in favor of instrumentalism that a number of critical theorists followed him in beating a hasty retreat from Marcuse's daring call for a reform of scientific-technical rationality. Recent work in social constructivism, described later, finally brings this episode to a close by removing any reason to concede the autonomy and neutrality of scientific-technical rationality.

21. Herbert Marcuse, *One-Dimensional Man: Studies in the Ideology of Advanced Industrial Society* (Boston: Beacon Press, 1964), 231–32.

22. Herbert Marcuse, *An Essay on Liberation* (Boston: Beacon Press, 1969), 45.

23. For a theory of cultural influences on technology, see Don Ihde, *Technology and the Lifeworld* (Bloomington and Indianapolis: Indiana University Press, 1990), chapters 6 and 7.

24. Michel Foucault, *Power/Knowledge*, ed. Colin Gordon, (New York: Pantheon, 1980), 81ff.

25. See Andrew Feenberg, "Subversive Rationalization: Technology, Power, and Democracy," *Inquiry* 35, (1992): 301–22.

26. See Bruno Latour, *Aramis ou l'amour des techniques* (Paris: La Decouverte, 1992); Trevor Pinch and Wiebe Bijker, "The Social Construction of Facts and Artefacts: Or How the Sociology of Science and the Sociology of Technology Might Benefit Each Other," *Social Studies of Science* 14 (1984): 399–441.

27. Langdon Winner, "Social Constructivism: Opening the Black Box and Finding It Empty," *Science as Culture* 16 (1992): 503–19.

28. Marcy Darnovsky, "Overhauling the Meaning Machines: An Interview with Donna Haraway," *Socialist Review* 21, 2 (1991): 65–84.

29. For examples, see my articles on clinical research techniques in relation to AIDS and the interactive evolution of computer technology: "On Being a Human Subject: Interest and Obligation in the Experimental Treatment of Incurable Disease," *Philosophical Forum* 23, 3 (1992): 213–30; "From Information to Communication: The French Experience with Videotex," in *The Contexts of Computer Mediated Communication*, ed. Martin Lea (London: Harvester-Wheatsheaf, 1992), 168–87.

Timothy J. Lukes

Mechanical Reproduction in the Age of Art: Marcuse and the Aesthetic Reduction of Technology

> On a cold, wet Canadian winter night, there's nothing like crawling into
> bed with your laptop and curling up with a good disk.
> —*Futurologist Frank Ogden*

A growing and mostly justifiable anxiety regarding the difficulties in safely, equitably, and sufficiently distributing essential goods and services has dampened utopian thinking. Marx's objections to utopian socialism focused on misdirected strategy. Those objections have been replaced with deeper concerns about the ability of the ecosystem, much less a particular political structure, to ever condone happiness. The response, by Habermas and his ilk, has been to cut losses and dig in.

This tactic has spawned detractors, thereby revitalizing admittedly fragile utopian considerations. In the wake of Habermas's ideal speech situation comes a nagging irritation with the tactic of partitioning free activity in an effort to preserve it. Notwithstanding the ecstasy of closet Aristotelians and incorrigible taxonomists, there is a growing suspicion that certain human activities are prematurely categorized as necessary evils, unnecessarily condemning normative constructs to permutations of a quasi-good life.

Herbert Marcuse, on the other hand, concedes nothing. His vision of a pacified existence does not tolerate dissonant partitions. While his discussions of a liberative technology foretell of a playful natural world, susceptible to and compatible with free human activity, his work on Freud dispels doubt that the human psyche could handle such freedom. What makes Marcuse's utopianism especially topical, however, is that he concedes as little to optimism as he does to premature resignation. That his intermittent utopian musings punctuate the most formidable and clinical assessments of the obstacles to human freedom should endear him to the new wave of restless pessimists.

In this essay I want to construct a high-technology bridge between the dissatisfaction with concessions to feasibility and the fragility of contemporary utopian thought. Although tempted to transport Marcuse's critical discussions to new and eminently legitimate anxieties regarding the proliferation of high technology, I choose to isolate hopeful developments that substantiate Marcuse's sometimes cryptic projections regarding the more sanguine possibilities of technology. That Marcuse's insights could simultaneously support wider reservations and renewed hope should not be surprising. After all, his mechanisms of qualitative change, whether psychic or political or cultural, are based consistently on the prospects of an escalating tension between the consciousness of enhanced possibilities and ever more formidable conventional obstacles.

Attempting to isolate within extant productive forces themselves the most potentially disruptive elements, Marcuse states that, "above all, the technification of domination undermines the foundation of domination."[1] Rather than inextricably linking technology and exploitation, Marcuse identifies aspects of technology that ultimately expose and resist repression: "Technification of domination means that if we rationally think through the technological processes to their end, we find that they are incompatible with capitalist institutions."[2]

Since Marcuse spoke those words, concrete developments in technology allow us to examine advances in technological processes without relying only on "thinking them through." I think that aspects of contemporary technification show an enhanced compatibility with, if not contribution to, pacification and thus to a renewed interest in utopian thinking.[3] From the promontory of Silicon Valley, I argue that recent developments in high technology render Marcuse's utopian musings more formidable in the face of popular reservations. Specifically, I want to show that technology is moving away from narcotic, ascetic, and elitist postures. Instead, technology is susceptible to what Marcuse calls an "aesthetic reduction," in which technology conforms to ontological rather than exploitative priorities.

Mickey Mouse Technology

Following Husserl, Hannah Arendt laments the contribution of technology to *The Human Condition*.[4] She argues that since the discovery of the telescope and the fracturing of the anthropocentric universe, we have been plagued by a debilitating disorientation that favors the self-contained validity of a mathematical formula to the ambiguity of considering an appropriate human existence. To assuage our existential doubt, we sacrifice thinking to making; we engineer human artifacts that reinforce the reliability of our calculations. We digitalize the sensuous and formularize the ambiguous.

Recall, painful as it might be, the day when the local pub's pinball, air hockey, and foosball apparatuses were displaced by black-and-white screens projecting images more granular than conglomerate feldspar. Pong, the electronic equivalent of Huxley's soma, pacifies its clientele in mindless, addictive, isolated encounters. The tradition is ably maintained by Nintendo and its clones. This is high technology as narcotic, as a retreat from life and its vicissitudes. Like life inside Zamiatin's Green Wall, insecurity and eccentricity are sacrificed to the replication of safe and familiar conventions.[5] We play Pong while Rome burns.

Technology as artificial cloister seems axiomatic to those of us whose first space odysseys involved pristine Zarathustrian waltzes through gleaming airlocks, with eerie libretto courtesy of an inaccessible digital cyclops. Yet, in popular culture at least, there is evidence that technology is percolating through increasingly porous partitions. Forsaking the clinical demeanor of HAL and Dave, Sigourney Weaver more recently cavorts in her underwear, flippantly allowing deviled poultry to dribble from its pouch onto her unprotected control panel. High technology no longer warrants the protection of the garage. Like the automobiles they replaced, our devices are left out on the driveway at night to collect the deposits of domesticity. The space shuttle is now greeted with fanfare reserved for a Greyhound pulling into Cleveland Terminal. For better or worse, technology is growing indistinguishable from its environment.

This damages Jean Baudrillard's colorful expansion of Husserl, Zamiatin, and Arendt. For Baudrillard, the lure of high technology is its ability to construct synthetic hyperreal alternatives to reality. Disneyland supplies the appropriate metaphor. Like Arendt's technology, Disneyland offers clean, safe, and simple simulations, designed to distract us from surrounding ambiguity. We need a separate technological universe, we are told, to provide sanctuary from the uncertain counterpart. The more tangible Disney sanctuary in Anaheim exists only to help convince us that its more pervasive cultural counterpart is something other than an artifact. If we have to visit Disneyland, we must not live in it. For Baudrillard, technology is Disneyland writ large.[6]

Yet just as the hermetic other of technology breaks down as *2001* evolves into *Alien*, so does the cachet of sovereignty and sanctuary erode as Disneyland becomes Disneyworld. The famous Orange County parking lot, providing protection and security to its regressing clientele, is replaced in Florida by a ring of golf courses and wetland habitats. Asphalt moat has become an unguarded buffer, as patrons lose track of boundaries. Simulations, although fanciful, are less frail. The attempt to distinguish reality from simulation, even if disingenuous, is fading—replaced by a new confidence in their compatibility.

The Aesthetic Reduction

Not that Herbert Marcuse would embrace Mickey Mouse under any circumstances. Marcuse does, however, anticipate the time when technology can no longer maintain its dependence on fables of an inscrutable and antagonistic natural world. Although often cataloging narcotic and diversionary propensities in high technology, Marcuse goes beyond Arendt and Baudrillard to anticipate the technological confrontation with more persistent concerns. According to Marcuse, the imminent but hardly monumental identity crisis of Disneyland technology can be averted by finally reducing technology to its fundamental *aesthetic* interest.[7]

That technique would ever serve art seems at first blush an outrageous proposition. Jacques Ellul, for instance, makes a compelling argument that, conversely, technique is preempting and eviscerating art.[8] He demonstrates that in the high-technology environment generality replaces idiosyncrasy, standard operating procedure replaces subjectivity, and permanence replaces transcendence. Marcuse, sympathetic, nevertheless extrapolates the bankruptcy of these phenomena, entertaining the proposition that this technological reduction of art will in turn provoke an *aes-*

thetic reduction of high technology,[9] whereby technology conforms to the aesthetic priorities of noninstrumentality, the imaginative recombination of reality, and the embracing of ambiguity. In so doing, technology "revalidates" aesthetics and metaphysics by contributing to the feasibility of their aspirations. The time is coming when technique will recapture its repressed connections to aesthetics and metaphysics.

Until now, nature, both human and external nature, has been too hostile and inscrutable to be treated consistently with the kind of noninstrumental posture necessary to consider possibilities and options beyond given preoccupations and deficiencies. Thus, whimsical projects are isolated in the museum or the soul, and scientific projects purify reality by subjecting it to debilitating formularization. Advances in technology, however, reduce the ominousness of nature, thereby delegitimizing the adversarial posture of technology. "The conquest[10] of Nature reduces the blindness, ferocity and fertility of Nature—which implies reducing the ferocity of man against Nature."[11] As technology supplies the ability to predict and replicate natural phenomena, it loses its defensive character and is free to join the aesthetic practice in the consideration of alternatives.

Technology thereby undergoes a *reduction* since it would be free of the unessential burden of resisting nature. Released from these external impositions, technology could return to its origins: "The rationality of domination has separated the Reason of science and the Reason of art, or, it has falsified the Reason of art by integrating art into the universe of domination. It was a separation because, from the beginning, science contained the aesthetic Reason, the free play and even the folly of imagination, the fantasy of transformation."[12] For Marcuse, science, purified of imposed instrumentalities, displays the same interests in unencumbered musing and imaginative transcendence that are now vicariously protected in aesthetic pursuits.

The Evidence

Indeed, there are signs that technology is being relieved of its responsibility to withdraw and fortify and is instead approaching and appreciating the ambiguities of existence in a way that brings an aesthetic reduction closer. Granted, the "personal" computer may offer seductive retreat, but like Pong, the personal computer is a relic of the past. With the burgeoning meld of computer and communications technology, devices and their operators can hardly stand alone and detached. Network technology has opened vast information resources, and participants are able to exchange opinions and questions at a breathtaking pace. Colleagues in the field of comparative politics knew of the attempted coup in Venezuela as it was happening, information provided via network by a participant observer. That the world has been rendered so accessible breaks down anxieties about its ultimate inaccessibility, if not its ultimate harmony.

Cockpit simulators, architectural imagers, and three-dimensional acoustic scanners embrace reality rather than escape it. It is hardly a formularized retreat from life when one of the most promising applications of virtual reality is to provide a congenial forum wherein those with and without physical disabilities can interact free of stigma and isolation. It is hardly a mathematical diversion when three-dimensional imagers are used to simulate the response of a disease-bearing enzyme to a new drug. And it is hardly a chasm between machine and organism when the newest generation of microprocessors consists of living, organic molecules, recently revealing a potential for employing human, "fuzzy" logic. Today, technological success is measured by the extent to which technology integrates ambiguity into its projects, not by the extent to which ambiguity is resisted.

Technology is undergoing a demystification. This is a symptom of the collapsing distinction between artifact and existence; we no longer are compelled to hide amid our formulas. Technology has facilitated the collapse. While admittedly producing its own dark and scary corners, it has illuminated and pacified sources of considerable anxiety. Fear of the forest has been replaced by remorse for not having fully appreciated its bounty. The yew tree gains new status as provider of anticarcinogens, inspiring investigation of the more than 95 percent of plant species that have never been tested for medicinal properties.

Technology is thus brought closer to the more honest and lasting concerns of humanity, which no longer seem alien to nature. Driven by a new impetus, "the rational transformation of the world could then lead to a reality formed by the aesthetic sensibility of man. Such a world could (in a literal sense!) embody, incorporate, the human faculties and desires to such an extent that they appear as part of the objective determinism of nature—coincidence of causality through nature and causality through freedom."[13] When arguments for the compartmentalization of technology can no longer be justified, the aesthetic reduction of technology provides an excellent framework within which the technical transformation of the world can be fruitfully investigated. No longer cloistered amid its pristine formulas, technology is showing signs of embracing, enveloping, and enhancing reality in ways previously reserved for the aesthetic oeuvre.

Technology and Sensuality

Perhaps the most distressing characteristic of "unreduced" technology is its association with asceticism. With shields depleted, warp drives wilted, and Klingons closing in, Captain Kirk inevitably solicits the cool, rational advice of his "science" officer, whose emotions have been vulcanized, save for a few human, "feminine" foibles. Sensuality, the Bones influence, is depicted as a diversion, an irritating disruption of technical efficiency. This is the efficiency of Ulysses, the great "strategist," who resists the seduction of the sirens by relying on his crew (in Freudian terms, the brother clan) to maintain his attachment to his ship and to the serious, technical work that awaits him.

Things weren't much different in *1984*,[14] in which sensuality is a mortal threat to the purveyors of technology and sensual encounters are undertaken only in the blink of Big Brother's eye. Society, as electronic circuit, discharges individual power with a relentless circulation of system messages. The body, then, as the clearest manifestation of individuality, surrenders to system logic and system maintenance. Confronted with the dreaded rats of Room 101, Winston imagines Julia's *body* as an alternative target for his phobia, and he begs for the exchange. In this painful forsaking of his confidant, he nevertheless appreciates the resistance capabilities of discrete, autonomous physical entities.

Although Marcuse consistently indicts technology for its role in separating "reason" from sensuality, again he reminds us that his dissection of technology is not condemnatory. "Is it still necessary to repeat that science and technology are the great vehicles of liberation, and that it is only their use and restriction in the repressive society which makes them into vehicles of domination?"[15] Having overcome the inscrutability of nature, technology could actually contribute to the legitimation of the sensate. "Already today, the achievements of science and technology permit the play of the productive imagination: experimentation with the possibilities of form and matter hitherto enclosed in the density of unmastered nature."[16] The aesthetic reduction of technology at once demands and facilitates the reduction of "the ferocity of nature," thereby condoning investment in human sensuality and distinctiveness. And, again, there is evidence of such progress.

Although I am not yet prepared to speak for the quality of the experiences, these days one is as likely to encounter high technology in the company of Bacchus as in the sterile temples of Apollo. (With exquisite irony, an underground collective of women science-fiction writers has expanded the relationship of Spock and Kirk into the realm of the carnal.) Technology promoters no longer demand the sacrifice of sensuality. The cybernerd, whose wilted libido surfaces only while inserting plasticine pen pack in its plaid polyester refuge, has been preempted by the cyberpunk, to whom technology is more a hothouse habitat for kinkiness. *Mondo 2000*, the slick journal that offers the neophyte a window into cyberpunk, promotes, among other things, smart drugs; unlike their predecessors, these drugs enhance the sensual by releasing rather than numbing the cerebral. Or one might be drawn to "Teledildonics: The Art of Virtual Sex," which discusses the sensual possibilities of virtual reality. Meanwhile, aspiring terminators chew on *Cybergenics* as they go through their paces on interactive treadmills, and new wave glitterati attend "raves," which mingle experimental music and laser spectaculars. Primitive and salacious as these phenomena may be, they nevertheless represent a cultural willingness to integrate the technological and the sensate.

And then there is the burgeoning integration of art and technology, which admittedly has developed unevenly. For years, high-tech art was conceived as a collaboration of distant interests. Robert Rauschenberg felt it necessary, in 1966, to collaborate with physicist Billy Klüver to produce *Nine Evenings: Theater and Engineering*. The project was a disappointment, as were most that were born of a mixture, rather than a compound, of expertise. Only when artists themselves, including Rauschenberg, began to feel more comfortable with their instruments did a more interesting product emerge. And now, postmodern artists await with informed eagerness the next generation of Silicon Graphics display terminals.

Jenny Holzer illuminates a Mitsubishi Diamond Vision 2000 screen, mounted on a tractor trailer, to broadcast her imaginative insights. Meanwhile, Lynn Hershman employs interactive videodisc technology in her art, inspiring infinite permutations of participatory creativity. Gretchen Berder surrounds her audience with provocative images from twenty-four computer monitors, three film screens, and eight video channels. Adele Shtern scans drawings into a personal computer, electronically manipulates the images, and produces the final product on a laser printer. Ulrike Rosenbach videorecords her responses to various images from history and popular culture. And perhaps the most famous of these technoartists, Laurie Anderson, fuses multiple technologies and art forms in her stunning performances.[17]

Of course, an animated technology is no panacea. If the stupor of Saturday night at the Dew Drop Inn continues to be the most popular and legitimate outlet for eros, there is little chance that technical avenues of sensual expression will be any more complex or intriguing than their more traditional predecessors. But then again, merely propagating outlets of sensual expression may be progressive. That human sensuality is presently so often absorbed in banal or exploitative pursuits may be partly due to the limited sensual releases available in contemporary technological society. That war games are the first prototypes of virtual reality ought not condemn technology's potential in a more liberated setting. Like art, technology is capable of complicating and sublimating sensuality. This is the key to Marcuse's ultimate integration of art and technology. Technology does not merely come to tolerate the senses; rather, it can play a crucial role in encouraging and enhancing them.

The Aesthetic Reduction of Power

Clearly, there is a possibility that certain vested interests can profit from an adversarial relationship with nature. Much of the vituperation of *One-Dimensional Man* is reserved for those who exploit the anxiety of inscrutable nature. It is no surprise, then, that Marcuse links the aesthetic reduction of technology to a "reduction of power."[18] No longer legitimized by their courageous domination of the fearful externality, the technological elite is ultimately vulnerable.

In his essay, "Some Social Implications of Modern Technology," Marcuse isolates the "one point at which the technological and the critical rationality seem to converge."[19] Although New Class harbingers caution a displacement of the industrial elite by a cadre of more refined technical experts, Marcuse anticipates the growth of technology leading to a "democratization of function," whereby the technological environment facilitates rather than undermines social equality. It begins with a highly circumscribed equality, tolerated only within a technological environment of strictly "limited personalities." However, the elite structure that imposes limits and maintains superior control becomes increasingly irrelevant to the technological environment, potentially weakening the control. Thus, there is room for technical democratization to diffuse into other areas:

> The standardization of production and consumption, the mechanization of labor, the improved facilities of transportation and communication, the extension of training, the general dissemination of knowledge—all of these factors seem to facilitate the exchangeability of functions. It is as if the basis were shrinking on which the pervasive distinction between "specialized (technical)" and "common knowledge" has been built and as if the authoritarian control of functions would prove increasingly foreign to the technological process.[20]

This metamorphosis of specialized into common knowledge defies New Class critiques, which hold that although the monumental personality may be in decline, the magnate has yielded to a more sober, deliberate, and cooperative plurality, whose capital is information and whose competitive edge is the glamourless study of markets and materials. The New Class argument maintains that, although capable of a "business" acumen and a passable familiarity with a simple product, captains of industry rely increasingly on specialized lieutenants when simpler products are inevitably displaced by sophisticated technological implements.

The key to the New Class argument is that complex technology encourages an ever-widening distance between those who can keep up and those who can't. This is a common anxiety. Cambridge University Press reissued the memoirs of one of England's last wheelwrights, undoubtedly intended to provoke comparisons.[21] George Sturt voices nostalgic pride at the convergence of craft, client, and artifact: "And so we got curiously intimate with the peculiar needs of the neighbourhood. In farm-waggon or dung-cart, barley-roller, plough, water-barrel or what not, the dimension we chose, the curves we followed (and almost every piece of timber was curved) were imposed upon us by the nature of the soil in this or that farm, the gradient of this or that hill, the temper of this or that customer or his choice perhaps in horseflesh."[22] Contrast this, we are asked, to the device of the present, which is too complicated to be understood by more than a handful of people and is so widely distributed that even if it could be understood by the consumer, it would lack any of the former connections between maker, user, and use. As a further example, John Kenneth Galbraith excavates the résumé of Henry Ford's collaborator, James Couzens, who in that simpler time could master the finer points not only of automobile production but of the locomotive and coal industries as well.[23]

Yet is there necessarily an intractable distinction between the technologist and the craftsperson? First of all, is the branch of a tree used by the wheelwright really all that primitive and simple? Does the average wheelwright have any idea of the importance of the tree's cambium layer, or of the complexity of the photosynthetic process? No doubt a botanist would argue vehemently for the sophistication of a plant over that of a microcircuit. In fact, complexity is often more a function of perception than reality, and it could be that technology bears the reputation for complexity only because it is not so familiar to us as is the tree branch. It follows, then, that as technology works its way into society, a chip will be perceived with about as much reverence as a two-by-four.

A promenade through Fry's electronic supermarket in Sunnyvale, California, is ample illustration. Just between the Hostess Twinkies and the *Hot Rod Review* is the newest in super VGA graphics boards. Math coprocessors are tossed around like so many bell peppers. (Is it accidental that Fry's is a subsidiary of a grocery store chain?) In part because the barrier of complexity is being broken, technology is being arranged in ways that clearly take into account the "gradient of the hill" of the prospective customer. Zen therapists, depositing their angst with the entry guard, boldly harvest components for a system sure to satisfy their creative idiosyncracies. It may not be so important, then, that the user understand fully the intricacies of the etched circuit as it is that the user is comfortable with the circuit and can adapt it to his or her purposes.

Alvin Gouldner, expanding on the work of Edward Shils, effectively isolates the "central ideals" of the New Class and, in so doing, illuminates the basis of its authority. The modern intellectuals, above all, hope to establish their "autonomy" and "self-groundedness," so that they may delineate and strengthen their burgeoning guild against the obsolescent but irritating competition of brute force, tradition, and irrational impulse. The political ammunition of the New Class is its "rules," so rigorous, complex, and esoteric that they demand ever more specialized and experienced interpreters. In fact, Gouldner asserts that the growth of these scientific rules inspires the creation of a separate language he calls "careful and critical discourse," which impresses in order to oppress.[24]

Yet Gouldner, Galbraith, and other New Class investigators do not fully appreciate the tenuousness of authority based on shibboleths rather than brute force. The prestige of the New Class lasts only as long as the popular perception that a hostile environment can be traversed safely only with the assistance of some gifted technological guru. Marcuse recognizes that there will be a point at which the "authoritative control of function," based on the belief that specialists are really special, will surrender to a "democratization of function," in which technological specialization remains but is no longer seen as anything extraordinary. Wide social deference becomes limited technical deference when advances in education, transportation, and communication promote a general familiarity with technology. Accessibility and acclimation prevent dominance by a privileged few.

In a 1988 Roper Organization survey, respondents were asked whether science could be trusted to solve major social problems. Only 24 percent of the general population responded positively. But more interesting yet, when technology practitioners (scientists, technicians, and teachers) were separated from the rest of the population, only 16 percent concurred that science can be trusted to solve social problems.[25] That technical expertise is perceived as insufficient to tackle contemporary problems, and that the perception is more prevalent among technocrats themselves, tends to disrupt assertions about the achievement of elite status—especially an elite status that is supposedly based on reputation.

238

The New Class has recently inspired renewed and anxious interest, and a new populism has been suggested as antidote.[26] For those interested in battling a mostly vanquished enemy, this battle may have appeal. Marcuse correctly detects in technocracy itself an ultimate propensity to participatory, "populist" manifestations. Indeed, the breakdown of technological aloofness may be most dramatic in the response to AIDS. Although one might expect the intimidating intransigence of the disease to rekindle patterns of meek deference to the technological community, AIDS patients, encouraged and enlightened by vast networks of informed sympathizers, resist technological objectification and participate in, rather than submit to, their treatment. "Their struggle represents a counter-tendency to the technocratic organization of medicine, an attempt at a recovery of its symbolic dimension and caring functions."[27] Clearly, this is the "authoritarian control of functions" proving to be "increasingly foreign to the technological process."[28]

Conclusion: Hyperindividuality

New developments in technology support the reduction of technological defensiveness, technological prudishness, and technological elitism. That does not mean there are not new concerns of some gravity. In fact, the aesthetic reduction of technology, anticipated by Marcuse, may challenge traditional justifications of the very formation of society. Kant argues that people are bound together in a shared system of morals and meanings out of the fear of an inscrutable natural surrounding and out of the satisfaction of imposing a human meaning on what is ultimately unfathomable. Our inability to capture "pure reason" prompts us to impose a "practical reason" on which we can base action. The more the system is shared, the more the subscribers feel secure that they are leading legitimate lives.

Interacting with a more predictable, less intimidating nature fosters security without the need for widespread concurrence. Technology is no longer seen as munitions with which armies of obedient citizens do battle with their antagonistic surroundings. Rather, technology assists in the release from an obligation to connect experiences in a monolithic, defensive structure of meanings. The result is not a collection of submissive drones but a cacophony of jitterbugs. Connections are shunned, attention spans are constantly strained, and time is superfluous. With Indiana Jones as archetype, the life of this hyperindividual can be severed at random and arbitrarily respliced without loss of continuity.

The hyperindividual is decidedly postmodern, refusing to judge one "text" as superior to another, instead arguing that meaning and value are only relevant within experiences rather than between them. Aspects of this individual have recently been described well by Allan Bloom, Saul Bellow, Robert Bellah, and other participants in the most recent episode of American self-flagellation. The accounts are less satisfying, however, when they attempt to isolate causes—political, educational, spiritual— with little or no attention paid to the social consequences of modern technology.

Marcuse can help move the debate about technology from obsolescent attention to its ascetic, elitist, or narcotic aspects to more legitimate concerns about connection and value. The latter, hardly accidentally, are the issues of postmodern theory, and, not surprisingly, Marcuse has a good deal to say about the allure of relativism and the deficiencies of what I call hyperindividuality. Thus, contributions to this volume from Paul Breines and Ben Agger, which address Marcuse's anticipation of postmodern dilemmas, ought to be read with an eye toward their excavation of new and formidable challenges to developments in technology. We do not have so much anxiety about high technology that we can afford to misdirect it.[29]

Notes

1. Herbert Marcuse, *Five Lectures: Psychoanalysis, Politics, and Utopia*, trans. Jeremy J. Shapiro and Shierry Weber (Boston: Beacon Press, 1970), 65–66.
2. Marcuse, *Five Lectures*, 78.
3. See Shierry Weber Nicholsen, "The Persistence of Passionate Subjectivity: Eros and Other in Marcuse, by Way of Adorno," in this volume.
4. Hannah Arendt, *The Human Condition* (Chicago: University of Chicago Press, 1958).
5. See Evgenii Zamiatin, *We*, trans. Gregory Zilboorg (New York: Dutton and Company, 1952).
6. Jean Baudrillard, *Simulations*, trans. Paul Foss, Paul Patton, and Philip Beitchman (New York: Semiotext(e), 1983), 25.
7. For a more thorough discussion of the meaning of aesthetic expression to

Marcuse, see Timothy J. Lukes, *The Flight into Inwardness: An Exposition and Critique of Herbert Marcuse's Theory of Liberative Aesthetics* (Selinsgrove, Pa., London, and Toronto: Associated University Presses, 1985).

8. Jacques Ellul, *The Technological Society*, trans. John Wilkinson (New York: Alfred A. Knopf, 1970), 340–49.

9. Douglas Kellner quite legitimately laments the superficial and infrequent attention paid to Marcuse's concept of the aesthetic reduction and its possible reflection in applications of high technology. Yet Kellner himself devotes less than three pages to the concept. See Douglas Kellner, *Herbert Marcuse and the Crisis of Marxism* (Berkeley: University of California Press, 1984), 334–37.

10. I prefer to interpret Marcuse's use of the term "conquest" here in the sense of a student "conquering" a subject rather than a monarch conquering a territory. However, there are times when Marcuse's language betrays his most daring proposals.

11. Herbert Marcuse, *One-Dimensional Man: Studies in the Ideology of Advanced Industrial Society* (Boston: Beacon Press, 1964), 240.

12. Marcuse, *One-Dimensional Man*, 228.

13. Herbert Marcuse, *An Essay on Liberation* (Boston: Beacon Press, 1969), 31.

14. George Orwell, *1984* (New York: New American Library of World Literature, 1964).

15. Marcuse, *An Essay on Liberation*, 12.

16. Ibid., 49.

17. While visual artists are becoming more comfortable with technology, there is a parallel movement in architecture to integrate sensual, noninstrumental, erotic priorities into what has become a mostly technical pursuit. See Alberto Perez-Gomez, *Polyphilo, or the Dark Forest Revisited: An Erotic Epiphany of Architecture* (Cambridge, Mass.: MIT Press, 1992).

18. Marcuse, *One-Dimensional Man*, 236.

19. Herbert Marcuse, "Some Social Implications of Modern Technology," *Studies in Philosophy and Social Science* 9, 3 (1941): 428.

20. Marcuse, "Some Social Implications of Modern Technology," 430.

21. A similar study was done on the shoemakers of Lynn, Massachusetts. See William Henry Mulligan, Jr., "The Family and Technological Change: The Shoemakers of Lynn, Massachusetts, during the Transition from Hand to Machine Production, 1850–1880," Ph.D. diss., Clark University, 1982.

22. George Sturt, *The Wheelwright's Shop* (New York: Cambridge University Press: 1974, first published in 1923), 17–18.

23. John Kenneth Galbraith, *The New Industrial State* (Boston: Houghton Mifflin, 1971), 15–16.

24. Alvin W. Gouldner, *The Future of Intellectuals and the Rise of the New Class* (New York: Seabury Press, 1979), 27, 34.

25. Significance at the .01 level, N = 1445. Data generated from the *General Social Survey, 1972–90*, National Opinion Research Center, subfile 1988 (machine-readable data file).

26. See *Telos* staff, "Populism vs. the New Class: The Second Elizabethtown *Telos* Conference (5–7 April 1991)," *Telos*, 88 (Summer 1991): 2–36.

27. Andrew Feenberg, "Subversive Rationalization: Technology, Power, and

Democracy," *Inquiry* 35 (1992): 319. Feenberg also discusses the Minitel project in France, whereby "the computer was politicized as soon as the government attempted to introduce a highly rationalistic information system to the general public. Users 'hacked' the network in which they were inserted and altered its functioning, introducing human communication on a vast scale where only the centralized distribution of information had been planned."

28. Marcuse, "Some Implications of Modern Technology," 430.

29. Thanks to Lori Bowman for her research assistance and to John Bokina for his always valuable editorial advice.

Part V

Revisiting Marcuse

Douglas Kellner

A Marcuse Renaissance?

Since his death in 1979, Herbert Marcuse's influence has been steadily waning. The extent to which his work is ignored in progressive circles is curious, for Marcuse was one of the most influential theorists of the day during the 1960s and his work continued to be a topic of interest and controversy during the 1970s. Although the quelling of the radical movements with which he was involved helps explain Marcuse's eclipse, a paucity of new texts and publications has also contributed. While there have been many new translations of Benjamin, Adorno, and Habermas during the past decade, there have been few new publications of material by Marcuse (although there has been a steady stream of books about him).[1] In addition, while there has been great interest in the writings of Foucault, Derrida, Baudrillard, Lyotard, and other French "postmodern" or "poststructuralist" theorists, Marcuse does not seem to fit into the fashionable debates concerning modern and postmodern thought.[2] Unlike Adorno, Marcuse did not anticipate the postmodern attacks on reason, and his dialectics were not "negative." Rather, he subscribed to the project of reconstructing reason and of positing utopian alternatives to the existing society—a dialectical imagination that has fallen out of favor in an era that rejects totalizing thought and grand visions of liberation and social reconstruction.

The neglect of Marcuse may be altered through the publication of a wealth of material that is found in the Herbert Marcuse archives in Frankfurt.[3] During visits to the archives from 1989 to the present, I went through the archival material and was astonished at the number of valuable unpublished texts. The Marcuse Archive is a treasure trove, and plans are shaping up to publish many volumes of this material. In this essay, I shall call attention to some of the most important archival material, concentrating on some extremely interesting manuscripts from the 1940s and some unpublished book manuscripts and articles from the 1960s and 1970s. I focus, in accord with the interests of this anthology, on how this new material can contribute to a Marcuse renaissance.

Philosophy and Politics:
Unpublished Papers from the 1940s

Some of the richest manuscripts result from Marcuse's work during the 1940s, when he was working for the U.S. government. The manuscripts include some fascinating studies of national socialism, a 1945 essay on art and politics in the totalitarian age, thirty-three theses on the contemporary era (which forecast the themes of *One-Dimensional Man*), and some manuscripts, coauthored with Franz Neumann, sketching out a book-length project on theories of social change.[4] These texts are important because they provide original analyses of the psychological, cultural, and technological conditions of totalitarian societies and the way that societies sell their citizens on the virtues of war. These topics are obviously relevant today during an era of increasing social administration in which U.S. military interventions like the Persian Gulf War can be orchestrated to manipulate individuals to consent to blind participation.

The unpublished manuscripts also suggest a revision of the received history of the Critical Theory[5] of the so-called Frankfurt School and provide material that mitigates the widespread opinion that the group was turning away from social practice and political action in the 1940s.[6] It has been hitherto unknown that Marcuse was collaborating with Franz Neumann during this period on a project entitled "Theory of Social Change."[7] In the Marcuse Archive in Frankfurt, there are three manuscripts that indicate that Marcuse and Neumann were working together to produce a systematic treatise on theories of social change in the Western tradition of political and social thought. One set of notes contains a short description of the project, and two drafts present overviews that indicate the scope, content, method, and goals. The short precis of the project describes it as:

> A historical and theoretical approach to the development of a positive theory of social change for contemporary society.
> The major historical changes of social systems, and the theories associated with them will be discussed. Particular attention will be paid to such transitions as those from feudalism to capitalism, from laissez-faire to organized industrial society, from capitalism to socialism and communism.

A note in Marcuse's handwriting on the themes of the study indicates that he and Neumann intended to analyze conflicting tendencies toward social change and social cohesion; forces of freedom and necessity in social change; subjective and objective factors that produce social change; patterns of social change, such as evolution and revolution; and directions of social change, such as progress, regression, and cycles. The project would have culminated in a "theory of social change for our society." A seventeen-page typed manuscript in the Marcuse Archive, entitled "A History of the Doctrine of Social Change," opens:

Since sociology as an independent science was not established before the 19th century, the theory of society up to that time was an integral part of philosophy or of those sciences (such as the economic or juristic) the conceptual structure of which was to a large extent based upon specific philosophical doctrines. This intrinsic connection between philosophy and the theory of society (a connection which will be explained in the text) formulates the pattern of all particular theories of social change occurring in the ancient world, in the middle ages, and in the commencement of modern times. One decisive result is the emphasis on the fact that social change cannot be interpreted within a particular social science, but must be understood within the social and natural totality of human life. This conception uses, to a large extent, psychological factors in the theories of social change. However, the derivation of social and political concepts from the "psyche" of man is not a psychological method in the modern sense but rather involves the negation of psychology as a special science. For the Greeks, psychological concepts were essentially ethical, social and political ones, to be integrated into the ultimate science of philosophy.[8]

This passage clearly reveals the typically Marcusean tendency—shared by other members of the Frankfurt School—to integrate philosophy, social theory, psychology, and politics. Although standard academic practice tended to separate these fields, Marcuse and his colleagues perceived their interrelation. Thus Marcuse and Neumann read ancient philosophy as containing a theory of social change that was basically determined by a search for the conditions that would produce the highest fulfillment of the individual. This project begins, they claimed, with the Sophists, for whom "social institutions are subject to the wants of the individuals for whose sake they have been established." The Sophists were thus prototypes of philosophers who protested against oppressive and congealed social conditions in the name of the interests of the individual. They did not, however, develop any systematic theories of social change or theories of laws of social change. Rather, their "oppositional" model was that of individuals who, realizing their true interests, changed society accordingly.

For Plato, the corruptions of private property and lack of a proper education rendered individuals incapable of "discovering unaided the correct form of social and political relations." It is up to the philosopher to discover the knowledge by virtue of which social and political life can be reordered to serve the true interests of the individual. Marcuse and Neumann read Plato, therefore, as elaborating "that form of social order which can best guarantee the development of human potentialities under the prevailing conditions." This involves, for Plato, conceptualization of the ideal forms of life by the philosopher and the reconstruction of society according to them: "The radical change of the traditional city state into the platonic state of estates implies a reconstruction of the economy in such a manner that the economic no longer determines the faculties and powers of man, but is rather determined by them."

Note that already Marcuse was contrasting true and false interests and claiming that only the philosopher can discover those true forms of social life that will make possible the full realization of human potentialities. Marcuse would later scandalize some on the Left by being sympathetic to the notion of the philosopher-king, who could see through the doxa and ideological confusion of everyday consciousness and perceive true needs, interests, and policies to reorder social life. This rather undemocratic political vision might be rooted in his early political thought and have its origins in his study of Plato.[9]

One notes also the distinctly Marxian reading of Plato, which stresses the negative impact of private property on human consciousness and values and the need to reorder the socio-economic system, as well as the state, to provide true happiness for humanity. There is also an emphasis in the section on Plato on the importance of restructuring the psyche and the equation of philosophy and psychology—reading psychology as "a kind of universal science and as such identical with philosophy"—that previews Marcuse's later turn to Freud and his particular philosophical reading of Freud.

According to Marcuse and Neumann, Aristotle was "the first philosopher who attempted to elaborate a general theory of social and political development." Aristotle's political philosophy was grounded in his metaphysics, in his theory of movement as progression from lower to higher potentialities. Historical movement, as opposed to natural movement, was a "conscious development in the course of which something actually new is produced, whereas change in the world of nature merely means a cycle in which identical things keep recurring." The state, in this vision, is the highest form in which the potentialities of a rational human being can be realized. As with Plato, the state can be judged according to whether it does or does not fulfill human potentialities. Thus both Plato and Aristotle have critical standards against which they can measure, criticize, and seek to transform existing social and political conditions. Unlike Plato, however, Aristotle did not believe that degeneration of all forms of political life was inevitable, and he instead argued that if "proportionate justice" in the state and society was maintained, social and political harmony could be preserved.

With the breakup of the Greek city-states, "political theory incorporated the concept of the equality and universality of human nature as the highest standard of social and political organization." With the Stoics and later Greek, Roman, and medieval philosophy, theories of natural law emerged which provided criteria for oppositional theories to criticize existing social and political forms of organization. The Epicurean school renounced theories of social and political development and focused instead on the production of individual happiness as the higher good.

In a brief sketch of medieval theories of social change, Marcuse and Neumann emphasized "radical social opposition inherent in the theology of the Church fathers" and "heretical religious doctrines," such as the teachings of Averroism, which "received practical, political and social significance . . . in the struggle between the church and the secular powers, in the disputes within the church, and, finally, in the discussion within the secular society caused by the disputed realm of temporal and secular powers." The oppositional force of this doctrine is discerned by contrasting it with Thomistic social philosophy, which attempted "to reconcile the natural law doctrine of the Stoics with the existing feudal, hierarchically organized estates." While Stoic natural law doctrines were often used against existing social formations, in Thomistic philosophy it was used to legitimate a hierarchical society.

Just as Marcuse and Neumann contrasted conservative and progressive medieval theories of social change, so too did they contrast modern theories, thus presenting theories of society as a contested terrain between opposing tendencies rather than as a monolithic bloc of domination. Generally, Marcuse and Neumann contrasted critical, materialist, and progressivist theories with more idealist and conservative ones. After some comments on how Machiavelli helped produce a secularization of theories of social change in the modern era, Marcuse and Neumann discussed trends of rationalist, empiricist, and materialist theories. Dominant rationalist theories (Hobbes, Spinoza, and Leibniz) are characterized as "positivistic . . . insofar as the prevailing structure of society provides the final framework for the analysis of social change." Empiricist philosophies share this positivist trend,[10] though there is a distinction, Marcuse and Neumann claimed, between optimistic and pessimistic trends. The former assume that humans are essentially good and therefore imply a theory of progress that asserts that human "potentialities can be fully developed in an orderly progress of society without revolution and retrogression" (Grotius, Locke, Shaftesbury, Jefferson, and so on). Pessimistic theories reject the possibilities of a harmonious progress and repudiate "any kind of social change which might endanger the existing social order" (the religious doctrines of Luther and Calvin as well as the counterrevolutionary theories of de Maistre, Mandeville, and Burke).

These trends are contrasted with a "strong non-conformist critical and predominantly materialist trend" which bases its criticism of society on the material needs of human beings. "To these, social change is equivalent to the complete transformation of society, particularly to a complete change of the system of private property. This materialistic criticism was the link unifying the philosophy of French enlightenment (Holbach, Helvetius, Morelly, Mably, Meslier, and Linguet) and was still operative in Rousseau's critique of the traditional society." The materialist critique achieved an "openly revolutionary character" in times of social disintegration (Munzer, the Anabaptists, and chiliastic trends in the Puritan revolution), though during the period in which the middle classes gained political and social power, materialist theories celebrated the existing capitalist economy, which was said to be governed by a preestablished harmony (the Physiocrats and classical economists).

Marcuse and Neumann presented Hegelian philosophy, much as Marcuse did in *Reason and Revolution*, as a critical rationalism that combines radical impulses with conservative ones. The dialectical method was praised "as an adequate theoretical structure capable of coping with the dynamic character of modern society. Social change is no longer a particular event within a rather static reality, but the primary reality itself from which all stasis must be explained. The interpretation of social change becomes identical with the theory of society." Marx was presented as the theorist who best develops Hegel's dialectical method in conceptualizing contemporary social antagonisms. For Marx, "the problem of social change is not a problem within the prevailing form of society, but of the substitution of this society for a socialist one." This Marxian position would guide Marcuse's thinking until the end of his life, and Neumann presumably shared this perspective at that time.

Marcuse and Neumann thus proposed a systematic examination of ancient, medieval, and modern theories of social change with a view toward developing a theory of social change for contemporary society. The distinctive feature of classical theories of social change for them was the interconnection of sociological, political, and psychological factors. "The true order of human life embraces all three realms," and "the laws ruling that order" are similar. They noted that modern sociology "has severed the intrinsic connection between the theory of society and philosophy which is still operative in Marxism and has treated the problem of social change as a particular sociological question." They proposed, by contrast, to integrate philosophy, sociology, and political theory in a theory of social change.

A larger, forty-seven-page manuscript, titled "A Theory of Social Change,"[11] presented a comprehensive analysis of some specific theories of social change, focusing on modern theories. Marcuse and Neumann offered detailed analyses of Vico, Montesquieu, French and British Enlightenment theories, the counterrevolution, idealist theories, administrative theories (Saint-Simon, Comte, and Spencer), dialectical theories (Hegel, Marx, and socialist theory), and the end of philosophically inspired theories of society and the beginning of "scientific" sociological ones in Lester Ward. As in the shorter prospectus, the framework contrasted earlier classical theories that combine philosophical, sociological, and political reflections with later doctrines that eliminate the philosophical components. Once again the dialectical and materialist perspectives of Marxism are privileged.[12]

This project is extremely interesting for the history of Critical Theory since it shows that in the 1940s there were two tendencies within Critical Theory: 1) the more pessimistic philosophical-cultural analysis of the trends of Western civilization being developed by Horkheimer and Adorno in *Dialectic of Enlightenment*; and 2) the more practical-political development of Critical Theory as a theory of social change anticipated by Marcuse and Neumann. For Marcuse and Neumann, Critical Theory was conceptualized as a theory of social change that would connect philosophy, social theory, and radical politics—precisely the project of 1930s Critical Theory that Horkheimer and Adorno were abandoning in the early 1940s in their turn toward philosophical and cultural criticism divorced from social theory and radical politics. Marcuse and Neumann, by contrast, were focusing precisely on the issue that Horkheimer and Adorno had neglected: the theory of social change.[13]

War, Totalitarianism, and the Fate of Socialism

Marcuse and Neumann became involved in antifascist work for the U.S. government during the Second World War, and their attention to the project was suspended; there is no evidence that they attempted to take it up again after the war. Meanwhile, Marcuse wrote some brilliant studies of fascism, including "The New German Mentality," "Presentation of the Enemy," and "On Psychological Neutrality."[14] "The New German Mentality" is an extremely rich sixty-three-page manuscript that analyzes the psychological components of the new fascist ideology and mentality, dissects its linguistic components, and presents an interesting concept of "counter-propaganda."

During his years of government service—from 1942 until the early 1950s—Marcuse continued to develop his Critical Theory and the themes that would become central to *One-Dimensional Man*. Although the Marcuse-Neumann project did not resume, archival material shows his continual commitment to connecting social theory and practice. In a 1947 essay that contained thirty-three theses on the current world situation, Marcuse sketched what he saw as the major social and political tendencies of the present moment.[15] The text was prepared for a possible relaunching of the Institute for Social Research journal, *Zeitschrift für Sozialforschung.* The plan was for Marcuse, Horkheimer, Neumann, Adorno, and others to write articles on contemporary philosophy, art, social theory, politics, and so on, but this project also failed to come to fruition—perhaps because of growing philosophical and political differences among the members of the institute. The return of Horkheimer, Adorno, and Pollock to Germany to reestablish the Institute for Social Research in Frankfurt might also have undermined the republication of their journal.

Marcuse's "Theses," like his later *One-Dimensional Man,* contain a Hegelian overview of the contemporary world situation that was deeply influenced by classical Marxism. It provides a sketch of the obstacles to social change that projects of radical social transformation, such as those envisaged in his work with Neumann, would face. In the theses, Marcuse introduced many of the key positions of *One-Dimensional Man,* including the integration of the proletariat, the stabilization of capitalism, the bureaucratization of socialism, the demise of the revolutionary Left, and the absence of genuine forces of progressive social change. In the first thesis, Marcuse wrote: "After the military defeat of Hitler-fascism (which was a premature and isolated form of capitalistic reorganization) the world is dividing itself into a neo-fascist and a soviet camp. The still existing remains of democratic-liberal forms within both camps are being rubbed away, or are being absorbed by them. The states, in which the old ruling class has survived the war economically and politically, will become fascist in a foreseeable time, while the others will enter into the soviet camp (Thesis 1)."

Marcuse feared a resurgence of fascism and escalating tension between neofascist capitalist countries and the Soviet Union. Anticipating *One-Dimensional Man,* he presented both blocs as being essentially antirevolutionary forms of domination and "hostile to a socialist development." Following a position he had argued in essays in the 1930s and in *Reason and Revolution* (1941), Marcuse claimed that liberal-democratic forms were being destroyed or absorbed into systems of domination. He also anticipated his later analyses of the militarization of the capitalist and socialist blocs in his suggestion that war between the Cold War antagonists was probable.

Producing his first written critique of Soviet Marxism,[16] Marcuse criticized the failure to create an emancipatory socialism in the Soviet Union and urged the defense of orthodox Marxist teaching against all compromises and deformations (Thesis 3). Previewing the analysis of the integration of the working class in *One-Dimensional Man*, Marcuse argued that the working class was becoming ever more absorbed into capitalist society and that there were no apparent forces of revolutionary opposition to the system. With the development of new war technologies, it is hopeless to project armed struggle against forces with powerful weapons at their disposal (Thesis 6). The *Verbürgerlichung* of the working class corresponds to deep structural changes in the capitalist economy and needs to be comprehensively theorized (Theses 11 and 12)—a task that Marcuse would undertake in succeeding years.

Despite the difficulties in pinpointing concrete revolutionary tendencies or movements, Marcuse continued to insist that the construction of socialism was a key goal for contemporary radical politics (Thesis 21) and that he himself held to the revolutionary tradition of Marxian theory, as he would indeed continue to do for the rest of his life. He conceived of the socialization of the means of production and their administration by the "immediate producers" as the key task of constructing socialism (Thesis 25). Although he envisaged economic democracy and the development of a classless society as part of his conception of socialism (Thesis 26), he did not sketch out an adequate model of a democratic socialism—an omission that represents a gap in his thought as a whole. Marcuse concluded with a view on the prospects for revolutionary theory and practice: "The political task consists in restoring the revolutionary theory in the communist parties and producing the corresponding revolutionary practice for them. This task appears impossible today. But perhaps the relative autonomy from the soviet dictatorship, which this task requires, is given as a possibility in the communist parties of Western Europe and West Germany (Thesis 33)."

Thus the thirty-three theses concretize in their contemporary era the revolutionary perspectives of *Reason and Revolution* and the project of "theories of social change," but in a rather pessimistic vein that anticipates *One-Dimensional Man*. Wiggershaus claims that Horkheimer never responded to Marcuse's theses,[17] and one imagines that the theoretical and political differences between them were now unbridgeable. And, in fact, the *Zeitschrift für Sozialforschung* was never to be relaunched; Horkheimer and Adorno soon returned to Germany to resurrect the Institute for Social Research, but Marcuse remained in the United States.

I conclude this section with a few remarks indicating how Marcuse perceived social change in the 1940s. As a Marxist, he conceived social change as a transition from capitalism to socialism and tended to downplay the importance of democracy—of constituting a democratic society as an essential feature of progressive social transformation. He seemed to assume that there can be no true democracy in a capitalist society and that socialism thus provides the necessary conditions for the democratization of society. Consequently, the theory of the transition to socialism is the fulcrum of his perspectives on social change. Indeed, Marcuse hardly mentions democracy in his major texts of the period and thus never develops a theory of democracy, a problem that remains a deficiency in his theory and in that of the first generation of the Frankfurt School.

The texts of the period also indicate that he believed mistakenly that capitalism would eventually lead to fascism if there were no socialist revolution to produce a socialist society. This is clear in the thirty-three theses and would reappear in many later studies, including the unpublished manuscript "Dilemmas of Bourgeois Democracy," in which he analyzed how the election of Richard Nixon in 1972 produced the preconditions for a new fascism in the United States. It is perhaps this fear that democracy could easily produce fascism—rooted in his experiences in 1920s Weimar Germany—that led Marcuse to be distrustful of democracy as a panacea for all social and political problems. Yet we must decide today what is needed—radical democracy, socialism, a combination of the two, or new political perspectives—to solve the problems of the present age. I shall return to this question in my conclusion.

Domination and Liberation:
The Marcusean Vision

In retrospect, the Marcusean vision perceives forces of domination and oppression yet envisages forms of liberation and alternatives to the existing society. Marcuse's vision of liberation was most compellingly sketched out in *Eros and Civilization* (1955), and some essays from the archives concretize the vision. An important 1945 essay, "Some Remarks on Aragon: Art and Politics in the Totalitarian Era," articulates his belief that love and erotic happiness are central to an emancipated existence. The essay contains some of his most detailed readings of literary texts and some fascinating philosophical reflections on art and liberation.[18] The aesthetic dimension was always an integral part of Marcuse's vision of liberation, and he always believed that great art inspired the quest for a better life, projecting visions of a freer and happier existence. The aesthetic dimension thus animated the Great Refusal of oppressive social conditions.

It is *One-Dimensional Man* (hereafter ODM) that provides Marcuse's most in-depth analysis of the forces of domination, and the archives contain many unpublished manuscripts that highlight the key ideas and the genesis of his most important analysis of contemporary society. A folder titled "Paris Lectures" from the early 1960s (Herbert Marcuse Archive #336) holds a fairly complete and systematic French version of ODM. Although some of the material was published in French journals during the period, and some of the text went into ODM itself, the Paris lectures offer a rather systematic and compelling articulation of Marcuse's vision of contemporary forces of domination in a more concentrated form than the later book manuscript. The text reveals Marcuse as a lecturer who illustrated his ideas with clear and compelling examples. Indeed, throughout the large collection of lectures in the archives, there are extremely concrete and lucid illustrations of some of his most complex ideas. These lectures often deal with topics, such as ecology, or concrete political events, such as the Vietnam War, that Marcuse never dealt with comprehensively in his published books. They thus help illuminate some of his key ideas or serve as important supplements to his major texts.

ODM provides a framework for analyzing contemporary society that was extremely useful during the Reagan and Bush years, in which a one-dimensional conservativism and rampant capitalism were hegemonic.[19] Yet there are obvious problems with the model of ODM that led Marcuse himself to overcome its overly totalizing view of social domination and its failure to articulate forces of social change. A 1968 lecture given at UCLA, "Beyond One-Dimensional Man," is one of the first expressions of his search for new theoretical perspectives during the 1960s. The text points to growing contradictions in contemporary capitalist societies and to new forms of social opposition, especially the New Left and the anti-war movement.

Marcuse described his new perspectives on society and social change in the 1969 text *An Essay on Liberation* (hereafter EL). One of the real finds in the archives is an untitled manuscript from the period immediately following EL of about ninety-five typescript pages (Herbert Marcuse Archive #406). This manuscript, found in a folder with the title "Cultural Revolution," had been edited anonymously. In retrospect, this work can be seen as the first version of *Counterrevolution and Revolt* (1972), though hardly any of the text actually appeared in the book. The manuscript is of interest because the philosophical-political vision of liberation is more fully developed there than in EL. The work is more explicitly grounded in Marxism than his other works of the period and yet is in many respects more systematically critical and reconstructive.

Marcuse opens "Cultural Revolution" with a list of the "deviations" from classical Marxian theory that are evident in the contemporary movements and developments. He also criticizes Marxism for neglecting the body, sensibility, nature, and the role of culture in the struggle for liberation. He offers an original reading of Marx's 1844 manuscripts and some reflections on the concepts of needs, cultural revolution, bourgeois culture, subjectivity, and aesthetics. Some of the ideas appeared in essays of the period, and some passages went into *Counterrevolution and Revolt*, but much of it is new and provides an interesting expression of his attempt to discover new perspectives on liberation. In fact, Marcuse never really successfully developed his perspectives on liberation, but they find integral articulation in this manuscript, which argues that cultural revolution is a central part of the process of emancipatory social transformation.

Another manuscript, titled "Historical Fate of Bourgeois Democracy" and written soon after the 1972 presidential victory of Richard Nixon over George McGovern, represents Marcuse's most detailed analysis of a specific historical conjuncture (Herbert Marcuse Archive #522). It is filled with sharp and passionate moral and political critique of the processes of bourgeois democracy that allowed Nixon, whom Marcuse regarded as a neofascist demagogue, to be reelected to the presidency: "The spectacle of the re-election of Nixon stands as the nightmarish epitome of the period in which the self-transformation of a bourgeois democracy into neo-fascism takes place—the highest stage so far of monopolistic state capitalism."[20]

Marcuse's manuscript was written before the Watergate hearings. Nixon's resignation partly validated his negative judgment of Nixon but also suggested that Marcuse exaggerated the threats to U.S. democracy.[21] In any case, Marcuse's text can be read as an attempt to revive the radical movements of the 1960s at a time when they faced demoralization and disintegration. Obviously, Marcuse was horrified by the reelection of Nixon and delivered a robust and often moving attack on the bourgeois democracy that could reelect such a sordid character. The manuscript contains much more detailed political analysis than was usual in Marcuse's published works and offers some interesting theoretical analyses: of the sadomasochistic character (using earlier institute analyses), of aggression, of the need for radical transformation of dominant personality structures, and of a new strategy for the Left in this situation. As in the previous manuscript and his published works of the era, Marcuse's political strategizing here seems to be the weakest part of the text—perhaps explaining why he never published it. Indeed, the text poignantly describes the dilemma of the radical intellectual who wants to relate theory to practice at a time when the bearers of the revolutionary hopes are in disarray and defeat. Obviously, nothing that anyone writes can solve the problem. Yet Marcuse tried repeatedly during this period to articulate a new politics and new revolutionary strategy.

Marcuse, Radical Ecology, and New Social Movements

Many other writings in the archives reveal Marcuse's attempts in the 1970s to link his work to the struggles of the day. There are several articles that relate his work to feminism, continue reflection on the fate of the New Left, and offer thoughts on the so-called new social movements, especially the peace and environmental movements to which Marcuse was deeply attracted. These works constitute a revision of his early, rather orthodox Marxian view that centered the fulcrum of social change in the transition from capitalism to socialism, rooted in the revolutionary struggles of the working class. Marcuse was an early theorist of the integration of the working class and had been seeking out new agents of social change for decades. Consequently, he turned attention in the 1960s to the New Left as a vehicle of radical social change and analyzed the potential of the "new social movements" throughout the 1970s.

Marcuse's essay "Ecology and the Critique of Modern Society," written in the late 1970s, shortly before his death, expresses his vision of liberation and his sense of the importance of the ecological movement for the radical project.[22] Marcuse argued that genuine ecology requires a transformation of human nature as well as the preservation and protection of external nature from capitalist and state-communist pollution and destruction. Basing his vision of human liberation in the Frankfurt School notion of the embeddedness of human beings in nature, Marcuse believed that until aggression and violence within human beings were diminished, there would necessarily be continued destruction of nature and continued violence against other human beings. Consequently, Marcuse stressed that it was radical psychology and the transformed inner nature that would ultimately preserve external nature and diminish violence in society.

Marcuse's ecological vision is rooted in his reflections on the early Marx. The author of one of the first reviews of Marx's *Economic and Philosophical Manuscripts of 1844*, Marcuse based his philosophy on Marx's early philosophical naturalism and humanism.[23] In Marx's anthropology, taken up and developed by Marcuse, the human being is a natural being, part and parcel of nature. Capitalism, in this view, produced an alienation of human beings by alienating individuals from many-sided activity and by forcing on them a specialized and one-sided capitalist division of labor. Under capitalism, life is organized around labor, around the production of commodities for private profit, and individuals are forced to engage in external, coercive, and one-sided activity. For Marx, by contrast, humans are many-sided, with a wealth of needs and potentialities suppressed under capitalism. The human being is both an individual and social being in Marx's view, and capitalism allows for neither the full development of individuality nor the possibility of diverse, social and cooperative relationships. Instead, it promotes greed, predation, and antisocial behavior.

Marcuse followed this early Marxian critique of capitalism throughout his life, focusing his analysis on how contemporary capitalism produced false needs and repressed both individuality and sociality. He also followed Marx's concept of human beings as desiring beings and conceptualized desire as part of nature, exemplified in both erotic desire for other human beings and instinctive needs for freedom and happiness. During the late 1940s and 1950s, Marcuse radicalized his anthropology, incorporating the Freudian instinct theory into his Marxist view of human nature and producing a version of Freudian Marxism to which he adhered until his death. This is evident in "Ecology and the Critique of Modern Society," which uses the Freudian instinct theory to criticize contemporary forms of ecological destruction.[24]

In a symposium on "Ecology and Revolution" in Paris in 1972, Marcuse argued that the most militant groups of the period were fighting "against the war crimes being committed against the Vietnamese people."[25] Yet he saw ecology as an important component of that struggle, since "the violation of the earth is a vital aspect of the counterrevolution."[26] For Marcuse, the United States was waging "ecocide" in Vietnam against the environment as well as genocide against the people: "It is no longer enough to do away with people living now; life must also be denied to those who aren't even born yet by burning and poisoning the earth, defoliating the forests, blowing up the dikes. This bloody insanity will not alter the ultimate course of the war but it is a very clear expression of where contemporary capitalism is at: the cruel waste of productive resources in the imperialist homeland goes hand in hand with the cruel waste of destructive forces and consumption of commodities of death manufactured by the war industry."[27]

In his major writings, Marcuse loyally followed the early Frankfurt School emphasis on reconciliation with nature as a vital element of human liberation, and he also stressed the importance of peace and harmony among human beings as the goal of an emancipated society. Marcuse frequently called for a new concept of socialism that made peace, joy, happiness, freedom, and oneness with nature primary components of an alternative society. Producing new institutions, social relations, and culture would make possible, in his liberatory vision, the sort of nonalienated labor, erotic relations, and harmonious community envisioned by Fourier and the utopian socialists. A radical ecology, then, that relentlessly criticized environmental destruction as well as the destruction of human beings and that struggled for a society without violence, destruction, and pollution was integral to Marcuse's vision of liberation.

Conclusion

The relevance of Marcuse's argument should also be apparent in the aftermath of the ecocide and genocide of the Persian Gulf War.[28] Indeed, the high-tech massacre in that region reveals the insanity of the Western project of the domination of nature, in which a military machine sees the economic and military infrastructure and the people of Iraq as objects to dominate and even destroy. The human and ecological holocaust discloses the importance of Marcuse's argument that individuals must change their very sensibilities and instinctual structure so that they can no longer commit or tolerate such atrocities against nature and other people. That the general population has exhibited such euphoria in destruction and widespread support of Persian Gulf war crimes committed by the United States shows the extent of societal regression during the conservative hegemony of the last years and the need for reeducation and humanization of the population. "Postmodern" cynicism and nihilism will not help us deal with such problems. Instead, we must look to the classical thinkers of the emancipatory tradition to guide us in the struggles ahead.

For this task, the works of Herbert Marcuse are especially relevant. Marcuse continually reconstructed radical social theory and politics according to the needs and developments of the moment. He provided dimensions missing within classical Marxism—psychology, anthropology, philosophy, culture, individual emancipation—and brought into his version of Marxism ideas from Freud, Nietzsche, Schiller, Baudelaire, and others whom he believed were relevant to the projects of liberation and social transformation. Marcuse was always open to new currents of radical thought and ready to modify his theory in the light of historical experience and new theoretical or political developments. Marxism was a dialectical theory for him, which meant a historical theory, always subject to revision and improvement. Although his theory of society and his vision of social change affirmed many theses of classical Marxism, Marcuse was always open to new social movements and new impulses for radical social critique and societal transformation.

Yet his writings on new social movements in the 1970s rarely discussed the theme of democracy or the democratization of society. Indeed, Marcuse continued to be skeptical as to whether democracy really existed in the United States and other advanced technological societies. Although he supported Tom Hayden's candidacy for the Senate in 1976, he cynically remarked: "We might ask: what is he doing running in the Democratic Party? Doesn't he know that democracy doesn't work anymore?"[29] Thus, Critical Theory today should place more emphasis on democracy and on multiculturalism to fill this space in Marcuse's theory.

Still, Herbert Marcuse provides an extremely valuable legacy for contemporary radical social theory and politics, and a return to Marcuse could help vitalize the radical project in a time of new hopes tempered by new problems and dangers. Marcuse is one of the first on the Left who developed a sharp critique of Soviet Marxism and yet foresaw the liberalizing trends in the Soviet Union.[30] After the uprisings in Poland and Hungary in 1956 were ruthlessly suppressed, many speculated that Khrushchev would have to roll back his program of de-Stalinization and crack down further. Marcuse, however, differed, writing in 1958: "The Eastern European events were likely to slow down and perhaps even reverse de-Stalinization in some fields; particularly in international strategy, a considerable 'hardening' has been apparent. However, if our analysis is correct, the fundamental trend will continue and reassert itself throughout such reversals. With respect to internal Soviet developments, this means at present continuation of 'collective leadership,' decline in the power of the secret police, decentralization, legal reforms, relaxation in censorship, liberalization in cultural life."[31]

In part as a response to the collapse of communism and in part as a result of new technological and economic conditions, the capitalist system has been undergoing disorganization and reorganization. Marcuse's loyalty to Marxism always led him to analyze new conditions within capitalist societies that had emerged since Marx. Social theory today can thus build on the Marcusean tradition by developing critical theories of contemporary society. For Marcuse, social theory was fundamentally historical and so must conceptualize the salient phenomena of the present age together with changes from previous social formations. Although the postmodern theories of Baudrillard and Lyotard claim to postulate a rupture in history, they fail to analyze the key constituents of changes, with Baudrillard even declaring the "end of political economy."[32] Marcuse, by contrast, continually attempted to analyze the shifting configurations of capitalism and to relate social and cultural changes to changes in the economy.

Moreover, Marcuse paid special attention to the important role of technology in organizing contemporary societies. With the emergence of new technologies in our time, the Marcusean emphasis on the relationship between technology, economy, and culture is especially important. Marcuse also was alert to new forms of culture and to the ways that culture provided instruments of both manipulation and liberation. The proliferation of new media technologies and cultural forms in recent years also demands a Marcusean perspective to capture both their potentialities for progressive social change and the possibilities of more streamlined forms of social domination. While postmodern theories also describe new technologies, Marcuse always related economy to technology and saw both emancipatory and dominating potentials in technology. By contrast, theorists such as Baudrillard are one-dimensional, often falling prey to technological determinism.

Finally, although some versions of postmodern theory have renounced radical politics, Marcuse always attempted to link his critical theory with the most radical political movements of the day. Thus I am suggesting that Marcuse's thought continues to be a resource and stimulus for radical theory and politics in the present age. Marcuse himself was open to new theoretical and political currents yet remained loyal to those theories that he believed provided inspiration and substance for the tasks of the present age. Consequently, as we confront our own theoretical and political problems, I believe that the works of Herbert Marcuse offer important resources for our current situation and that a Marcuse renaissance will inspire new theories and politics for the contemporary era. The Marcuse Archive can contribute to a rebirth in Marcusean thought because its treasure of unpublished material demonstrates the richness of his theory, its relevance to contemporary concerns, and the broad theoretical and political vision that informs his work. As the contributions to this book document, Marcuse continues to be a living force today. A Marcuse renaissance can only enrich contemporary social theory and radical politics.[33]

Douglas Kellner

Notes

1. Significant texts on Marcuse during the past decade include Douglas Kellner, *Herbert Marcuse and the Crisis of Marxism* (London: Macmillan Press; Berkeley: University of California Press, 1984); C. Fred Alford, *Science and the Revenge of Nature: Marcuse and Habermas* (Gainesville: University Presses of Florida, 1985); Timothy J. Lukes, *The Flight into Inwardness: An Exposition and Critique of Herbert Marcuse's Theory of Liberative Aesthetics* (Cranbury, N.J., London, and Toronto: Associated University Presses, 1986); Alain Martineau, *Herbert Marcuse's Utopia* (Montreal: Harvest House, 1986); Hauke Brunkhorst and Gertrud Koch, *Herbert Marcuse zur Einführung* (Hamburg: Junius Verlag, 1987); Heinz Jansohn et al., "Herbert Marcuse", *Text + Kritik* 98 (April 1988): 3–23; Robert Pippin, Andrew Feenberg, and Charles P. Webel, eds., *Marcuse: Critical Theory and the Promise of Utopia* (South Hadley, Mass.: Bergin and Garvey Publishers, 1988); Gerard Raulet, "Fait-il Oublier Marcuse?" *Archives de Philosophie* 52, 3 (July–September 1989): 363–480; Reinhard Brunner and Inka Thunecke, "Politik und Asthetik am Ende der Industriegesellschaft. Zur Aktualität von Herbert Marcuse," *Tüte*, Sonderheft (September 1989): 3–75; Peter-Erwin Jansen, ed., *Befreiung denken—Ein politischer Imperativ* (Offenbach: Verlag 2000, 1990); Bernard Gorlich, *Die Wette mit Freud. Drei Studien zu Herbert Marcuse* (Frankfurt: Nexus, 1991); and Institute for Social Research, *Kritik und Utopie im Werk von Herbert Marcuse* (Frankfurt: Suhrkamp, 1992).

2. In the Marcuse Archive, I found an ad for one of Derrida's books with a contemptuous scrawl over it in Marcuse's handwriting: "This is what passes for philosophy today!" There are no references that I have found in Marcuse's texts, letters, or other manuscripts to the major French theorists I just noted. Although Marcuse spent some years in France, which he frequently visited, and kept up with many currents of French thought, he seems to have had little interest in the trends identified with poststructuralist or postmodern theory.

3. Generally speaking, one could categorize the most important texts from the Marcuse *Nachlass* in the following manner: unpublished book manuscripts and articles; lecture and conference papers; letters, notes, and fragments; excerpt collections; and lecture notes. At least six volumes of this material will be published in the United States during the coming years under my editorship. Negotiations are under way with several U.S. publishers to bring out new editions of Marcuse's unpublished and uncollected writings and with Suhrkamp press to publish a German edition.

4. I plan to publish this material under the rubric *Technology, War, and Fascism: The Unknown Marcuse*.

5. I am capitalizing "Critical Theory" to denote the theoretical project of the so-called Frankfurt School and to distinguish their project from other forms of critical theory. See my book *Critical Theory, Marxism, and Modernity* (Cambridge: Polity Press; Baltimore: Johns Hopkins University Press, 1988). On postmodern theory, see my books *Jean Baudrillard: From Marxism to Postmodernism and Beyond* (Cambridge: Polity Press; Stanford, Calif.: Stanford University Press, 1988) and (with Steven Best) *Postmodern Theory: Critical Interrogations* (London: Macmillan Press; New York: Guilford Press, 1991).

6. Claims that the Frankfurt School was abandoning radical politics in the 1940s are made by Martin Jay in *The Dialectical Imagination* (Boston: Little, Brown, and Company, 1973) and appear in most other standard accounts of the Institute for Social Research.

7. Herbert Marcuse and Franz Neumann, "Theory of Social Change,"; unpublished text in the Marcuse Archive #118.00, #118.01, #118.04, no date. The Marcuse Archive opened in Frankfurt in the Stadtsbibliothek in October 1990; I shall refer to the number of the manuscript according to the bibliographical system established in the archive.

8. Herbert Marcuse and Franz Neumann, "A History of the Doctrine of Social Change," unpublished text in Marcuse Archive #118.00, no date.

9. Obviously, Marcuse's attraction to the Lukács of *History and Class Consciousness* [Georg Lukács, *History and Class Consciousness: Studies in Marxist Dialectics*, trans. Rodney Livingstone (Cambridge, Mass.: MIT Press, 1971)] and his celebration of the party and dictatorship of the proletariat as the subject-object of history also influenced his inclination to support a philosophical dictatorship, as did his belief in the failures of bourgeois democracy, which I shall discuss later.

10. Marcuse and Neumann are employing the term "positivist" as Marcuse used it in *Reason and Revolution: Hegel and the Rise of Social Theory* (Boston: Beacon Press, 1960) to denote social theories that were "positive" toward existing society, as opposed to "negative" and critical social theories.

11. Herbert Marcuse and Franz Neumann, "A Theory of Social Change," Marcuse Archive #118.04, forty-seven-page unpublished manuscript, no date.

12. Anticipating the standard Institute for Social Research line, Marcuse constantly emphasized the importance of philosophy for social theory. In an article titled "On the Critique of Sociology," Marcuse reviewed a 1929 book on sociology by Siegfried Landshut and argued that "the essential characteristics, laws, and forms of social being as a fundamental mode of human being can be probed only by philosophy." The article was originally published in 1931 and was translated by Annette Kuhlmann and David Smith, *Mid-American Review of Sociology* 16, 2 (1992): 19.

13. In *The Origins of Negative Dialectics* (New York: Free Press, 1977), Susan Buck-Morss argues that in the 1930s there were two distinct tendencies of Critical Theory: the attempt by Marcuse, Horkheimer, and others to develop a Critical Theory of contemporary society and the attempt to develop a radical cultural criticism by Theodor W. Adorno and Walter Benjamin. The discovery of the manuscripts by Marcuse and Neumann on theories of social change suggests that there were also two distinct tendencies within Critical Theory in the 1940s.

14. Herbert Marcuse, "The New German Mentality," Marcuse Archive #119.00; "Presentation of the Enemy," Marcuse Archive #129.00; and "On Psychological Neutrality," Marcuse Archive #129.01.

15. Herbert Marcuse, unpublished manuscript with no title, dated February 1947, in the Marcuse Archive. For a discussion of the manuscript's history, see Rolf Wiggershaus, *Die Frankfurter Schule* (München: Hanser, 1986), 429ff.

16. Herbert Marcuse, *Soviet Marxism: A Critical Analysis* (New York: Columbia University Press, 1985; new paperback edition with introduction by Douglas Kellner). This critique is interesting because, as Helmut Dubiel argues in *Theory*

and Politics (Cambridge, Mass.: MIT Press, 1985), the institute had previously eschewed criticizing the Soviet Union. Thus Marcuse presents here the first sustained critical analysis of the Soviet Union from the perspective of Critical Theory.

17. Wiggershaus, *Die Frankfurter Schule*, 436ff.

18. This article will be published in 1993 in *Theory, Culture, and Society*, in a special section on Critical Theory.

19. The text was conceived and partly written during a conservative period in the 1950s, though the upheavals of the 1960s caused Marcuse to modify some of his theses. For detailed analysis of the genesis and reception of the book, and of Marcuse's later modification of some of its theses, see my book *Herbert Marcuse and the Crisis of Marxism*. For an analysis of the relevance of Marcuse's ODM during the past epoch of conservative rule, see my "Introduction to the Second Edition" of Marcuse's *One-Dimensional Man: Studies in the Ideology of Advanced Industrial Society*, 2d ed. (Boston: Beacon Press, 1991), xi-xxxix.

20. Marcuse, "Historical Fate of Bourgeois Democracy," in Marcuse Archives #522, quote on p. 16.

21. The Watergate affair, however, is still contested, with some interpreting the event as evidence that U.S. democracy was still functional and others arguing that the degree of Nixon's violation of the democratic rules of the game shows the fragility of democracy in the United States. Still others claim that Nixon was subject to a coup from the Right, orchestrated by conservative Republicans for whom Nixon was an embarrassment and other right-wingers who strongly disagreed with some of his policies.

22. This article was published in *Capitalism, Nature, Socialism* 3, 3 (September 1992): 1-48, with commentaries by myself, Andrew Feenberg, and Joel Kovel.

23. See Marcuse's "Foundations of Historical Materialism," in *Studies in Critical Philosophy*, trans. Joris De Bres (Boston: Beacon Press, 1973; originally published in 1932), 1-48. I discuss this essay and other elements of Marcuse's theory in *Herbert Marcuse and the Crisis of Marxism*, 77ff.

24. One might criticize Marcuse's orthodox and somewhat mechanistic use of the Freudian instinct theory in this article. Yet debates over which Freud or which version of psychoanalytic theory should be appropriated by Critical Theory still rage on; see the articles by Horowitz and Alford in this volume for some of the current positions.

25. Parts of the symposium were translated in *Liberation* [Herbert Marcuse, "Ecology and Revolution: A Symposium," *Liberation* 17, 6 (New York: September, 1972): 10-12].

26. Ibid.

27. Ibid.

28. See my book *The Persian Gulf TV War* (Boulder, Colo.: Westview Press, 1992).

29. Quoted in *Newsweek*, 7 June 1976.

30. See the 1985 edition of *Soviet Marxism*, to which I contribute an introduction. In the light of the collapse of Soviet communism, Marcuse should be appreciated as one of the few who saw the depth of the liberalizing trends in the country, though he did not predict its collapse. See Peter Marcuse's essay in this volume.

31. Marcuse, *Soviet Marxism*, 174.

32. See the discussion in Kellner, *Jean Baudrillard*.

33. For helpful remarks on earlier versions of this text, I would like to thank Helmut Dubiel, Jürgen Habermas, and other members of the 1989 Marcuse conference held at the Institute for Social Research in Frankfurt. For helpful remarks and editing of this version, I am thankful to Stephen Bronner, Timothy Lukes, Danny Postol, and Renan Rapallo.

The Contributors

Ben Agger is professor and chair of the Department of Sociology at SUNY–Buffalo. He has published ten books, including *Socio(onto)logy*; *Fast Capitalism: A Critical Theory of Significance*; *The Decline of Discourse: Reading, Writing, and Resistance in Postmodern Capitalism*; *The Discourse of Domination: From the Frankfurt School to Postmodernism*; and *Gender, Culture and Power: Toward a Feminist Postmodern Critical Theory*.

C. Fred Alford is professor of government at the University of Maryland. His books include *The Self in Social Theory: A Psychoanalytic Interpretation of Its Construction in Plato, Hobbes, Locke, Rousseau, and Rawls*; *Melanie Klein and Critical Social Theory: An Account of Politics, Art, and Reason Based on Her Psychoanalytic Theory*; *Narcissism: Socrates, the Frankfurt School, and Psychoanalytic Theory*; and *Science and the Revenge of Nature: Marcuse and Habermas*.

Isaac D. Balbus is professor of political science at the University of Illinois at Chicago. He teaches psychoanalytically informed social theory and is the author of *The Dialectics of Legal Repression* and *Marxism and Domination*. He is currently working on a synthesis of feminist mothering theory and psychoanalytic theories of narcissism, the necessity for which was discovered in the course of his own coparenting practice.

Carol Becker is associate dean and professor of liberal arts at the School of the Art Institute of Chicago. She received her Ph.D. in literature from the University of California, San Diego, where she worked closely with Herbert Marcuse. She is the author of *The Invisible Drama: Women and the Anxiety of Change* and of a forthcoming book on the responsibility of the artist to society and society to the artist.

John Bokina is professor of political science at the University of Texas–Pan American. His doctoral dissertation was on "The Young Marcuse" (University of Illinois–Urbana, 1979). His essays on critical theory and the politics of art have appeared in *Telos, International Political Science Review, Cultural Critique,* and several books. He is completing a book on the politics of opera.

Paul Breines is associate professor of history at Boston College. In 1970, he edited and contributed to *Critical Interruptions: New Left Perspectives on Herbert Marcuse.* In addition to numerous essays, he is also the author of *The Young Lukács and the Origins of Western Marxism* (with Andrew Arato) and *Tough Jews: Political Fantasies and the Moral Dilemma of American Jewry.*

Terrell Carver is reader in political theory at the University of Bristol. He is the author of textual and biographical studies of Marx and Engels, including books for students. His works have been translated into Japanese, Chinese, and Spanish, and he has held visiting appointments in the United States, Australia, New Zealand, and Japan. He also works with European researchers on interpretive methodology and theories of gender.

Andrew Feenberg is professor of philosophy at San Diego State University. He is the author of *Lukács, Marx, and the Sources of Critical Theory* and *Critical Theory of Technology*; he is coeditor of *Marcuse: Critical Theory and the Promise of Utopia* and *Technology, Democracy, and the Politics of Knowledge* (forthcoming).

Gad Horowitz is professor of political science at the University of Toronto. His publications include *Repression: Basic and Surplus Repression in Psychoanalytic Theory: Freud, Reich, Marcuse; Everywhere They Are in Chains: Political Theory from Rousseau to Marx;* "The Foucaultian Impasse: No Sex, No Self, No Revolution" (*Political Theory* [February 1987]); and "Groundless Democracy," in *Shadow of Spirit: Postmodernism and Religion,* edited by P. Berry and A. Wernick.

Douglas Kellner is professor of philosophy at the University of Texas at Austin. He is the author of *Herbert Marcuse and the Crisis of Marxism; Critical Theory, Marxism, and Modernity; Jean Baudrillard: From Marxism to Postmodernism and Beyond; Postmodern Theory* (with Steven Best); and other books and articles on social theory, culture, and politics. He will be editing forthcoming volumes of the unpublished works of Herbert Marcuse.

Timothy W. Luke is professor of political science at Virginia Polytechnic Institute and State University. His most recent publications are *Shows of Force: Power, Politics, and Ideology in Art Exhibitions*; *Social Theory and Modernity: Critique, Dissent and Revolution*; and *Screens of Power: Ideology, Domination, and Resistance in Informational Society.*

Timothy J. Lukes is associate professor and chair of the Department of Political Science at Santa Clara University. His books include *The Flight into Inwardness: An Exposition and Critique of Herbert Marcuse's Theory of Liberative Aesthetics*; *Japanese Legacy: Farming and Community Life in California's Santa Clara Valley* (with Gary Y. Okihiro; 1987 Book Award of the Association for Asian American Studies); and *American Politics in a Changing World* (with Janet Flammang, Dennis Gordon, and Kenneth Smorsten; 1991 Book Award of the Women's Caucus of the American Political Science Association).

Peter Marcuse, a lawyer and city planner, is now professor of urban planning at Columbia University in New York City. His interest in the aspect of his father's work represented by this contribution was whetted by a year in East Germany, 1989–1990, which also resulted in a book, *Missing Marx*. He has also published several articles on the process of "de-Stalinization" in that country in *Nation, Leviathan, Lingua Franca*, and elsewhere.

Shierry Weber Nicholsen is an interdisciplinary core faculty member of Antioch University's School for Adult and Experiential Learning. She works primarily with graduate students in SAEL's nontraditional Individualized Master of Arts Program. She has translated numerous works by members of the Frankfurt School, most recently Adorno's *Notes to Literature* and *Hegel: Three Studies*. She writes of Frankfurt School aesthetics, and is beginning to extend her interests to environmental philosophy.

Trudy Steuernagel is professor of political science at Kent State University. She is currently at work on two books dealing with women and public policy and women and political participation. She is coeditor of *Foundations for a Feminist Restructuring of the Academic Disciplines* and is coauthor of "More than Pink and Blue: Gender, Occupational Stratification, and Political Attitudes," in *Women in Politics*, edited by Lois Lovelace Duke.

Index

Index

Index

Marcuse, Herbert (*continued*)
210, 240, 258–61, 263 (*see also* Ecology;
Social change; Technology; *under* Feminism); U.S. government work, 252; writings, 1, 16, 29, 36, 37, 57, 191, 236, 256
(*see also individual titles*); writings, unpublished, 5, 245, 247, 252, 255, 256,
257, 263; writings about, 245, 264(nl);
writings banned in Soviet Union, 62;
writing style, 35. *See also* Aesthetics;
Beauty; Body; Critical theory; Fascism;
Frankfurt School; Imagination; New
Left; Pacification of existence; Revolution; Sensuality
Marcuse, Peter, 4, 9
Marcuse Archive (Frankfurt), 3, 5, 20, 245,
263
Marginalization, 92–93, 95, 100, 222
Marx, Karl, 1, 53, 60, 68, 77, 109, 191,
192, 193, 200, 208, 214, 216, 251;
culture hero (*see* Prometheus)
Marxism, 8, 9–10, 27, 28, 29, 31, 214,
227, 253, 257, 258; analytical/rational
choice, 73–75, 76–78, 80–83; and capitalism, 215, 216, 259; critical, 217; humanist, 42, 77, 259; and non-Marxist methods, 10; post-, 38; pseudo-, 59;
revolutionary tradition of, 254; Soviet-style, 2, 9, 59–64, 65–66 (*see also under*
Marcuse, Herbert). *See also* Western
Marxism
Marxists (Mills), 36
Mass media, 34
Maurras, Charles, 52
May movement, 34
Mbuti pygmies, 128
Means of production, 2, 9, 60, 62; socialization of, 254
Mechanization, 216
Medical treatment, 19, 219, 223, 232
Mellos, Koula, 190
Merchant, Carolyn, 203
Meslier, Jean, 250
Metapsychology, 14, 194, 199
Michels, Roberto, 52
Micropolitics, 221, 222
Middle-class, 1–2, 93, 250
Midgeley, Mary, 165–66
Mill, John Stuart, 99
Miller, Mark Crispin, 28–29
Mills, C. Wright, 36
Mitchell, Stephen, 121, 122
Modernity, 210–11, 215–16, 219

"Modernity versus Postmodernity" (Habermas), 32
Mondo 2000 (journal), 234
Montesquieu, Charles, 251
Motherhood, 95, 118–19, 123, 128–29,
140–41
Movies, 35
Multiculturalism, 6, 262
Munzer, Thomas, 250

Naess, Arne, 203
Narcissism, 119, 120, 137, 138
Narcissus, 11, 47, 52, 136–37
Nash, Roderick, 203
National Consumer Law Center, 164
National Women's Studies Association, 97–
98
Natural law, 249–50
Nature, 163, 164, 166, 168, 190, 191, 192,
199, 201, 204, 231, 234, 257, 259, 260.
See also under Domination
Neep, Victor, 176
Negative dialectics, 27, 31
Negative Dialectics (Adorno), 36
Neo-Freudian revisionists, 121, 138
Neumann, Franz, 3, 21, 246, 247, 248, 249,
250, 251, 252, 253
New Class technical experts, 20, 236, 238–
39
"New German Mentality, The" (Marcuse),
252
New Left, 41, 203, 209; and Adorno, 16;
characterization of, 1, 5, 22, 42, 45, 49,
50; critique of, 8, 45–48; defeat of, 18,
22, 42, 118, 189, 210; factionalism, 22;
guru, 36; ideology, 2–3, 5, 6, 8, 18, 34,
42, 190; and Marcuse, 15, 36, 190, 210,
245, 257, 258, 259; post-, 49; and poststructuralism, 8; and transformation of
society, 35
New Philosophers, 8
New rationality, 106, 109, 110
New science. *See* Technology, and liberalization
New sensibility, 30–31, 32, 41, 92, 94, 106,
109, 110, 111, 112, 113–14, 189, 198,
199, 200–202, 204
Nicholsen, Sherry Weber, 4, 16
Nielsen, Kai, 75
Nietzsche, Friedrich, 6, 32, 33, 55, 261
Nine Evenings: Theater and Engineering,
234
Nineteen sixties, 34, 41, 42; as commodi-

278

Index

Rauschenberg, Robert, 234
Reality principle, 135, 137, 173, 174, 175–76, 178, 179, 209
Reason, 132, 204, 215, 245; aesthetic, 231; and emotion, 13, 15, 107, 109–10, 111, 133, 150, 192; and needs, 31; transformation of, 137, 231. *See also under* Sensuality
Reason and Revolution (Marcuse), 36, 77, 251, 253, 254
Reich, Wilhelm, 44, 45, 49, 50, 118, 126
Relationships, 14, 122, 131, 137–38, 139–40, 142–43
Relativism, 7, 240
Repression, 62, 63, 64, 69, 119–20, 123, 129, 134, 135, 173, 185, 195, 199; Freudian, 135; resistance to, 138, 179; surplus, 120, 121, 124, 125, 134, 200
Repressive reality principle, 123, 127. *See also* Performance principle
Resistance politics, 23, 48–49, 203, 221
Revolution, 7, 48–49, 138, 254, 258; and women's movement, 12, 89; and working class, 12, 91, 94, 133, 254
Revolutionary consciousness, 5, 6, 91–93, 96, 100
Revolutionary hope, 21–22, 23
Revolutionary Left, 253
Rimbaud, Arthur, 177
Robinson, Paul A., 49, 50, 51
Roemer, John, 74
Roheim, Geza, 50
Romanticism, 17
Roper Organization, survey on science and social problems (1988), 238
Rosenbach, Ulrike, 235
Rousseau, Jean Jacques, 250
Ruling majority, 2
Ryan, Michael, 35

Saint-Just, Louis-Antoine de, 209
Saint-Simon, Claude, 251
Sale, Kirkpatrick, 203
Satisfaction, 139, 193
Schiller, Johann, 1, 15, 261
Schoolman, Morton, 191
Schumacher, E. F., 203
Science and technology. *See* Technology
Science fiction, 234
SDS, 36
Self-censorship, 194
Semiotics, 6, 7
Sensibility, 257
Sensuality, 2, 11, 15, 110, 111, 113, 114, 136, 151, 156, 159, 160, 161, 162, 164, 166, 168, 180, 204, 256, 260; and art, 180, 182, 235; and reason, 15, 150, 151, 155, 159, 160, 233
Sessions, George, 203
Sexism, 7, 8, 96
Sexual Dissidence: Augustine to Wilde, Freud to Foucault (Dollimore), 50
Sexuality, 2, 11, 13, 14, 30, 33, 53–55, 79–80, 118, 121–22, 129; antirepressive struggle, 45, 50; and identity, 51, 53–54, 124
Sexual politics, 42, 45
Shaftsbury, Anthony, 250
Shils, Edward, 238
Shtern, Adele, 235
Simulations (Baudrillard), 29
Skolimowski, Henryk, 203
Social action, 112–13, 138
Social change, 31, 33, 35, 59–64, 106, 159, 200, 219, 246–49, 250, 251–52, 255, 257, 259, 263
Socialism, 2, 7, 8, 9, 41, 57, 66, 67, 106, 110, 209, 253; democratic, 254; and object relations theory, 14; new, 260; pseudo- and proto-, reality, 59; and radical politics, 254; transition to, 58, 60, 246, 255, 258; utopian, 227, 260
Socialist transformation, 110–11, 251, 255
Social movements, 36, 37, 44, 214, 258, 259, 261–62
Social reconstruction, 30–31
Social theory, 13, 33, 75–76, 82, 106, 214, 247, 249, 251, 252–53, 261, 262, 263; self-reflexive, 107, 112–16
Sociology, 251
"Some Remarks on Aragon: Art and Politics in the Totalitarian Era" (Marcuse), 256
"Some Social Implications of Modern Technology" (Marcuse), 236
Sommers, Christina Hoff, 98
Sontag, Susan, 185
Sophists, 247–48
Sorel, Georges, 52
Soviet Marxism: A Critical Analysis (Marcuse), 57, 58, 59, 61–62, 64, 254
Soviet Union, 5, 8, 9, 57, 65, 68, 209, 253; bureaucracy, 61, 62, 66, 67–68; militarization, 61; nationalization, 60, 61; and reform, 9, 58, 262; social transformation in, 60–64, 69; and the West, 62, 70. *See also* Communism; Marxism; Marcuse, Herbert, and Soviet-style Marxist theory

280